INDUSTRIAL GOVERNMENT

THE MACMILLAN COMPANY
NEW YORK · BOSTON · CHICAGO · DALLAS
ATLANTA · SAN FRANCISCO

MACMILLAN & CO., Limited
LONDON · BOMBAY · CALCUTTA
MELBOURNE

THE MACMILLAN COMPANY
OF CANADA, Limited
TORONTO

INDUSTRIAL GOVERNMENT

BY

JOHN R. COMMONS

WILLIS WISLER, ALFRED P. HAAKE, O. F. CARPENTER, JENNIE
McMULLIN TURNER, ETHEL B. DIETRICH, JEAN DAVIS,
MALCOLM SHARP, JOHN A. COMMONS,
UNIVERSITY OF WISCONSIN

New York
THE MACMILLAN COMPANY
1929

FERRIS
PRINTING COMPANY
NEW YORK CITY

PREFACE

WE visited some thirty establishments from July to September, 1919, and Wisconsin to Maine. We prepared by studying industrial government in books, papers and pamphlets from Russia to Australia. We selected as large variety of types that had successful experience as we could find. America has examples of every kind, from industrial autocracy to the farthest left wing of revolutionary democracy.

We specialized somewhat and had different points of view, which accounts for differences noticeable in the "Inferences." One of us took constitutional government in industry; another took the employer's scheme of management; another the wage-earner's scheme of democracy; another the procedure in settling grievances; another shop representation of employees. We spent from one to five days together in each establishment, with the managers and with the employees. Individuals followed up with separate inquiries, in one case spending two months at one place. The four Wisconsin manufacturers, Messrs. F. J. Sensenbrenner, M. O. Wertheimer, D. E. Everest, and Judson Rosebush, who financed the bulk of our traveling expenses, and Maj. E. A. Fitzpatrick, of the State Board of Education, who aided us greatly, wished to know the best practice in dealings with labor that the country affords. We avoided fresh experiments and selected those that had a record going back before the war. When we came back to Madison each one of our party was made responsible for certain chapters, but the others contributed, and the whole is as nearly a cooperative product as any collaboration can be. Certain of the chapters were used by *The Independent,* one by the U. S. Bureau of Labor Statistics in its *Monthly Labor Review,* another by *Industrial Management,* and are here reprinted with permission.

We saw that each establishment visited was experimental. Each was looking for experiments elsewhere. Nothing is settled in the field of labor, but everything is being settled every day. We naturally distinguished personality from system. But we found that even that distinction was treacherous. Gradually certain establishments began to stand out as distinctive. Each had something that was unique. Sometimes its distinction sprang from its system of organization; sometimes from a dominating personality that seemed to override system. Yet even that personality had a system.

We tried to find something on which to hang the facts in each business concern. One of the concerns stood out as a struggle for power of organized capital and organized labor, resulting in an equilibrium which we named due process of law; another was just plain health and happiness for its workers; another was faith in people of all sorts and conditions; several were faith in the management; another was getting employees to think about the future of the business; another was cooperative speeding-up; another was minute measurement of human motives in terms of money; another was emancipation from absentee owners, and government by the imaginative minds active in the business. The only cash profit-sharing system that we found, which looked good to us at the time, broke down sixteen months later, when prices dropped.

All of them, of course, had features in common, but these ruling ideas stood out rather clearly as we neared the end of our journey when we could look back and compare them one with another.

All of them were very alive and were making great changes in short periods, both in system and personality. One was passing from autocracy into government by employees; another from scientific management into unionism; another from welfare into self-government; another from political to industrial form of government.

One interesting fact was found: the sudden or gradual moral conversion of an employer from business to humanity. Employees noted it, and could not at first believe it, or were still incredulous, and told us about it, and so did the employer himself. In some cases it was unionism or strikes that did it. In others it was business foresight of the labor problem. In others it was sermons by an industrial evangelist.

We noted also certain obvious contrasts. In one case, not however included in this book, output had fallen off two-thirds, wages had doubled and high prices took care of both. In others efficiency had increased nearly as much as wages, so that the increased cost of living was nearly paid for by increased output per man. In some cases wages had not kept up with the cost of living; in others they had exceeded the increased cost. In some cases labor-turnover was down at astonishingly low figures compared with the

industrial world in general. In some cases seasonal
industries had been stabilized so that no employee is
laid off. In others a reserve army is depended on for
elasticity. In others the rapid growth of the business
has overcome instability of employment.

We give here only eighteen of these experiments in
Industrial Government, out of the thirty visited. We
do not say "Industrial Democracy." We find widely
different things done in the name of Democracy. The
main thing is that they are being done by very vigorous
men and women, who are going after things, and are
making things buzz. Every one of them is a live idea
getting itself into action. Forms of government are
adapting themselves to ideas and conditions.

Yet we were not under illusions. We looked up experts in industrial government. It is astonishing what
easy marks for experts many employers had become in
the summer of 1919. From all sides and several vo-
cations these experts were coming in and setting themselves up. They got long-distance calls from employers to hurry up and come at once. They lifted the
employers' pocket-book at will. One would think that
the capitalistic system was crumbling, in that employers had lost the power of discipline. In some cases we
found that they had actually abdicated and turned the
labor end of their business over to professors. Just
what it all portended was a puzzle. Certainly the temporary scarcity of labor was a leading fact, and employers began to regain their independence, to reduce
wages and lay off the professors in 1920.

Naturally we began to put together our conclusions
and to draw up some general statements, based, not
only on these eighteen establishments, but also on oth-

ers. We are not ready, however, to call them Conclusions. Things are too uncertain in labor matters.
We content ourselves with calling them "Inferences."
Our first eighteen chapters, then, describe the selected
establishments. Our last five chapters are our "Inferences."

January, 1921.

CONTENTS

xi

PART I. ESTABLISHMENTS

I

THINKING AND PLANNING

THE manager was attending a committee meeting. He would be back in his office in about an hour.

The offices might all be schoolrooms. Plain tables, many chairs, walls hung with charts and diagrams—that is the academic and utilitarian background for the transaction of business at The White Motor Company of Cleveland, Ohio.

The time of waiting passed quickly. We were making a rather furtive inspection of the charts and blueprints on the walls when a dark, energetic-looking man came forward and offered to explain any of them which we did not understand. We expressed surprise at the unusual spectacle of a company posting for public consumption the facts which are usually held as inviolate secrets. It was almost embarrassing to have thus boldly thrust upon us information the like of which we had sought always modestly, often vainly, and had usually received only in the strictest confidence. We might even have been rival manufacturers, for all the company knew of us, diligently inquiring into their trade secrets.

We also expressed our interest in the prominent

place given in the diagrams to the Department of Industrial Relations.

The dark young man thereupon introduced himself as the Director of Industrial Relations. We recognized him at once as a departure from the ordinary run of things—a new type of Industrial Director. We had heard of him before from labor officials in the city; he was formerly President of the Cleveland Federation of Labor. And apparently he is still greatly respected by his former co-workers in the labor movement.

We were deep in his theories of the part the worker should play in management and in responsibility for producing, when the General Manager came in abruptly. He was quite taken, he told us, with an idea that had just occurred to him and which he wished he had thought of in time to take up with his men. Unfortunately the committee had disbanded and the men had gone back to the shops. So there was nothing for him to do but wait until it should meet again two weeks later. He turned to us with the same eagerness to give and to take which he must have had in the meeting just dismissed. The committee, as he explained to us, is composed of from twenty to fifty employees, each one of whom has been elected by a group of ten fellow employees to be part of a giant shop committee, to attend meetings for one year, and to report back to his constituents as much information as he is able to absorb and impart.

The "shop committee" as it appears here is a unique institution. It is not a union committee; it is not a workmen's council; it is not a "company union." It lays no claim to being a form of "industrial democracy," and it has nothing to do with collective bargaining. It is simply one of the essential parts—perhaps the most important part—of the great big scheme of thinking and planning for the future which makes the White Motor worth thinking about and writing about. The "shop committee" is just a mammoth forum, divided up into sections which meet every alternate week to talk over with the manager or his assistants any part of the whole industrial problem from the situation in Russia and Australia to the answer to the question, "Where will the White Motor be when the conditions change?"

Some kind of readjustment, declare the management, is bound to come. It does not make much difference what kind of a change is coming if we are only ready for it. White Motor wants to be ready. Anybody, be he capitalist, socialist, radical, or trade union agitator, is welcome to come in and tell the management what kind of a change *he* thinks is coming. The manager invites information and goes after it. He searches the papers, radical and reactionary, foreign and American. He gets every slant possible on human thought and action. And he seems to have here in his plant a germ of almost every great movement which is shaking the world to-day. Whichever one of these ideas wins out, the White Motor has a chance of passing over gradually into the new régime without any violent upheaval.

We asked this unusual manager to consider us one of his committee and give us exactly the kind of thing he had been handing out to his men the hour before, or previous hours. He agreed, and this is what he gave us:

"We do not know which way the country is going.
A financial readjustment is certain to come. But
whatever the result White Motor wants to survive,
and wants to govern itself and not be dictated to by
outsiders. How can we survive and keep control of
this business among ourselves whichever way the
country goes? And what is there in it for you to
have the White Motor keep on in the way it has started,
regardless of what happens outside?

"Let us see. There are three hundred manufacturers of motor trucks in America. A large number
of them will go to the wall. We manufacture about
ten per cent of the total output of the country. We
want to keep that ten per cent. If we do we shall have
to keep on absorbing our ten per cent of all those that
go under. That means that we shall need to double our
plant in, say two years, and triple it in five years.
Now, if we double or triple our plant what will it
mean for us?

"Well, we doubled it during the past five years and
here is what it meant:

"While our plant value increased from $1,879,000
in 1914 to $3,650,000 in 1919 our production value
increased from $9,000,000 in 1914 to over $35,000,000
in 1919. This means that five years ago for every
dollar we invested on our plant we produced about
$4.80 worth of motor trucks, and this year for every
dollar in the plant we produced $9.60 worth of trucks.

"The number of employees has more than doubled.
The average number of men in 1914 was 2202; now
it is 5475. The production per man in 1914 was
1-92/100 trucks; in 1919, it was 2-75/100 trucks,
an increase of 43 per cent.

"We have increased the earnings of our employees from an average of $15.03 a week in 1914 to $31.64 in 1919, or an increase of 111 per cent. Our total pay roll for factory employees in 1914 was $1,688,000, now it is $8,835,000.

"All this has been done without any material increase in the price to the purchaser of our trucks. Our price has been increased only 10 per cent, at a time when all prices, wages, and cost of material have gone up 50 per cent, 100 per cent, or more.

"Looks wonderful, doesn't it? Can we keep it up? See where we must be to double in two years and triple in five years, if we can keep it up. The figures given below show the estimated factory value of production for each of the next five years:

FACTORY VALUE OF PRODUCTION

1920	$51,961,350
1921	67,244,100
1922	82,526,850
1923	97,809,600
1924	113,092,350

"The big thing is, where are we going to get the capital in order to expand? The business that does not expand is really falling behind. We must expand further than our competitors, or else we are falling behind. If we take five years we can probably build up our plant out of earnings. If we have to go too fast in order to take up our share of the business of those who fail we may have to go and get outside capital. As long as we have the present control you can be certain that the present labor policy will be carried out.

Our policy has been in the past and is now, to limit payment of dividends to 8 per cent on capital stock."

On what devices does the White Motor depend for keeping up and increasing production?

The White Motor has neither any system of bonuses, premiums or piece rates. Everything is a straight day wage. No time and motion studies, no specific inducements to individuals to increase their output.

There is, of course, a very careful system of scheduling the work through the factory and there is a standard output figured out for a year ahead showing how many trucks must be made if they keep up to the plan of expansion. The year's output has been narrowed down to four types of motor trucks, with some variations within the types, and all models are scheduled for erection daily. The figure of each day's output of completed trucks is filed with the various superintendents so that the organization is familiar with the result of each day's work and the production both of completed trucks and the main assemblies, such as engines, axles, and transmissions, is published each month in the regular issue of the White-Book so that the workmen are kept informed concerning the product of the factory. No individual is speeded up by a piece rate, bonus or premium—the whole factory is simply watching that the schedule is met or exceeded. Then, if a department falls behind, or if the whole factory falls behind, the fifty-eight hundred employees want to know where the fault lies. The committees and the management begin to inquire. Cases come along occasionally where the men in a department freeze out a loafer. The management is proud of the fact that they seldom fire a man, and, most of all, that the men seldom quit.

The turnover records are astonishing. During the year 1919 the rate was about 24½ per cent. It got as low as 1.23 per cent in February; as high as 2.65 per cent in May. In 1916 the turnover was the highest—77 per cent for the year; in 1917 it was 66 per cent; in 1918, it was 63 per cent, but this should come down to 54 per cent after deducting army enlistments. The average for other factories that year in Cleveland and vicinity was stated by the company to have been about 300 per cent.

To sum it all up, what are the White Motor's substitutes for the motion studies, piece work, profit sharing and all the other scientific methods of appealing to the individual for increased product.

Isn't it something like this? Thinking and planning for the future. Keeping the mind of every man away from whatever there is of dullness and monotony in his task. Just touching the imagination; arousing in every heart zeal for progress and pride in a great common enterprise; lighting up the most menial and stupefying task with the rays of a great industrial vision.

But all this is not as easy as it may sound. How are you going to get a good red-blooded workman to sit down and be lectured to on the subject of a great industrial vision? How are you going to get him to believe that expansion has something in it for him?

The White Motor Management does it by the policy of honesty and openness. It furnishes copies of its annual report to all employees requesting it, and sets forth in the White-Book the essential facts contained in the report. The White-Book is sent every month into the homes of every employee and it forces information about itself not only on the men but also on their wives and families. It shows what they have to fear and what they have to hope, and then promises to keep faith with them in sharing prosperity with them.

It does not offer all this information in the name of industrial democracy. The shop committee in the White Motor Company was started neither as a grievance committee nor a legislative body. The idea back of it was not in any sense the idea back of the inside organization of workmen which union men are accustomed to designate with greater or less scorn as "a company union." The company has never made any attempt to give the employees any degree of industrial self-government. One of the objects of this committee was apparently exactly the opposite—it was that some day employees may assume a greater or less degree of self-government, and if this company is going to be one of those which survive it must prepare the workmen to exercise intelligently whatever degree of power they may have. It is not for the company to give power, it is for it to give the information which may save it when the workmen have power. The company is not trying to determine the form of organization under which the power may sometime be wielded. The company keeps in its employ strong, responsible, intelligent leaders of every variety of organization which is likely ever to be in control. This seems to be all that it cares to do toward securing a safe transition into any form of industrial government which may come. Which form this industrial government will take is still a question.

Many trades are to be found in the factory, most of them at least partially organized. Cleveland is one of the most highly organized cities in the country, so that although White Motor has an open shop policy, a large part of the men probably are or have been at some time members of the union of their trade. No union, however, has ever presented a demand to the company. Informal shop committees have asked for wage increases or other changes in conditions, and their requests have been listened to, but the unions have not interfered in the question of wages. Only once have they shown any great degree of activity and that was when the men got an idea that a change of management was impending. Then how can the White Motor Company get production like this on a straight hourly rate?

In the long run, according to the officials of the company, time rather than piece rates will prove to be the cheapest. It costs too much to hurry. It is more economical to employ a young man and keep him until he grows old, than to wear out a man, or lose him when he is still young. They point to their average age of over thirty-five and their annual turnover of 24½ per cent in connection with their increased per capita production figures. Time and motion studies, they maintain, are almost necessarily liable to grave error. They are not elastic enough. In order to be fairly accurate they need to be taken on very hot days and comfortable days; early in the morning and just before closing time; early in the week and late in the week; during periods of political and industrial turmoil, and during periods of political and industrial calm. They vary under conditions of domestic dif-

ficulty and domestic tranquillity. Human beings are
not constant in their ability to perform. Their at-
tainments must be measured over reasonably long periods.

Is there any other factor that can help to account
for increasing per capita production on an hourly rate?

When you offer desirable conditions you get your
pick of employees.

As might be expected there is never any lack of applicants for work at the White Motor. As a matter
of fact, the employment department takes about one
out of every thirty or forty applicants. Two conditions are required of each one who is employed; he
must live in Cleveland and he must have taken out his
first citizenship papers. Preference is given to married men and returned soldiers. The word "he" is
used literally here. It means what it says. The company aims to pay a family wage and endeavors to employ family men. Much of the work could be performed by women, but it is the intention of the company to use only men.

There is in the White Motor plant a considerable
amount of "service work." It takes the usual forms
of furnishing lunch and medical aid. Then there is
the consultation bureau where legal aid and other
forms of advice are dispensed on company time. The
company shows that this is no loss to them since it
furnishes a convenient place to transact the necessary
business for which employees might otherwise have to
lay off during working hours. And it is on record
that the men themselves once petitioned to have more
men in the Industrial Service Department to answer

their requests in order that they need not spend so much time away from their work.

The foremen and all executives get a special kind of service work. It is one hour a day in the gymnasium, on company time, and it is mandatory. If a foreman cannot arrange his work so as to be away from it for an hour, he is not the kind of a foreman they want. This is the White Motor course of instruction for foremen and executives—it gets them acquainted with each other undressed; it keeps them in splendid physique; and it keeps them from indigestion and getting cross and sour with their workmen; it keeps them at the top notch of initiative and pep.

The educational work does not stop with the shop. There are in addition the classes of Americanization. Suspicion need not be aroused here with regard to employers' propaganda. The man at the head of Americanization is a man of liberal thought. He attends national Socialist conferences and he is first of all a teacher and an American. He has lived in this country twenty years. There are only thirty men out of fifty-eight hundred employees who have not taken out their first papers, and that is because they intend to go back to Europe soon. The teacher in Americanization has connected up with the public schools and three hundred men are in the classes an hour a day on their own time. The company gives them fifteen minutes on company time to wash up and reach the Public School.

The cost of all this work is figured out for the men and they see that it takes eight cents a day from their possible wages. But they see that it adds much to their actual wages.

Is anything more needed to explain why they work as they do? What is back of it all? Not a strong union with power to secure for the men the benefits of increased production. Not industrial democracy. Not a premium or a bonus.

Nothing but a knowledge of all the facts which the company itself possesses; the company's verbal assurance that it will do certain things in the future; the company's reputation for keeping faith with employees in the past; for not having tried to "put anything over," and, added to this, the knowledge that the company has not weeded out of its employ all those who disagree with the present industrial system. On the contrary, it has deliberately encouraged the presence of strong and trusted leaders of the people, in whom they have confidence and on whose judgment and intentions they can rely. Real power is here—potential largely, but power which makes it possible for the men at the White Motor to accept their responsibility and satisfaction in thinking and planning for the future.

II

FAITH IN PEOPLE

"THE industrial miracle of the age," John D. Rockefeller is reported to have said of the Ford Motor Company. He might have added, the psychological miracle
of the age. The industrial end is amazing enough.
Three completed cars moving off every minute on their
own gasoline. The breadwinners of a city of two
hundred and fifty thousand at work in one factory.

But the psychological miracle is equally miraculous.
Ford reversed the ordinary psychology of industry.
Instead of sharing profits with employees at the end
of the year he shared them before they were earned.
Instead of carefully selecting employees at the gates
he takes them as they come—gets a cross-section of the
community—has a theory that he must carry his share
of the maimed, blind, and criminal, because somebody
has to do it anyhow—believes in ordinary plain people as they come along.

This is not scientific and is not business. According to the usual ideas Ford ought to break. They
tried to prove in court that he was a very ignorant
man and could scarcely even read and write. He
needs somebody to protect him against himself. And
that is what his employees are doing.

Ford says, in effect, to anybody who gets into his
works, "How much do you think you are worth?"

Well, the man thinks he is worth a little more than he has been getting elsewhere. "Why," says Ford, "that's nothing. Here is the biggest thing in the world. We are going to sell a million cars a year and give every family in America a 'Lizzie.' If you get into the game you are worth twice as much, ten times as much, as you have been getting. We will pay you that in advance. Now go to it."

And just the ordinary, everyday man rises up out of himself and sees himself twice as big, ten times as big, as he had ever thought possible. He goes to it.

That is why even men with a prison record have done big things at Ford's. There are 400 of them and the majority making good.

Two thousand men go around with labels, "For light work only." A blind man does the work of three men. The fact is, everybody turns in and protects Ford against himself. He is positively too democratic for this world. One man is just as good as another, he thinks. That certainly is not business. But behold, you see ordinary, common men doing big things at Ford's.

Of course, they make mistakes. Ford took his sociologists out of the ranks, and they certainly did raw work for a while. Ford somewhere had gotten an idea that what he wanted as workers in his factory were men who were living clean and wholesome and constructive lives. So he did not care to have employees examined as to their efficiency—efficiency was to be a by-product of the clean and wholesome life. He was going to share his profits, not with those who got out the work, but with those who led a clean and wholesome life. So he picked out his sociologists from the ranks to investigate and find out. And they went into the homes, investigating and re-investigating everybody. They had an idea that that was the clean, wholesome and constructive life.

Well, after about three years, Ford called in Dr. Marquis, Dean of the Episcopal Cathedral, and spoke in this wise: "There is too much of this snooping around in private affairs. We'll change this from a Sociology Department to an Education Department— you take charge. You know what I want—clean and constructive life—but cut out these investigations all except those that really need further assistance and advice."

And that is what Dr. Marquis has been doing. He has about fifty men on that job.

Then about the 400 with prison records. Ford had an idea that if he could save men from the penitentiary they would make good. All they needed was a chance. But the idea did not work. They had a different idea. This was just another chance to get off, and so they took advantage of it and went on with their criminality. Now this has been changed. The Education Department takes on no convicted delinquent until after he has served his term, or at least an appreciable part of it. He must take his medicine. Then he may have his chance to make good. These four hundred are assigned to a confidential adviser— a kind of unofficial parole officer attached to the Education Department of the factory. So Ford tried out his theory of faith in human nature, and his Education Department learned how to protect Ford against himself.

People say, "Oh yes, Ford can do these things because he has such an enormous business. There is nothing at Ford's that can teach other employers anything in any ordinary business subject to competition."

Wrong again. Ford got his enormous business because he did these other things first. Ford is really a plunger—a plunger in social psychology. When he started his profit-sharing scheme in 1914, he had 14,000 employees. He doubled their wages with a bang— that is, he doubled the wages of those who could pass his sociology examination on the clean and wholesome life. In August, 1919, his 14,000 men had become 53,000, and were growing at the rate of 1200, on an average, a month. The first year after he doubled their wages he made more net profit than he did the year before.

How was it? The labor turnover. In order to keep his force of 14,000 men he had to fill the places of those who quit with new men, at the rate of 50,000 a year. The next year after he put in his new plan he had to hire only 6508. If the old rate of labor turnover were to keep going now he would be hiring 196,000 men a year to keep up a force of 53,000. But he only hires at the rate of 23,000 to replace those who quit. We were told by another employer in Detroit that the turnover in foundries that summer had been 20 per cent a month. In Ford's foundry of 7000 workers it was running at 6 per cent to 8 per cent a month. The average turnover for all departments ranged from 3 per cent to 6 per cent a month.

Now, the cost of labor turnover is something huge. There is the hiring and examination of applicants, the files of records, the breakage and accidents of new employees, the teaching and training and fitting them into the job, most of all, the slowing up of production. It is a big overhead cost, added to the wages. You might credit almost the entire increase in efficiency to that item. If you have 1000 men in a single gang then the speed of the 1000 is limited by the speed of the slowest. And if 3700 new men, the former proportion at Ford's, are coming into that gang of 1000 every year and 3700 are leaving, there certainly must be a lot of slow men holding them up. But, if only five hundred or less, the new proportion in a gang of 1000, are coming and going for a year then you begin to get team work and can reduce the size of the gang, and move the stuff along.

That is what you see at Ford's. That is the industrial miracle. It follows the psychological miracle. Innumerable trolleys, conveyor belts, tractors and trailers, carrying multitudes of castings to appointed foregatherings with other castings and parts. Waist-high assembly carriers do away with lifting and bending. In the foundry, usually the bugbear of employment managers, endless chains, overhead trolleys, sustain the weight of ladles; sand-hoppers in the ceiling do away with back-breaking shoveling; electric and magnetic hoists "hustle the pigs." In the cylinder-casting department three men pour what scarce yesterday required a hundred.

Throughout the factory seven hundred men are detailed to the exclusive task of keeping the place "policed up," to use the military phrase. A squad of painters, window-washers, accident-preventers, keep things fresh and safe. The machine shop floor is as clean as a kitchen. Rough stock, though accessible to the operator, is piled clear of the aisles. True, many of the workers are close together where detail jobs are contemporaneous. Yet the entire air-content is changed every twelve minutes. In the foundry powerful down-drafts and sucking blowers carry off the smoke and gas.

Some people say that the men are "driven" at Ford's. A scientific manager who had come up through machine shops elsewhere had told us he never saw such speeding up. So we looked for it. We had had some experience ourselves. The only place where we found it was in some parts of the foundry. There one might say they were speeding up. The machinery did it, not the boss. But those 7000 foundry workers are nearly all new men. In October, 1918, the foundry had only 700 men. Six thousand farmhands from Europe learning a foundry job might look very active, while 6000 who have got their pace would look easy. And there were so many of them who were easily at work that the driven ones caught your eye as exceptions.

Anyhow, why shouldn't strong men work hard for eight hours at 75 cents an hour? The Steel Corporation pays the same class of labor 40 cents an hour for twelve hours. One does not like to see them work that hard in the steel mills. And the enormous turnover shows that the steel workers do not keep it up. The foundry is a hard job anyhow—the hardest of all. The turnover there, at Ford's, is 8 per cent a month, when the average for other shops in the works is 4, 5 or 6 per cent. If a foundry turnover, for men who have been employed on the average only six months can be kept down to that figure, at a time when

labor was in such demand as it was in the summer
of 1919, it would seem that the appearance of over-
speeding was not to be taken too seriously. Of course,
men work hard if they are paid enough.

The output certainly has been increased. Hours
were reduced and profit-sharing began in 1914. Here
are typical results from four departments, figured on
the comparative performance of the same number of
men before and after.

Motor—100 in nine hours, 120 in eight hours.

Radiator—100 in nine hours, 169 in eight hours.

Fender—100 in nine hours, 155 in eight hours.

Gasoline tank—100 in nine hours, 150 in eight hours.

That profit-sharing scheme is a curious one. Really
that is a wrong name for it. The Ford people now
call it "prosperity sharing." That is hardly correct
either. It does not depend on the work a man does.
It depends on the way he lives outside working hours.
It ought to be called a citizenship fund, a community-
development fund, a home-maker's fund. It is 15
cents an hour devoted to faith in human nature.

It is the payment of a fixed amount to each worker,
not a percentage of his wages, nor a pro-rated distribution of the profits of the concern. It has strings
to it, but these strings are different from any ever tied
to profit-sharing. It does not depend on output, nor
upon skill, nor upon length of service. It is based
upon the value of the individual in citizenship and in
society. It is not based on how much a man brings up
the average production of the factory, but upon how
much he brings up the average standards of the community, in living, in thrift, in good American citizenship. If he is good in these he may receive today in

advance the profits the company believes he will bring
in tomorrow. The idea is that every man wants to be
a sober, capable, industrious citizen, and that such a
man is the best investment the company can make.

Married men, living with and taking good care of
their families, receive this bonus for frugality. Lads
under eighteen may also receive it if they are the support of some next of kin. Single men of eighteen years
who are known to be living wholesomely and constructively are eligible. Women share as well as men. All
that is required is to meet the company's specifications
of good citizenship. The Education Department attends to it. The standards are not petty. When the
plan took effect, sixty per cent of the workers immediately shared profits. At the end of six months seventy-
five per cent were sharing; after one year, eighty-seven
per cent, and at the present time all but a fraction of
one per cent are receiving profits.

In October, 1913, the men were first really classified
according to their skill. Previously there had been
sixty different wage rates. November, 1912, saw a
labor turnover of forty-two per cent for the month.
The month following the change it was but eight. The
men had been freed from the favoritism and partiality
of the foremen. At the time that the sharing system
was introduced, the lowest wage in the shop was thirty-
four cents an hour, and the scale ran up to eighty cents
an hour. The division of the "profits" being primarily
to raise the standards of living of each to a good level,
twenty-eight and one-half cents an hour was given to
the lowest skilled, and seven and one-half to the highest
skilled. It was presumed that the totally unskilled
needed more elevation than the man who was getting

a higher rate. This extreme discrepancy afterwards was abandoned. On January 1, 1919, the minimum hourly rate was raised to fifty cents. Sharing profits was then changed to a fixed and equal amount to every man regardless of skill, and determined by dividing the total hourly division of profits on the old basis by the number receiving them. Thus the average share was given each man. The schedule adopted in May, 1919, and given in the table below,[1] was a minimum hourly rate of sixty cents, a profit payment of fifteen cents an hour, and a classification of but nine different grades of skill.

In order to find whether a man was entitled to receive profits or not, a probationary period of six months in the employ of the company was at first required. At the end of that time, if there was promise of worth, or intention and desire to "get ahead," the newcomer began to get profits. This period was changed in July, 1919, to thirty days. It was found that accurate measurement of the character of the man could be made in that time, and the delay of six months was thought to discourage some of the probationers. For the administration of the scheme a Sociological Department was organized with two hundred "investigators" drawn directly from the working force.

[1]

WAGE SCHEDULE.

Effective May 24, 1919.

Wage	HOURLY		DAILY			MONTHLY (25 days)		
	Profits	Total	Wage	Profits	Total	Wage	Profits	Total
.60	.15	.75	4.80	1.20	6.00	120.00	30.00	150.00
.65	.15	.80	5.20	1.20	6.40	130.00	30.00	160.00
.70	.15	.85	5.60	1.20	6.80	140.00	30.00	170.00
.75	.15	.90	6.00	1.20	7.20	150.00	30.00	180.00
.80	.15	.95	6.40	1.20	7.60	160.00	30.00	190.00
.85	.15	1.00	6.80	1.20	8.00	170.00	30.00	200.00
.90	.15	1.05	7.20	1.20	8.40	180.00	30.00	210.00
.95	.15	1.10	7.60	1.20	8.80	190.00	30.00	220.00
1.00	.15	1.15	8.00	1.20	9.20	200.00	30.00	230.00

Subsequently the name of the department was changed to Educational, and the investigators became "advisors" because of the hint, conveyed by the former terms, of prying and delving into the intimate relations of the home. The number of advisors was reduced.

These advisors have been trained through actual work and selected as a permanent force through examination for originality, personality, tact, clear understanding of their duties and of the ideals of the plan. They interview the new employee after he has already been hired by the employment department. After being hired, this newcomer is questioned by the advisor as to his financial, domestic, and legal status, an estimate is made of his character, and he is told to report for work the following morning. The next day the advisor goes to his home, getting further information of household conditions, life of the children, habits of the breadwinner, in fact all about the family as members of society. The employee and his wife are then shown how to improve their conditions and their mode of living, and the benefits to be derived are set forth to them. Photographs are shown them of clean, well-ordered Ford homes. If, at the end of thirty days, they show evidence of desire to lay up for the future, sharing of the profits ensues. At first, investigations to check up followed on the average of once a month, but at the present time, unless special complaint from one source or another indicates that there is something wrong, only three in all are given. These are the examination at hiring, or within thirty days thereafter, the one five months later, and one eighteen months after hiring.

In case a man slips below the specifications, using

destructively rather than constructively the money he
receives, he is penalized through refused profits. If he
"comes back" at the end of thirty days he loses nothing. If it takes two months, he loses 25 per cent of
the profits for the period, three months fifty per cent,
and so on. If at the end of six months he shows no
indication of reforming to methods of thrift and so-
briety, his discharge is automatic. The money exacted
in these penalties goes into a charity fund for the
alleviation of cases of especial misfortune.

The activities of the advisors and the Educational
Department are extensive. A chart of their investigations for the period from March 31 to June 30, 1919,
gives the analysis of 14,988 cases. These come under
108 different subjects and were provoked from twenty-
two different sources in public institutions, in the
company, and among the friends and families of the
workers. Thirty-one cases entailed the rendering of
advice and various sorts of aid; twenty were cases of
domestic difficulties, nineteen were violations of law
and of company rules, while 7,700 cases were new and
rehired men and 1,558 were reinvestigations. The
many other cases ranged from legal advice all the way
to financial relief. One employee came to the company
saddled with a $900 debt. The company was helping
him with that when the first of four expensive and
quickly successive surgical operations took him from
work. He finally became practically paralyzed and
was indebted to the concern over $2,000. About the
middle of last September, this was being wiped off
the books, the man was being sent to expert medical
attention for his serious condition, and efforts were

being made to help the wife and mother to help herself, a suitable position being given her in the factory.

The Ford scheme of industrial government has nothing of unionism, or shop committees, or collective bargaining, or "industrial democracy." It is just old-fashioned industrial autocracy tempered by faith in human nature. It is plain that no scientific systematizer laid out that labor department. The labor department is not a department, it is a lot of independent activities that were started wherever something was not going just right, and so somebody was picked out of the factory to specialize on that point. There is, for example, a little department of about thirty men that does not know what to call itself, whether a grievance committee, or a supervisor of foremen, or a training school or a transfer department, or a branch of an educational department, or a trouble department. It just grew up as a specialty in dealing with troubles between foremen and employees. An employee cannot be discharged from the Ford works without great formality and final action by a committee representing the education department and the general management. During the year 1919 only 118 men were discharged. Hence, if a foreman wants to get rid of a man it is liable to involve the whole factory clear up to the top. Somebody must look into the matter and fix it up with the foreman, or find another foreman to take the man, or talk with the man. So this trouble-man becomes a labor adjuster, a personal-relation expert, and he has a staff and an office and clerks with files, and the files give a line on each one of the 2,000 foremen, and the foreman who has trouble looms up, and the general management begins to inquire whether he is fit to be a foreman. Thus the grievance department evolves into an investigating bureau, an advisory board to the general superintendent on the qualifications of foremen, and advisory to the education department on whether the workman is living the clean and wholesome life.

Why should there be any industrial democracy or workmen's grievance committee, or labor organizations, when nobody can be fired anyhow, and when this advisory committee of thirty is always on the job investigating trouble long before it ripens, and when the management always has a line on the foremen who have too much trouble? It all goes back to faith in people and ends in a trouble department to make repairs where something goes wrong in the exercise of faith.

III

FROM SCIENTIFIC MANAGEMENT TO
PERSONAL RELATIONS

THE American business man is usually thought of
as hard-headed, intensely practical and unsentimental.
As a matter of fact he is probably ruled by sentiment,
even by religion, to a far greater extent than we
realize.

Witness the Link-Belt Company of Philadelphia,
Chicago, and Indianapolis, where there has been a conscious development from pure scientific management
to humanism in management; from figures to feelings
as the instruments of control.

We visited the Philadelphia establishment. Twenty
years ago this concern was one of the first to introduce the Taylor system of scientific management, under
the supervision of Frederick W. Taylor himself; with
some modifications, to be sure, owing to the fact that
this concern manufactures special orders and not staple
products, but essentially the Taylor system with its
functional foremen, time and motion study, minute
cost determinations and the rest.

The nine hundred and odd workmen were scientifi-
cally adjusted to their jobs, shop routine was carefully
and thoroughly established, and the men worked at a
swift, steady pace. The worker who failed to come
up to the standard of performance found that his

earnings were so small that he did not wait to be discharged. He quit and sought work where he could go it at a slower pace. The worker who remained produced in large quantities and made better than average earnings.

Costs were kept in such minute detail that operations of so little duration as 105 seconds were recorded as separate units. Labor-hour costs were recorded at their actual cash costs. Value of buildings, equipment, tools and machinery, were allocated to separate workmen and unit processes with accuracy. Every instruction was written and carefully recorded. Orders and results passed by writing, and even human relations were controlled finally by paper forms. For every act and process there was a form which required careful filling out. The processes and relations were as mechanical as the Taylor system could make them.

This required an immense amount of work, rewriting bills of material, making thousands of entries; costs were always at least a week behind the labor date. A thorough study of their methods and recognition of faults resulted in a number of changes: the use of a single bill of materials, a distinctive time card for each separate form of production labor, and a uniform, general method of distributing indirect expenses. Selling costs were kept apart from the rest. Thus the work was materially reduced and accuracy sufficient for practical purposes retained.

While they still have scientific management it is so modified that it can no longer be called the Taylor system. It is the Link-Belt system.

In the planning department there have been probably the fewest changes. Here we find scientific management par excellence, likewise in the cost-accounting and stores departments. The work is carefully planned, instructions are made out in copies sufficient for each of the employed workers on each job, and accurate time studies are made and recorded. Their purpose, however, is more to make possible intelligible cost accounts and job estimates than to maintain rigorous paper control over the shops.

The greatest variation from scientific management has probably been in the personal relations with the men. This plant has always tried to give the workers a consciousness that the management was interested in their welfare and a fair deal for everyone : the effort has always been apparent to give the men all that is coming to them, to recognize their interest in the plant. It is easy to understand, therefore, that the management would early feel that the Taylor system went too far with its functionalization, particularly with respect to foremen. And they returned to the system of a single superintendent with general foremen and sub-foremen, each in complete charge of his particular group of workmen.

This foreman has all the functions of the old type of foreman, with slightly less emphasis on the personal relation side. He can recommend for discharge, but his discharge is not final. He is still the gang boss, with the responsibility of "getting out the goods," but is primarily an instructor and executive.

The interesting development in this concern is the changed type of superintendent. Contrary to general practice, he is not the technical type of man. He did not forge his way up through the ranks of factory workers to his present position. He was a cost accountant with an attractive personality, a man of impelling presence. He is superintendent, not because he knows the technical side of manufacturing, but because he knows and can handle men, because of his great and evident human sympathy. The responsibility for matters technical is left to his foremen and subforemen.

His training school for this present position was a Sunday School. He was a whirlwind of a superintendent there. His school was live and interesting. Mothers sent their sons to him. He reformed recalcitrants. He built his whole soul on making everyone feel happy, contented, and anxious to do things.

So when the management of the Link-Belt Company saw, a few years ago, that they were facing a peculiarly difficult labor situation, they decided that they must change their tactics. They decided to pin their faith on the man who showed that he could inspire and lead his fellows, who could preach a sermonette to an imported workman in greasy overalls without evoking indifferent suspicion in response. The technical side of the problem could be left to his lieutenants. It was subordinated to the human relations aspect of the general manufacturing problem.

Not that this factory has become a revival camp meeting with a chorus of "Glory Halleluiahs" for every achievement in production. Far from it. Enthusiasm has not replaced, it has supplemented hard sense and technical skill. The superintendent with his foremen meet every morning, and at this meeting each man reports the progress of work in his department. Technical difficulties, failures to hold up to the schedule, failures to coördinate—these and more are discussed to the end that each knows just what the rest are doing, just where he stands, and what is expected of him. It would go hard with the foreman who showed in these meetings any shortcomings as a technician.

The technical side of the work is foundational. On it rests all else. But it is the peculiar function of the superintendent, through these meetings and through personal contacts with the workmen themselves, to build and maintain a high esprit de corps, to keep the machinery of production, including the human element, well coördinated, running at high speed and without friction.

Once a week the same group holds a meeting to take up pure labor questions, such as welfare, accidents, discipline. This is a non-technical meeting for the discussion of human relations, and through it the superintendent aims to build up his sub-executives as managers of men—and at the same time keep himself informed and fit.

The foremen do not fire. That is left for the superintendent. A workman was caught manipulating his time card. They pay both hour and piece rates, the latter for the higher and better-paying types of work. This workman so made out his time card that it showed a less number of hour-rate jobs and larger number of piece-rate jobs than he had actually performed. Of course he was detected. He was called before the superintendent and given a lecture on stealing, lying, and cheating. He was told that he would be given another chance and no more. The men in the shop were given to understand that this man was on probation, and he went back to work, with a hearty slap on the shoulder from the superintendent.

A little later he was again detected in the same trick. This time he was called in, reminded of his former offense, and the warning then given him, and discharged. Notice of his discharge and the reason for it were given the men. Appeals from the discharged worker's family failed to move the superintendent. "He had his chance, he was warned, and if I did not stick to my word the whole organization would go to pieces." This was final.

The superintendent walks out through the shops, calling men by their first names. He takes a personal interest in their personal problems. Mothers who meet him in church send him their boys and he employs them. He is the great, pulsing heart of the management, carrying its interest in the men directly to them, building a great family in the factory.

And the result? Over eight hundred workers steadily on the job—at increased wages to be sure—but also with increased output. The turnover is low.

Where is the union all this time? There isn't any, officially. Although this company, in one of its four plants, operates a shop closed against union men, because of the aggressive attitude of certain unions, here in Philadelphia it finds the unions less objectionable. It operates an open shop, making no discrimination between union and non-union men.

The management here takes the position that men cannot at all times be loyal to both their employers and their union, and in the past has put it up to the men on just this basis. A group of workers came and expressed the desire to organize.

"Why?" asked the management. Well, the men did not exactly know, but they thought they wanted a union.

"Suppose the union officials out of town order you to strike, even though you have no grievance against this management? What would you do?" asked the manager.

The men protested that they would stick to the company.

"And be disloyal to your union?" said the manager. "If you are disloyal to your union, how can we be sure you will not be disloyal to us? Be union men, if you must, but you are through here." The men were surprised, but saw the point. The matter was dropped.

The less aggressive policy of the unions in Philadelphia may be explained by the fact that the men are well paid. The general labor situation is better than elsewhere, wages having kept pace with the cost of living. Wages in this plant run as high as $3,000 per annum for ordinary skilled workers, $1,800 being a common wage.

The interest of the management in its workers as humans is undoubtedly a factor in the healthy situation in this plant. Effort is being made constantly to evoke a more earnest interest in the business and this interest is rewarded. Absentee ownership is recognized as an evil, and conscious effort is being made to retain control of the plant within the ranks of those actively engaged in it. They are planning to divide profits with their employees on a stock-participation basis. This, briefly, is the plan.

They have a property capitalized at six and a half million dollars. The physical value of the property is at least nine million dollars. The reason for this is that there never has been any water in the stock. They have always paid not to exceed eight per cent on the investment. The result is that they have a big property account which is far in excess of their capitalization. This they have accomplished by putting profits back into the business instead of out as dividends, thereby expanding and developing the business out of earnings.

There is here apparently no attempt to camouflage. There is no industrial democracy with a lot of strings attached, no committee system. It is a strict open shop, paying no attention to labor unions. but endeavoring at all times to maintain close human relationship between men and management.

The general manager does not barricade himself in a private office with a screen of clerks and secretaries. He sits in a large office with several hundred executives and clerks. He has a kind of horseshoe desk on a platform at one end of the room and everybody can tell whether he is on the job or not. He is accessible.

The superintendent mixes personally with the men. Their troubles are his troubles. No grievance is strangled. Everyone gets a fair hearing, and through the daily meetings of the foremen a splendid esprit de corps is maintained.

How far an executive may wisely go in this policy of slapping shoulders and calling men by their first names is an open question. The president of the company is concerned over it. At another plant of this company there is a superintendent who is anything but a human nature expert. He cannot bring himself to be familiar with his workers, to speak to them as he goes through the plant. He is a keen technician, his eyes miss little, he is a splendid organizer of technical details, he is fair and just, but he is not a good fellow with the men. Yet his plant runs smoothly, and production is maintained. He avoids the suspicion that he is trying to slip something over by smooth talk, and if there is less of fellowship in his reign, there is better discipline, and a general conviction that the men will get a square deal.

The two experiments are going on; the management is watching. The verdict is not yet declared.

IV

MEASUREMENT OF MOTIVES

In a great, well-lighted structure, nimble fingers are guiding hundreds of garments under the needles of power-driven sewing machines. A quick turn, a break of the thread, a toss to the left while picking up another garment at the right, and each girl bends forward again as the cloth speeds through the machine. In rapid succession girl after girl arises from her place, carries the bundle of garments she has sewed over to a nearby table, walks to the control board in the center of her division, has her work recorded and receives another batch of garments to work on.

They work hard, these girls, and they work steadily. The garments literally flow through the shop in an unbroken stream. One gains the impression that some omniscient being has arranged all the machinery, so delicately adjusting its parts that everything operates in perfect coördination and balance with every other part.

For this group of six hundred workers, most of whom are women and girls, the turnover for employees, after the probation period of five days, has averaged about 5 per cent per month over a period of six years, the range being between 33.5 per cent and 67.02 per cent per year. The absentees average about 2 per cent per day, and many of the women are married and have their own homes. More than two-thirds of the entire group have been employed here more than a year, while over 15 per cent have served ten years or longer. The workers are healthy, their appearance is neat and business-like. There are no strikes, production has steadily mounted, and wages have increased more than the increase in labor costs. The factory runs with the full force the year around.

Joseph & Feiss, Cleveland, Ohio, understood the art of designing clothes and measuring cloth to fit the pattern so as to utilize most of the cloth. Likewise, they designed the kind of an operative force they needed for their business and proceeded to measure the human beings to fit the design.

They needed work done in large quantities. It had to be well done. It had to meet competition. It had to be produced at low costs. They needed to produce garments which would sell.

If the factory could be kept running without lay-offs one great source of loss could be overcome; it would mean less waste of overhead expense and smaller turnover of labor. But it was difficult to accomplish this so long as dealers bought goods in season and so long as changes of style made over-production an ever-present menace.

They proceeded to educate their salesmen and their trade. First their materials and later their styles were standardized to meet a certain extensive conservative demand, principally for the more serviceable and everyday men's clothing. These models change very little, standardization lowers the cost, and it becomes feasible to manufacture the garments before they are actually sold rather than wait for orders. They develop their market to absorb a year-round production and make possible the economies of continuous production.

Fitting the operative force to the production design meant a measurement of human motives. How can you induce Lizzie Meyers to fit herself in with a scheme of scientific production, appear for work on time every morning and work steadily for the entire day? How can you get her to keep the quality up and the stream of production unimpeded, at the same time keeping her happy and loyal, willing to remain in your employ even when another employer tries to attract her to his company?

Lizzie is a bundle of motives and if you appeal to the proper motives with just the requisite appeal you win; if not you lose.

But you cannot measure motives with a yard stick as you can cloth. Incentives, motives, human willingness to do things, all grow out of mental states. It was discovered, however, that you can measure motives in terms of dollars and cents. For money makes possible the gratification of most desires and provides a measure of the attitude of human beings to each other.

The management of Joseph & Feiss found that inequalities in pay among their workers rankled even more than the fact of larger pay elsewhere. The girls who felt that they were discriminated against lost interest in their work; they talked, and the dissatisfaction which resulted lowered the morale of the shop.

Justice, then, is one of the motives which needs to be measured. Instead of leaving the hiring, firing and promotion to forty different foremen with forty different standards and all manner of prejudices and favoritisms, a single department, the Employment and Service Department, with a single standard for all workers, supervises relationship between the company and its employees. An open channel to the manager through their own elected representative provides the machinery for hearing complaints. With the removal of all signs of inequality and discrimination, providing the same measure of rewards for all employees, the dissatisfaction of Miss Lizzie Meyers and her kind disappears.

It was recognized that work must be paid for in accordance with the difficulty involved, the skill required, the degree of agreeableness or disagreeableness and the importance. The management further recognized that the basic amount to be paid was a question for bargaining, since judgment as to difficulty or disagreeableness or importance varies with the individual. So they arrived through investigation and discussion at what was believed to be a fair wage per hour for each kind of work. In 1914, the average for men— excepting cutters, markers and trimmers—was $13.35 per week. In 1918 the average was $24.37. In 1919, it was $28.09. Women's average earnings were $9.28 in 1914, $15.90 in 1918, and $18.25 in 1919. These are actual earnings determined by dividing the total annual earnings by fifty-two; and so include vacation week, sickness, and any shutdown or lay-off. The earnings for markers, cutters, and trimmers are appreciably higher.

Suppose we say that a coat baster should receive 60 cents per hour. But on the *amount of work* to be done to earn the 60 cents, the firm was not willing to bargain. This was not a matter of judgment or higgling;

it was a matter for measurement. An actual test showed how many operations could be performed in an hour. Allowance is made for interruptions, personal needs and the like, and a standard performance determined. Thus while Miss Lizzie Meyers might have produced fourteen basted coats in an hour, due allowance would lower the amount set as a standard, let us say to ten. The rate of pay then becomes six cents per garment, and the standard worker, producing her ten garments per hour, earns the agreed-upon sixty cents.

The worker who actually meets the standard, however, is given additional compensation in the shape of a 20 per cent "production bonus," and she would earn seventy-two cents instead of sixty cents. The company states that at the present time over 70 per cent of the workers are making the production bonus regularly.

There is also a "quality bonus." For each kind of work there is determined a maximum number of rejections to be allowed the worker, the number depending upon the speed and kind of operation. If the worker exceeds this schedule, that is, falls below the standard of quality required, she is paid no quality bonus. If she reaches or passes the standard she is paid a bonus up to 10 per cent of her earnings for perfect performance. She need not maintain the standard continuously to earn a bonus, but is paid a bonus for the aggregate of the hours for which she attains or exceeds the standard.

In order to keep the workers interested in pursuing the prize the management helps them to qualify in skill, or to find the kind of work for which their natural aptitude will fit them. A business-like young woman, who has the position of supervisor of production, keeps in close touch with the workers all day, encouraging, helping where she can.

College-trained women fill many of the executive positions. The management has learned that the higher type of executive, with the necessary ability and the mind trained to gauge human motives, is often developed more easily from the product of the college class-room than from the ranks of experienced operatives in the industry. Given the same opportunity, and possessing the perseverance essential to acquiring practical experience, the college-trained aspirant is likely to win out.

The worker during the first weeks of employment is likely to become discouraged, and if paid by the piece would not earn enough to pay her board for several weeks. To meet this discouragement, the management divides the pay of the worker into two parts, called the "Retainer" and the "Expectancy." Suppose a girl is put on an operation worth fifty cents per hour. Being a beginner she is not expected to produce the amount of work which would entitle her to the pay, but she is expected to earn part of it. So they pay her, let us say, thirty cents per hour for a "retainer" and expect her to earn twenty cents at the piece rate for that operation. The twenty cents is called "expectancy," and is earned in whole or part as the worker measures up to the learning standard. As the worker progresses the "retainer" goes down and the "expectancy" increases, that is, the guaranteed rate decreases and the standard of performance is raised.

The same method is used when a girl is taught a

new operation. For, mind you, the management is bent upon having every worker familiar with several operations, so that the absence of a worker does not prevent her operation from being performed. This scheme makes possible the balancing of all departments so that the flow of work is continuous and regular in quantity: which would not be the case if Department A were fully manned while Department B had only one-half its force at work.

The worker, while being taught this new operation, is not penalized for loss of production, but is given a "retainer" to compensate for the possible loss. Again, increasing familiarity with the operation reduces the "retainer" and increases the "expectancy." This "retainer" is in effect an instruction bonus.

An "attendance bonus" invokes regularity and helps to keep the productive machinery balanced. For each unbroken consecutive day of work the worker gets a bonus of fifty cents. For each absence, she fails to make the fifty cents attendance bonus for the first day following the absence. Thus, if Lizzie Meyers worked on Monday, Tuesday and Wednesday, she received fifty cents bonus for each day. But if she is absent on Thursday, works on Friday and also on Saturday, she loses her Thursday bonus, by reason of being absent on that day, and loses also her Friday bonus, the first day of her attendance, but earns her bonus on Saturday.

There is additional inducement offered in the "excuse bonus." It may be that Lizzie was sick on Thursday and called up the firm before nine in the morning; or she may have had to stay home and help with the washing, or wanted to go to a funeral, and knowing this, secured an excuse from her foreman and the Service Department. Or she may have gone home without completing the day's work, but secured an excuse for her absence. In any of these cases half of her attendance bonus is given her on Friday, that is, the "excuse bonus" nets her twenty-five cents.

Economic superiority, especially if it is earned, provides basis for social standing in the group. The aristocrats of this body of workers are the people who have served many years, earn regularly the production bonus and quality bonus, and are able to perform a large number of operations. The badge of superiority in each instance is not a blue ribbon, or the listing of a name at the head of a typewritten sheet, but cold cash. It has its physical counterpart in clothes, hats, shoes; a higher standard of living.

What if these workers could be made to feel that every day in the service of Joseph & Feiss made more certain provision for their old age; if they could be convinced that long service with the company, instead of exploiting them of their youth and strength, leaving them worn out and useless in their old age, would guarantee provision against want and suffering?

The "service bonus" does it. For each year of service the worker gets a bonus of five cents per day, up to thirty years of service, beyond which time the rate does not increase, although the payment continues. Lizzie Meyers has now been with the company for four years, and is getting a service bonus of twenty cents per day, paid every day, in addition to the other bonuses she earns.

But this bonus is not to be wasted, and the company reserves the right to deposit the bonus, agreeing to turn over the bank book when the employee leaves the service. It is intended to be educational towards thrift. In effect it is similar to a pension fund, but has the advantage of being actually seen to grow with each pay period out of the employees own steadfastness, instead of mysteriously appearing out of the company's benevolence upon the incapacity or old age of the worker.

There is still another bonus. The management is not content with having measured economic desire, esteem, desire for justice, security of employment, power and dignity, pleasantness of work, congeniality of the group, merely for the sake of greater production and steadiness of service. It also utilizes these to forestall termination of service. If the worker has decided to leave she can secure her pay up to the minute that she quits. But if she gives notice of her intention to leave she gets a bonus of a day's pay for each week of notice up to six weeks' notice. Six weeks' notice would entitle her to an extra week's pay, when leaving, but it would give the firm that much time to adjust its organization, and to discover whether any solution may be found which will make it possible for the worker to remain. It is surprising how easily personal difficulties may be surmounted when an experienced person analyzes them.

But the very backbone of this whole system of measurement is the piece-rate system—the system which has probably received as general condemnation by organized labor as any one method of wage measurement. Under it have developed the evils of rate-cutting, speeding-up, the tenseness of application which so often exact heavy toll, physical and mental, of the worker. And here we have the piece-rate system probably as highly refined as it will be found anywhere in the country. There is not merely a simple measurement of wages by piece production, but additional measurement for bonus, quality, attendance, length of service, promptness and notice of resignation.

On the other hand the evils that usually accompany the piece-rate system are decidedly mitigated. The low rate of turnover shows it. The operatives are required to work only forty-four hours a week, as short a period as will be found for regular day work anywhere. The speeding-up which becomes really serious only for long work periods is thus ameliorated by the shortness of the working hours. If a division completes its task before the day is done the girls can go home; and many of them finish before 5 o'clock.

Systematic organization of their time, the avoidance of delays in getting work to the operatives, the occasional rising from a sitting posture to walking over and getting fresh batches of work, the manifest effort of the management to maintain exact justice—make for contentment and increased productivity and earning power.

They are paid well; the rates once made are not cut unless some mechanical improvement or change of task justifies the cut and causes the worker no loss. The company provides a lunch room with wholesome food at low cost, rest room, visiting nurse, a dispensary.

But the crowning stroke in the use of motive measurement and bonus incentives is the play hour. We watched them at play. The stout woman at the end of the line slipped the loop about her waist and strained her weight against the rope. Twenty other married women in front of her laid strong hands on the rope and dug their feet into the ground, while on the other half of the rope twenty-one unmarried women strained in the opposite direction. A signal from the umpire and the tug-of-war was on. Mixed in the crowd, hatless and coatless like the rest, cheering and laughing and finally wiping the beads of perspiration from his face, the manager of the factory could scarcely have been recognized as the same man who had talked to us on his philosophy of management for several hours the day before.

Today it was a tug-of-war, tomorrow it will be baseball, day after tomorrow something else; but every day it is something, and the management takes the opportunity to achieve a common footing with the rest of the organization. Nowhere else have we found either such minute measurement of motives in terms of pecuniary incentive, or such careful attention toward preventing any ill-effects that are often charged against it. The management is thoroughly convinced that motive measurement and bonus incentive, as applied in their organization, has the opposite of ill-effects. We figure the reason to be, that they do not leave it to operate itself like a machine once wound up and let go, but the whole management is always on the job attending every minute to the wear and tear of the system, and improving it at any point as soon as a defect appears. Little points which we found in August were not there the following March. Improvements made in March, 1920, were just beginning to be thought of the preceding August. Even yet, they tell us, much remains to be done. Theirs is, indeed, the greatest experimental laboratory of industrial psychology that we have found in America.

V

HEALTH AND HAPPINESS

THE Filene store in Boston has always been recognized as a great experiment station in industrial government. The machinery here is of an amazing variety. Long before industrial democracy became a fetish, Filene's had all the forms which fertile brains have been thinking out in the last year or two under that name. The representative lawmaking body of employees, the paid executive "business agent" elected by the employees, the Board of Arbitration, even the employee members of the Board of Directors—Filene's have them all and more. They had worked it all out gradually before most places had thought about starting.

Mary Smith thinks that she would like to work at Filene's. She has heard that it is a mighty good place. Inexperienced girls start to work there for a minimum wage of $9 a week, but with the commissions they say that beginners—sales girls—seldom make less than $16 or $18. Experienced sales people are paid a minimum of $15 to start—in addition to commissions. The girls who start at $9 (and they are very few nowadays, as most of them begin at $10 or $12) are assured of an automatic increase up to $15 within two years.

Then they say that they are always treated well at Filene's. You can't be imposed on by a customer or somebody above you. If a customer accuses you of short changing and you know you didn't, you can take your case to the Board of Arbitration and you are sure of a fair hearing, and sure to get justice. The department heads are pretty decent. They have to be or you will complain to the Board of Arbitration. The board is elected *solely by the employees* and is very likely, if it has had a lot of trouble from the department headed by any particular person, to tell the company they had better remove that person and put in someone else whom the girls will stand for.

These are only a few of the reasons why Mary Smith —and there are thousands of Mary Smiths in Greater Boston—wants to work at Filene's. The girls say they have awfully good times there. They have parties and plays and picnics and concerts. The three thousand employees run their own cafeteria at cost, and they have their own club rooms. If you are ambitious there is a good chance, too. The employees' own organization— The Filene Coöperative Association (F. C. A. for short)—maintains a lot of classes—courses for general culture and courses for improvement in business ability. According to the plan of the F. C. A., you are supposed to go with your group and listen to lectures from members of the store force who know all about different branches of the business. On Monday morning, or Tuesday morning, or some time when the store is not very busy, one of the teachers whom the store employs comes into your department and talks over with the whole sales force the problems that bother you and the best methods of building up sales, increasing the business or selecting goods.

If you like politics, they say you can get all you want

here. Great is the excitement when the campaign is on
for election of the president and council of the F. C. A.
and for the Board of Arbitration. You come down
early before opening time and stay after closing time.
The candidates and their lieutenants hold executive
meetings around the store. The speakers are eloquent.
So are the candy and cigars bought from a generous
campaign fund.

Mary Smith does not care particularly about politics,
but the whole thing sounds pretty good—the fun, and
everybody good-natured—and all. So she applies at
the employment office and gets a job.

Now she has become a part of the employees' organization—the F. C. A.—the "company union" as
critics might call it.

Just how much of a union is it? What does it
amount to anyway? Well, that depends on Mary
Smith—and all the other Mary Smiths in the store.
There are a great many of them—girls to whom
Filene's looks good. There are almost too many of
them, in fact, for the effective working of this same
machinery of freedom from autocratic control and
supervision. For after one Mary Smith and all the
other Mary Smiths get in, there is just as much democracy at Filene's as they themselves make—just as much
freedom from autocratic control as they are willing
and able to assert.

No, that is not true. We must not forget the Board
of Managers whose democracy has invited that of the
employees. Otherwise there would be no F. C. A., no
legislative body, no Board of Arbitration, no employee
members of the Board of Directors. These do not exist because Mary Smith and her friends asked for

them, but because the Filenes had an idea that Mary Smith and Jane Sullivan and Bill Johnson and all the others *ought* to want them and *would* be democratic if they only knew what fun it was.

How about it? What good are they getting from their machinery of "democracy"?

Take the organization—the Filene Coöperative Association. To begin with, they manage all their own "welfare work," a savings bank with a loan department; a health and accident insurance plan; a coöperative store through which they can buy food, meat, and other articles; a lunch room of their own which serves three meals a day and caters for their parties and dances; a clinic; a choral club; a musical comedy once each year; a department of athletics, and a newspaper. Everything but the clinic is supposed to be self-supporting. If anything fails to be, they go into the pockets of the company.

These activities are supervised by committees of the council and administered by the executive secretary of the F. C. A., who is paid by the store, but appointed by the president of the F. C. A. and confirmed by five-sixths of the council. Making the company foot the bill seems to be a favorite pastime of the F. C. A. They even went so far one time as to employ an expert to go over the books of the company to check up certain facts which they wanted in connection with a profit-sharing plan, and presented the bill to the company.

The legislative body for the employees is the council, which consists of twenty-four members, one member elected from each of the twelve sections of the store; the presidents of the Men's, Women's and Girls' clubs, members ex-officio, and the president, vice-president, secretary and treasurer.

Through the council, the F. C. A. exerts power to make the rules that affect the discipline or working conditions of the employees of the store. Through the council the employees make wage agreements with the company, and carry on, by means of committees, the social and other activities of the employees.

The Board of Arbitration is the strangest thing in the whole category of strange things at Filene's. A board of twelve members *consisting entirely of employees,* elected one from each section of the store, with a chairman appointed from the council by the president of the F. C. A.; it passes on all appeals affecting differences between the firm or the management and the employees—questions of dismissal, wages, position in the store, missing sales, short change, lost packages and damages to goods. *The decision of the board is final.*

The firm can hire Mary Smith, but if it keeps her two weeks it cannot fire her without a possible "come back." She has a right of appeal to the Board of Arbitration and if the majority of these twelve employees say that the firm has shown no good reason for firing her, she cannot be dismissed. On the other hand, the Board may carry its decision further than simply declaring that Mary Smith is to be retained. It may decide that the trouble was not due to the fault of Mary Smith, but of someone higher up. It may even go so far as to recommend that the firm dismiss the department head. This sometimes happens when a lot of complaints from various persons in the same department lead to the suspicion that the trouble is not with Mary Smith.

It is the Arbitration Board, in fact, which is the real efficiency committee for the firm. It is the body which discovers the weak spots and the sore spots in the store. It is the body which is the closest to the employees, the most cherished by them and the most popular for aspiring candidates at election time. Election to this board is considered a great honor. The fortunate ones who are elected take their work very seriously. They realize that they are making decisions momentous to the persons involved and to be followed as precedents for the future.

If the Board of Arbitration is unique, yet, in one other venture Filene's takes first prize. So far as we are able to find out, it was the first firm in the United States to admit non-stockholding employees, elected by the employees, to membership in the Board of Directors; and one of only three firms in the country at this writing. Four out of the eleven members are thus chosen, and two more employee members are chosen by the firm.

Filene's is a gold mine for A, who wants arguments in favor of this plan, so much debated today, provided for in the law of Massachusetts, and proposed by at least one other state legislature. It is just as much of a "find" for B, who wants arguments against the system of employee representation on the Board of Directors.

B, for example, studies the present employee membership of the Board of Directors and tells you that it is very evident that the employees take little interest in it. Not a single employee representative is a real salesman on the floor. They are all taken from the "higher-ups"; two merchandise managers, a division manager and the paid executive secretary of the F. C. A. "You see," says B, "give them a chance and they don't make the most of it. They don't trust each other and they have to turn, after all, to the high executives when it comes to managing the business."

"Why," says A, "what's the matter with you? Here you have the best argument in the world in favor of allowing the employees to select some of the members. This simply shows their good judgment. The point is that the people whom they do select are responsible to them and must come back to them for reëlection, and if the voters don't like their representatives they simply won't vote for them again. If the store force wants information and their representatives don't give it to them, it is up to them to put in representatives who will do what they want."

"But," says B, "look at the difference between the way they act about the director business and the eagerness with which they scramble for seats on the Board of Arbitration. There they have four salesgirls, one salesman, one merchandise man, one buyer, the head of the telephone girls, a girl member of the educational force of the store, a minor executive and a store detective. *There* is where their heart is—in the Board of Arbitration, not in the Board of Directors. The employees don't *want* to run the business."

"On the other hand," says A, "the firm considers this Board of Arbitration a real efficiency board. It is here that you get a lot of the skeletons in the closet—the secrets that the firm and the Board of Directors can't get at. They have to depend on the Arbitration Board to give *them* information and advice about the weak spots in the store management, and after they've had a little taste of it, these board members who engaged in such a scramble for office, become pretty well sobered. They begin to feel a heavy weight on them and to move as cautiously as if they really were on the Board of Directors."

Let it go at that. Anyhow, Filene's have the two big things that are advocated these days for labor participation in management. They have the so-called Arbitration Board, which is miscalled, for there is no representative of the employers on the board and no provision for calling in a disinterested party to arbitrate. It is elected solely by the employees and is the final authority in the store on every question affecting any or all employees. It is more than collective bargaining, or collective government, it is a Supreme Court of Employees. And, in addition, employees have four of the nine members of the Board of Directors.

How are Filene's going to be rated when the roll of industrial government is called? Have we here simply a "company union" founded by enthusiastic employers and tolerated by indifferent employees? Is the whole thing a trick to get more and better work out of the employees, or does it flow from a real desire to hasten self-government in industry? Is there any real democracy here? If you should take away the two Filenes and the other managers, could the employees keep the business going as it ought to go?

That is asking a good deal. You must remember that this is a big specialty store. A large percentage of the employees are women—girls who are young and love to dance and play and look for husbands, and women who no longer dance and play and whose first and last thought is to keep the job, in order that they may care for those who are dependent on them; all of them women who long for the beautiful things which they pass daily across the counter to those who can afford to buy them. It is no easy or brief task to stir the ambition of these women to the point where they thrill at the thought of sharing in the management of a great business.

Anyhow, do they need democracy and self-government when they have such democratic management? Efficiency here is evidently a by-product of health and happiness. But even though democracy here started from above, is not the democratic attitude of management a reflection of the democracy of the whole store? Although the Board of Arbitration has actually at times reinstated employees whose dismissal has been approved by the management, the management say now that the Board was right, and it was a good thing for them, as individuals, to be overruled by the employees collectively. They had made a mistake, and they were protected in the store against their own mistakes. Surely it would seem that almost any manager would cultivate and acquire a winning personality toward employees if they had a veto on him like that.

Further light, perhaps, may be thrown upon some of these questions by the attitude of some of the leaders in a matter which has received a great deal of attention of late, namely, the question of affiliation with national labor organizations. Several departments in the concern, including the factory, are already affiliated with national labor unions. The Filenes recognize these unions and make agreements with them. The company is apparently taking no stand on the question whether the F. C. A. shall join the Federation of Labor. It leaves the employees to settle it among themselves. Discussions are heated. The heat is not spent, however, upon the spirit and object of national unions, with which Filene employees seem to be in entire sympathy. The agreement against affiliation is entirely a local one; namely, that with their F. C. A. they can obtain more than they can obtain through any other union; that the F. C. A. is *really in advance of any union.* Affiliated with an outside union, they would be held down to its level, which is a lower level than the one which they have achieved. The problem as seen by the Filene employee is to wake up and use the power he has and not trade it off before he has discovered its value and learn to make the most of it.

If you study all the machinery of organization on paper, you may get the idea that here is Industrial Democracy personified. If you look only at the record of social activities, you may conclude that here is simply another "company union" made up of employees who are indifferent to their own real interests. You see a scattering of energy, a great deal of activity spent upon having a good time which you might think could be spent to greater advantage upon the vital problems of greater efficiency in sales and fairer distribution. But you see, also, if you make a fair analysis of the place, that in spite of distractions, there is here much greater attention given to these fundamental problems than in other places where the pursuit of happiness seems to be lacking. It seems logical that if they were a little less gay, they might accomplish more to their own interest. The only trouble with the idea is, that in other places where they are less gay, they do not seem to have accomplished as much! Whatever else one may say of the men and women at Filene's, they are a lively group and they at least have leaders who are far more alive to their own interests than are the average sales people. Of the employers it is pretty safe to say that while health and happiness of the employees is with them a great object, they are intensely interested in the development of self-government in the store.

VI

GOVERNMENT BY IMAGINATION

DENNISON for the Dennisons! Not the Dennison Family, but the Dennison Workers. Every stockholder, every director, every officer of the Dennison Manufacturing Company, Framingham, Mass., is an actual, active employee of the company. There are other stockholders—preferred stockholders—but they have no voting power.

Seventy-five years ago the great-grandfather of the Dennison family began to make paper boxes in his kitchen. A knife, a scissors, a pot of paste, a slab of wood, were his factory.

His jewelry boxes were in great demand. He added other paper products. Today the company manufactures 10,000 separate articles, sends its products to all parts of the country and many parts of the world, sells millions of tags and baggage checks to large railway companies, millions of Christmas cards to small retailers.

A splendid organization, several valuable patents, a few monopolies, big dividends, the period of risk and development has passed and the company is as safe as any industrial investment may be.

But prosperity brought its perils. There were certain stockholders who saw the Dennison industry merely as a means to an end, the end being profits and

58

then some more profits, with the absentee owners in the saddle in unchallenged enjoyment of money and power.

The president of the company, himself a Dennison, saw another vision. He saw the Dennison equipment and the Dennison workers as something more than engines for turning out more profits. He saw them also as instruments for manufacturing paper boxes and tags, and paper napkins and 10,000 like articles, and sell them to railroads and people who use them up in making the world richer. He determined that while he had control he would fix it up so that those who looked at the industry in his own broad-minded fashion should always keep control. And that is how there came to be government by imagination.

Who is it that creates the profits of the Dennison Manufacturing Company? It certainly is not the absentee stockholders. The original Dennison evidently had a creative imagination. His imagination was used in making boxes that nobody ever thought of before, and creating markets that nobody ever imagined could be created.

Who, then, are the real descendants of the original Dennison? Shall we say they are the workers? The original Dennison was a worker. But it was not his work that built up this magnificent business—this going concern that lives on fifty years after he died. It was his creative imagination. He *hired* the workers and they did what he told them to do, after his imagination had told *him* what to do and how to do it.

The real descendants of the original Dennison are those of the 3,000 workers who work primarily with creative imagination. It is by imagination that the Dennison Company has developed 10,000 separate ar-

ticles, and it will be imagination that will make and sell
the innumerable new articles and the better old ones
that it must make and sell if the concern is to keep going another seventy-five years.

If not all of these three thousand work with imagination how shall we discover those who do? Shall we
appoint a committee and give it power to pick and
choose? No, that will leave too much room for favoritism. Favoritism will discourage imagination.

An automatic method of choosing was first sought
by means of the pay envelope and the length of service
record. Men who stick and rise would seem to have
imagination. So $1,200 a year and seven years' service
were hit upon as the boundary line where imagination
crosses over. Then came the war and the unstable
dollar, and a change seemed desirable. Of the change
finally adopted, a company booklet says:

Eventually the tremendous changes in the value of the
dollar, and more especially the irregular application of
these changes among various classes of employees, entirely destroyed the salary line as a true dividing line between those of the employees whose effects upon profits were
important and appreciable and those whose effects upon our
net profits account were remote and heavily conditioned by
the policies of the management. Principal employees are
now limited to those who have had five years or more of
service and whose position with the company requires the
exercise of managing ability and control over methods of
manufacturing and marketing, such as any executive, department head, principal foreman, chief clerk, branch manager, or principal salesman; or whose work shows the use
of a high degree of imagination, tact or business judgment
—those qualities upon which we believe the constant earning of profits to depend. To the directors is left the application of this rule, but the industrial partnership stockholders

may from year to year pass votes further defining the directors' methods of choosing.

In 1913 there were 167 principal employees. In 1919 the number had risen to 320, about one-ninth of the total force. One-ninth are employees with creative imagination. They are the real industrial descendants of the great-grandfather of the Dennisons. It is they who "produce" the profits, and keep the concern going. The other eight-ninths produce wages.

Profits are in the future. It requires imagination to see them. Wages are paid every week in cash. These are paid for jobs which need but little imagination. Many of the employees are girls whose industrial life is soon over—two or three years in the factory after schooling time is past, in which to put by something for family or for self. Their imagination is more bound up with anticipations of romance than devoted to solving the perplexities of production.

For them, and all the others whom it has been thought advisable to keep on the other side of the industrial partnership line, weekly wages are deemed the accurate measure of their value to the company. They are paid mostly by the piece. Their performance can be seen and measured as they go along. Theirs is not the field of the creative imagination, of profit creation, nor should theirs be the reward.

Having discovered the one-ninth whose imagination creates the unseen profits, how shall they be put in control of the profits which they expect to create?

The absentees own the property. The absentees simply must be bought off. How much will they take to get out and in what currency will they accept payment?

A simple matter, once it has been done. But it was a big imagination that conceived it and did it.

Induce the absentees to turn over their common stock *with* voting power to the imaginative workers and accept preferred stock *without* voting power. Clever enough. But the imaginative workers had to pay. They paid $4,500,000 in preferred stock at 8 per cent —a permanent charge on the business of $360,000 a year, where the dividends on the common stock had been running something like $200,000 to $250,000.

The preferred stock is doubly secure. If the workers fail to pay that full $360,000 a year for a period of four years, then the preferred stock automatically gets back its voting power and the absentee owners step into control. The preferred stockholders are virtually bondholders but are saved the trouble of legal foreclosure if interest is defaulted.

Now about the common stock. They call it "industrial partnership stock." Where does it come from? By March, 1913, 15,122 shares had been issued to the 167 principal employees. The issue amounted to about one-third of the total salary-roll of the principal employees. Thirty-three and one-third per cent profit for imagination!

But it was not cash, of course. It was just that amount of profits put back into the machinery and buildings and business. In 1919, thirty thousand shares of industrial partnership stock were issued—45 per cent of the payroll of 320 principal employees—all of it going back into the business. A good depreciation account and several reserve funds have been built up for lean years and emergencies.

Besides, the industrial partnership stock has been getting dividends in cash—as high as 15 per cent in 1919. This dividend must always amount to at least five per cent in cash before any additional stock can be issued.

Finally, another clever thing—in fact the heart of the whole thing—an industrial partner cannot sell, or give away, or bequeath, or even take away his industrial partnership stock, for every share of it is a reward for the continual exercise of creative imagination on the job in the interest of an ever-expanding and improving Dennison industry. Not the investment it represents but its conferring of power on one who has been selected to help keep alight the Dennison imagination, this is the real significance of a share of industrial partnership stock.

If an individual partner severs his connections with the concern the reward for the use of imagination in the past is, of course, made secure. The company may pay immediately for his stock either at par or cash or by the issuance of a second preferred stock of equal face value which can be sold, given away, bequeathed, and taken away, but which *has no voting power*. On some other Dennison worker will descend in time the mantle of power as a reward for imagination, which this new absorbed industrial partnership stock used to hold.

That is the reason why every member of the board of directors is a worker.

The president of the board is president of the company. The vice-president exercises general supervision over the retail stores. The treasurer watches over manufacturing, warehousing, and shipping. The other members of the board are in charge, respectively, of foreign sales, purchasing and merchandizing, and selling personnel.

Not even a banker, or financier, or dummy director, or absentee of any kind on the board! All of them workers with the Dennison imagination!

What does it mean for the 320 industrial partners? Take an illustration: Suppose John Doe is head of a department with $4,000 salary. Here is what it would have meant for him during the past three years, even though his salary had not been increased:

Year	Salary	I. P. Stock Issued % of Salary	Amt.	Total Stk. held before
1916	$4,000	25%	$1,000	.....
1917	4,000	75%	3,000	$1,000
1918	4,000	30%	1,333	4,000
1919	4,000	45%	1,800	5,333

	Dividends on previously held stock	Total Income
1916	none	$4,000
1917	(10%) $100	4,100
1918	(10%) 400	4,400
1919	(15%) 800	4,800

Suppose he were to remain in the service of the company for another ten years even without an increase in salary, and that each year the stock dividend should amount to only 25 per cent of his salary, which is the smallest issue to date, and that the dividends on already issued stock would amount to only 10 per cent, the situation of John Doe in 1929 would be like this:

Salary	I. P. Stock Issued % of salary	Amount	Total I. P. Stock Earn- ing Dividends
$4,000	25%	$1,000	$16,133
	Dividends on stock (10%) $1,613	Total Income $5,613	

At the end of seven more years, a total service of not more than twenty-seven years, John Doe would hold industrial partnership stock to the amount of $23,133. Should he at that time decide to leave the employ of the company his income on the second preferred stock taken in exchange would amount to something over $1,600 per year. Thus, even though he had saved not a penny of his salary or dividends in all his years of service, John Doe would be assured an income on which to retire.

Surely this looks promising for the workers with imagination! No absentee can ever get control if they continue to make the profits. The control is secure against the speculation of the manipulator, the financier.

But how about the 2,700 wage workers? Is it not just as bad to be governed by industrial imagination in the shop as by financial imagination on Wall Street? Is it quite fair, after all, or even wise, to reward imagination for creative plans, and offer no incentive for extra effort, elimination of waste and for coöperation on the part of ordinary wage workers?

The Dennison management faced this question frankly. The answer is two-fold.

The Dennison Company has been an outstanding pioneer in regularizing employment. In 1919 they had set aside $100,000 as a starter for "unemployment insurance," thereby making an important beginning in the direction of making the Dennison workers' future secure.

The management recognized that we live for the present as well as the future, that we like to see the ounces of energy which we are expending transform themselves visibly into a reward which makes possible a higher standard of comfort. So they asked the 2,700 workers to propose something. The 2,700 appointed a committee of sixty. This committee formulated a plan. They submitted this plan to the management. Details were worked out and the following scheme determined.

Hereafter, instead of all the net profits above what are necessary to satisfy the First Preferred Stock, going to the Principal Employees, they are to be divided. One-third of the total fund to be distributed is set aside as the Employees' Industrial Partnership fund; the remaining two-thirds goes to the Principal Employees.

Every employee, other than a principal employee, actually employed in the plant, who has had at least two years' continuous service prior to January 1 of any year in which profits are shared shall participate. Resignation or discharge from the company terminates all rights as an Employee Industrial Partner. The worker may be reinstated upon re-entering the service of the company, but loses credit for the years of service prior to his separation.

The basis of distribution is simple. It recognizes no differences in kind of service, department or rank,

other than the differences already reflected in regular
wages. The workers are all classified into six groups,
based purely on length of service. Thus:

Group 1—Less than 5 yrs............. 10 points
Group 2—5 yrs. to 10 yrs. .... 12 points
Group 3—10 yrs. to 15 yrs. .... 15 points
Group 4—15 yrs. to 20 yrs. .... 18 points
Group 5—20 yrs. to 25 yrs. .... 21 points
Group 6—25 yrs. and over............. 24 points

The individual member of each group is each to receive a uniform sum which bears the ratio to sums
received by individual members of each of the other
groups as indicated by the number of points for each
group.

Thus, let us suppose there are twelve workers in
Group 1, ten in 2, eight in 3, six in 4, four in 5, and
two in 6. The total fund available for distribution
is $36,000, of which the workers get one-third, or
$12,000.

Group	No. of Workers	Point Index	Total points for the group
1	12	10	120
2	10	12	120
3	8	15	120
4	6	18	108
5	4	21	84
6	2	24	48
Total			600

Since the total share is $12,000 and the total points is
600, the share per point is twenty dollars, and the

share of each worker in the several groups would be
$20.00 per point, or as follows:

Group	Share for each member of group
1	$200
2	240
3	300
4	360
5	420
6	480

The fund is then to be distributed in the form, not
of cash, but of non-transferable, non-voting stock,
known as "Dennison Employees Industrial Partnership Stock" with par value of ten dollars. Amounts
of less than ten dollars are to be distributed in cash.

Thus each member of the above "group one" would
receive twenty shares of stock, each member of "group
two" would receive twenty-four shares, and so on. If
the fund had been such as to amount to $20.50 per
point, each member of group one would receive twenty
shares of stock and five dollars in cash, and members
of the other groups in proportion.

This stock is held by the workers only so long as
employed, drawing the same rate of dividends as the
original Industrial Partnership Stock. If the worker
should leave the company he is given either cash at
par for the stock, or it is converted into Second Preferred Stock at the rate of ten shares to one, since
the latter has a par value of one hundred dollars.

The administration of the fund and its apportion-
ment is democratic, being in charge of a committee
consisting of the chairman of the General Works Committee on Operation, in which the President of the

Company sits for these cases only, and its decision is final.

It is significant that this Employees' Industrial Partnership Stock is non-voting. Thus while one-third of all common stock issues go to the lower grade workers, the control of the company remains in the hands of the "imagination" group of executives; subject to such influence as is exerted by the workers' committees in the ordinary course of affairs.

However, the workers are rewarded for extra effort, for elimination of waste, and superior coöperation. They get their share of the surplus earnings—the way to participation in control is open to them through promotion within the company. It may be that in time they will develop, through exercise of their opportunities and increased interest in the business, the qualities which will fit them for more active participation in the management.

VII

COÖPERATIVE SPEEDING-UP

The Packard Piano Company had won the strike in 1912. But the workers who came back were sullen, production was low, harmony gone. In the midst of this distressing situation the president of the company, Albert S. Bond, chanced to hear John Leitch deliver a lecture on industrial democracy. Leitch is an industrial evangelist. He converted Mr. Bond. Bond saw the error of his ways. He had been a salesman but he had not applied the psychology of salesmanship to his employees. He had been "driving" them, not "selling" them the Packard piano. Forthwith he changed his character and attitude toward labor. He accepted at once the four corner stones of Leitch's Industrial Democracy—Justice, Coöperation, Economy, Energy and the capstone, Service.

Next he induced Leitch to come over and convert his workmen. Mass meetings were held on company time. At first the men were cold and skeptical. They wondered what the management was trying to "put over." But after a few meetings they, too, were converted. When the psychological hour arrived, Leitch offered his resolution and it was adopted:

"We, the employees, officers and directors of the Packard Piano Company, recognizing that Justice is the greatest good and Injustice the greatest evil, do hereby lay, and sub-

70

scribe to, as the first Corner Stone of our Policy, this greatest of all good."

We talked with Mr. Bond and thirty or more employees. They have unbounded faith in Industrial Democracy. They speak the common language of Justice. The firm that makes the best men will make the best pianos. The great end of Justice is "to construct broader character as individuals," as the foundation of "broader commerce as an institution."

Coöperation was the second corner stone laid by John Leitch. Coöperation is the way to obtain Justice. In the other Leitch plants which we visited we found the whole machinery of representative democracy according to the Constitution of the United States—a Cabinet, a Senate, a House of Representatives. But the Packard Company did not find it necessary to have representative bodies for a force of less than 300. So everybody attends the meetings.

In the beginning they held a meeting every week; now about once a month. Factory problems are discussed and decided by the Committee of the Whole. If an investigation is necessary, a special committee of five, three elected by the employees and two appointed by the management, makes the investigation and report to the next meeting.

The factory was hard hit in 1914, following the outbreak of the World War. A cabinet maker arose in the Committee of the Whole and suggested that they work three days a week and spread the unemployment over the entire force instead of concentrating it. The foremen volunteered to reduce their own salaries twenty-five per cent. The Committee of the Whole agreed to operate three days a week, but the management was able to assure them four days.

A backmaker is stated to have told how coöperation worked in his department. "When I started in this work," he said, "it took two men ten hours to make six backs. That's the same as one man working ten hours to make three backs—or a back every three and a third hours. Now one man can complete a back in an hour, and the work is much easier than it ever was in the past. How did we do it? Well, it was because the Packard Piano Policy got us to do it. The men at the head said to us, 'Now, boys, we all want to do our best, and sometimes doing our best doesn't mean working our heads off. The easier our work becomes, the better specialists we become—so try to see if there aren't better ways of doing things.' And what I have told you about this department shows what coöperation can do."

While we sat in the president's office, several workers came to the door, which is kept open without any sign, "Private." The workers halted when they saw us. In every case Mr. Bond excused himself and gave priority to the workers. These interviews cover every subject —shop problems, domestic, financial problems. It is the latter that give to the president his opportunity to win the confidence of the workers.

Economy is the third corner-stone. The "Collective Economy Dividend" is John Leitch's inducement to economy. "I take the cost of a unit of production in the period preceding the introduction of Industrial Democracy," says Leitch, "and compare that cost with results after Democracy has gone into effect. If there is a saving, then one-half that aggregate saving is the amount of the economy dividend for the period and is paid to the men as an added percentage to wages."

In the Packard Piano Company it is simplified as follows: Three hundred pianos a month are the standard. If the factory turns out 300 pianos, the employees get 5 per cent dividend added to their wages, and 2½ per cent additional for every 25 in excess of 300. The dividend is paid the first pay day in the following month. Every day the bulletin board announces the number of pianos for the day before and the number up to that day for the month. This bulletin board is the focus of every eager eye in the factory. It tells them whether they are approaching or losing that cooperative economy dividend. Individually they are paid piece-rates. Collectively they get this added collective piece-rate.

The economy dividend is really the superstructure that holds together the three corner-stones, Coöperation, Economy, Energy. It works wonders. During three months in the fall of 1913, an average of 242 employees, working ten hours a day, turned out 746 pianos. For the corresponding months in 1919, an average of 235 employees, working eight hours a day, turned out 1,100 pianos. The increase in efficiency amounts to 45 per cent on the basis of plant output, and reduces overhead proportionately, while the increase in efficiency is 86 per cent on the basis of workman's output per hour, and increases wages more than proportionately. The average rate of wages per hour, for the same periods, advanced from 28 cents to 58 cents, an increase of 106 per cent, due entirely to increased output and economy dividend.

See how it works. Every employee is directly interested in the efficiency of his fellow-worker. Absenteeism cuts down the economy dividend. Slow work cuts it down. Wasteful work cuts it down. Careless shop planning and routing of materials and pianos through the factory cuts it down. A dozen placards on the walls tell us "200 scientific managers in this factory." Every employee is a scientific manager. It was an efficiency engineer brought in from the outside, whose scientific time and motion studies provoked the strike of 1912. That outside expert is gone, but industrial democracy and the economy dividend filled the workers in the shop with the spirit of scientific management. The evidence of it is everywhere. Not long after the efficiency engineer left the plant, they had reduced the hours to nine. Five months later they came down to eight, and on each reduction in hours production was increased.

Furthermore, the corner-stones, Justice and Coöperation, prevent the piece-rate from being cut arbitrarily. Every worker is secure in earning as much as he can at piece-rates, for he knows that the rate will not be cut without his consent. The president cited one instance of a voluntary cut in the piece-rate from 42 cents to 11 cents. The workers could earn more at the new rate than formerly at the old rate.

The foreman is no longer a "boss." He is one of the coöperators. Here is where the other corner-stones, Economy and Energy, come in. Piece-rates fixed by coöperation on the principles of Justice; economy dividend added to piece-rates on the principles of Economy and Energy—this is the greatest combination of inducements to output that we have found anywhere, measured by results. In no place have we found the men working with greater initiative, energy and speed. They are completely absorbed in their work. Courteous, willing to talk with visitors, proud of both their principles of democracy and of their hard, speedy work, they keep on working while they talk. No boss stands over them; no outsider times their motions; they speed themselves up coöperatively.

This is the only place we found where pure efficiency outran the increased cost of living. In other places piece-rates have been advanced. Here they have, in some cases, been reduced, in others equalized, but not generally advanced; yet their earnings per hour, the correct unit of efficiency, have increased 106 per cent, while their earnings per day have increased 66 per cent. Assuming that the increase in cost of living had been 80 per cent in 1919, the workers' daily earnings indeed had not kept up with the cost of living, but they had swallowed the difference in the increased leisure per day.

This comes about in two ways, partly by greater output per individual at the same or even lower piece-rates, and partly by the economy dividend, or collective piece-rate, added on to their individual earnings. It is not increased rates of pay, but increased output per man that has increased their earnings.

The workers say that they work hard. But with it they keep up their enthusiasm and devotion to Industrial Democracy. The company prides itself on what an old cabinet worker said who had worked there forty years, "Nobody ever cheats on work around here. I can tell you that every one of the boys likes to do his best, and why shouldn't he?" During the war the company obtained a contract for making airplane propellers. The race with Ludendorf was close, and the government was driven to getting machines regardless of cost. The Packard Company was compelled to pay war wages to airplane workers brought in from the outside. Trade unionists twitted the Packard Family about the wage differential under the same roof—war wages on airplanes, peace wages on pianos. But never a ripple on the placid stream! Justice, Energy, and Coöperation prevailed over any resentment against wage inequality.

That the profits of the company have greatly increased is evident. Even without an increase in price to the consumer the economy-dividend has added its share to profits as well as wages, against which should, of course, be set the increased prices of raw material. The economy-dividend has the further advantage that it does away with any necessity of letting the workers in to the financial affairs or profits of the company. It is not profit-sharing; it is economy-sharing.

Lastly the capstone of industrial democracy is Service. In a way each worker can see his contribution to the music of the world, as the growing piano moves along through the factory. "Quality shall always be the first element of our service, and quantity shall ever be the second consideration." Each worker is an inspector of his own and the work of others. At the very last, before the instrument leaves the factory, the highly skilled piano tuners epitomize the motto of the business: "If there is no harmony in the factory, there will be none in the piano."

VIII

"INDUSTRIAL DEMOCRACY"

"WE took as a sample the United States government, which, having been successfully established and carried out for over 140 years, seemed like a pretty fair guide to go by."

The Cabinet and Senate hold their places by virtue of their positions in the business. The Cabinet is composed of the chief executives of the company; the Senate of the foremen and heads of departments. The House of Representatives is the only elected body, elected by the employees by secret ballot, approximately one representative to every 30 workers. The only qualifications for membership in the House are ability to speak and understand the English language, employment in the works for at least one year, and "on the level."

The United States government has no provision for collective bargaining. When the Demuth House of Representatives began to talk about wages the Cabinet replied that they could increase their wages by increasing production, since increased production would increase the collective-economy-dividend.

John Leitch had not worked out an accounting system to back up his collective-economy-dividend. The Company did not know for any month just what the increase in efficiency or collective savings had been,

and was obliged to approximate the amount every two
weeks. The employees finally detected this defect and
lost their zeal for speeding up. But, at first, it worked.
The first employees' dividend was 6½ per cent. As
high as 17½ per cent was paid. Contests were worked
up between departments, the prize being a large American flag. A department winning the highest efficiency
honors the third time in succession was dined by the
other departments. The losing departments began to
put pressure on their loafers and slackers. A committee was appointed by the House to work out a penal
code for careless, tardy and shirking workers. "You
are stealing my dividends," said the worker to the
shirker. The latter were gradually squeezed out.

Yet the Company, at the end of two years, could not
say definitely whether or not Industrial Democracy had
reduced the costs of production, although convinced
that under the old system they would have had a much
more rapidly rising scale of wages and the other difficulties suffered by other firms.

No plan of industrial government that we have found
has accomplished more in the way of increasing the
output than the John Leitch plan of Industrial Democracy and collective-economy-dividend. We saw in the
Packard Piano Company that it had almost doubled
the efficiency of the workers. But the limit had apparently been reached at Demuth's in the summer of 1919
when it had added something less than 50 per cent to
wages.

Yet the cost of living had gone up 80 per cent.

The workers at Demuth's could see about them in
Brooklyn and New York that other workers had increased their wages 80 per cent, even 100 per cent,

without increasing their efficiency and without Industrial Democracy. Somebody in the House of Representatives suggested an increase without waiting for a further increase in the economy-dividend.

But the remarkable success of Industrial Democracy smothered the suggestion. About that time the Company printed a statement of one of the representatives elected by the workers. He said,

"I have seen Industrial Democracy in operation at this factory for the past two years, and the main reason I am for it, heart and soul, is because I know that through it I can always get a square deal.

"When a man in my department has a grievance, he comes to me and tells me about it and he knows that I will take the question up at the next meeting of the House of Representatives, and consequently the foremen in the Senate and the 'Bosses' in the Cabinet will know about it. They will act on it one way or another and my experience has been that every question has been settled fairly.

"Before we had Industrial Democracy a man with any cause for dissatisfaction would most likely keep it to himself or tell the other workers about it. Perhaps the manager would be too busy to listen to him, so he would nurse his grievance and very likely he would quit. Industrial Democracy prevents just such little troubles before they get big.

"Nowadays at the plant you never hear a foreman urging the men to get on the job. There is no need for it. We all know that by doing our best all the time we are increasing our own dividends. Now whenever a man 'knocks off' early, comes in late or takes a holiday, it is the other men and women workers whose dividends he is lowering. Before Industrial Democracy was put into effect, it was every man for himself; now, it is all for one and one for all. I have been in this shop for twenty years and I have never seen the desire to coöperate with the other departments and help the other fellow out so strong as it is now.

"Years ago if a worker had a grudge against the foreman he would probably lay down on the job whenever he thought he wasn't being watched; but that is a thing of the past, for whatever complaints a man has are now always quickly settled in a way satisfactory to everybody.

"And another thing. Industrial Democracy has proven that some of our men had stored up in their minds ideas for new machinery and other labor saving devices; but they kept these plans to themselves because they were not sure of their reception by the management. Now, a man with a good idea knows that not only will his suggestion be welcome, but that if practicable it will be rewarded. In our plant today, labor and time saving machinery invented by the men is lowering the costs, increasing production, and thus earning dividends.

"Industrial Democracy has given us our say in the management of the shop; it has reduced our working hours per week from 53 to 48; it has given us insurance; it has given us a lunch room where we can get good meals for twenty cents; it has made this shop a better place to work in; it is teaching English to our foreigners and helping them to become Americans; it has taught us that the firm has troubles and worries just the same as we have, and that by working and coöperating together, we all benefit.

"That is what I think of Industrial Democracy as I see it at the Demuth plant and I think that all of the nine hundred workers here agree with me."

This was in the spring of 1919. Each one of the four cornerstones and the capstone of Leitch's Industrial Democracy—Justice, Coöperation, Economy, Energy and Service—apparently was solid and in its place. But wages were not keeping up with the cost of living.

Really, it was too much to expect. If every factory and firm in the United States had adopted Industrial Democracy and doubled its output, prices would still have gone up, if the world's supply of gold, paper money, and credit instruments had more than doubled. We know that all of them did not adopt Industrial Democracy nor double their output, and so, much less than double the supply of money and credit was needed to double the prices.

Industrial Democracy at Demuth's might have sailed triumphant, had John Leitch grasped the currency situation. As it was, when some one suggested an increase of wages, he only answered the House of Representatives in effect: "See what you have already done. You have increased your earnings 50 per cent and reduced your hours from 53 to 48! Industrial Democracy is no longer an experiment. You have it in your own power to increase your earnings 70, 80 and 100 per cent. And see the service you have rendered to Society. You have increased earnings 50 per cent but Society is not compelled to pay any more for smoking pipes on that account. The labor-cost of a pipe has not increased. Keep it up. Raise your wages 100 per cent, but do not force us to raise the price of pipes."

The House of Representatives could not answer this appeal. The Representatives were silenced. Democracy was a success, and they knew it. But, somehow, democracy was not keeping pace with the cost of living. Other places without democracy were keeping pace. It was puzzling. Other places were doing even better. In the clothing trades, immigrants like themselves, Jews, Poles, Lithuanians and a dozen nationalities, had gained 44 hours a week, and much more than 50 per cent increase in earnings.

The acquiescence of the House was bringing it into discredit. Representatives were taunted. They began to drop out of the meetings. Mistakes had been made.

In 1918 twenty-five men in a certain department desired an increase in wages. An outsider agitator was urging them to strike, but they submitted their case to the House. A committee of the House investigated. It denounced the twenty-five, charging that they were "absolutely unfair in their demands." The House accepted the report. The company published it as a triumph of "Industrial Democracy." It was really a "handle" for the trade union organizer.

While the House was dormant on the wage question, the union organizers were at work. The union promised action and results. Workers began transferring their allegiance to the Smoking-Pipe Workers' Union, not affiliated with the American Federation of Labor. The House was spurred to action. This time it was the 44-hour week. The spokesman of the company in the House denounced it as Bolshevism and gave high praise to the American Federation of Labor and Samuel Gompers, who, he said, stood for the American 48-hour week. The "Bolshevists" were voted down.

But this did not end the discussion. The House again broke silence and demanded both the 44-hour week and 20 per cent advance in wages.

The company came forward with a compromise. They would grant the 44 hours. By Economy, Cooperation and Efficiency, as much could be produced in 44 hours as in 48 hours. Former reductions in hours had actually increased the output. So would this.

But the 20 per cent increase in piece-rates would compel the company to increase the price of pipes to Society and this was contrary to the capstone, Service. Besides, Society would buy less pipes. This meant less work. This meant unemployment and less earnings. No. The employees must earn their increase in wages by greater production and thus maintain the capstone, Service.

A deadlock followed. The union gained. Industrial Democracy was set aside. The strike began. The company countered with a lockout. The union came to the aid of the strikers with strike benefits. Then, after six or seven weeks, the other companies ordered their employees to stop support of the Demuth workers. Then the general strike.

The Demuth Company resumed after two weeks of lockout. Many of the old workers returned. The union claimed that one-third had quit for good. The company claimed that it had eliminated the undesirable element.

Industrial Democracy was resumed, with few changes. The minutes of the meetings are now posted in the shop. Each employee is given a copy of the plan and required to sign a pledge to abide by and uphold Industrial Democracy. No person not speaking English and not a citizen, by fact or declaration, is employed. A 12½ per cent increase in wages is granted.

It is no reproach on Industrial Democracy that it should have failed to cope with the jumping cost of living. Democracy, autocracy, collective bargaining, all of them fail, when the dollar runs amuck. We visited John Leuch. He had so many calls from employers that he could not listen to our query. He referred us to his book. He is not an institution. He cannot delegate his methods to a staff of subordinates. He must go in person. His is the heart-to-heart method—the method of the industrial revivalist—the John the Baptist of Industry. He converts first the employer in person, then the employees in mass. He stays with them at least one day a week. Hence his clientele is limited.

For many years he went from job to job, on his own wages, seeking an answer to his question. He saw "employees come and go, live and die, without a thought on the part of employers as to their welfare." He saw "employees show an equal lack of interest in the employers, and demonstrated their disinterestedness by pointedly doing just as little as they possibly could for their wages." He could find "no relation between work and wages. The employer paid the lowest wage at which he could get men, and the worker gave the smallest return which he could possibly give and still get the highest wages." Inside each business concern he found "ruinous competition between labor and capital—the one to get more, the other to give less." "Out of that first-hand investigation," he goes on, "pursued without theories and without a knowledge of philosophy, came a gradual comprehension that there could be a better way. Seeking the why and the how led me into philosophy—into the causes behind what we call results—and step by step unfolded that which I now call Industrial Democracy."

At last he found his opportunity. He was superintendent of a small plant, without a labor union. He held mass meetings. They "talked over the management of the factory, better ways of doing work, etc."

It worked. His "fundamental ideas were right." "The men liked the meetings; they liked the chance to air their troubles, to have it out over anything that did not satisfy them; and gradually it dawned on me that this desire to talk and to have a say in things was the bubbling to the surface of the innate spirit of democracy—of the desire which is in almost every man to have a voice in his own destiny and a means for self-expression. Analyzing my personal work, I found that what I had really done was to capitalize fair play— to sell the management to the men, to convince them that their meetings were of importance and not merely opportunities to blow off steam."

The next quest was to find a method of industrial organization that would make these meetings a fixed part of the business. So far Industrial Democracy was only "a state of mind." It must have a body and a constitution. This was the final discovery. "The organization of any factory or other business institution into a little democratic state, with a representative government which shall have both its legislative and executive phases." There was but one such model—the Constitution of the United States. So he seized upon it. "I am taking as settled without argument," he exclaimed, "that American principles of democracy are right and then making application of these principles to the governing of a factory."

So it came about that Industrial Democracy is modeled on the Constitution of the United States. It has its Cabinet—the President and Chiefs of the Business; its Senate—the foremen and heads of departments; its House of Representatives—the workers elected by their fellow-workers on a basis of equal suffrage in each department or section of the shop.

Thus Industrial Democracy is the repetition of Political Democracy—with two important exceptions—

the President and Senate are not elected by the people. Yet, such as it was it grew many years in the mind of John Leitch, and finally, when he came out of the wilderness of competition, he had it full ready to proclaim, "The Kingdom of Democracy is at Hand." Some of the seed fell upon stony places and sprang up but withered away, because the employer saw only another device to put something over on his workers. Some fell into good ground and brought forth justice and efficiency because the employer's heart was reached and he was completely converted. And some fell among thorns; and the high cost of living sprang up and choked them.

IX

FROM POLITICAL TO INDUSTRIAL GOVERNMENT

In 1914 John Leitch "sold" the idea of "Industrial Democracy" to the management and employees of the Printz-Biederman Company, Cleveland, Ohio. The shop organization has had all the features of the Leitch system: A senate, a house of representatives, a cabinet, and a collective economy dividend.

In his book [1] Leitch assumed "as settled without argument that American principles of democracy are right," and made "application of these principles to the government of a factory." He defined industrial democracy as "the organization of any factory or other business institution into a little democratic state, with a representative government which shall have both its legislative and executive phases." An examination of the Leitch plan, however, reveals considerable differences between it and the United States Government. The latter is made up of representatives from one body —the citizens of the Republic. Representatives, Senators, President, all come from and represent the same great constituency, while in industry there are capital and labor to be represented. Leitch met this dualism by giving the employees a house of representatives and by giving the management a Senate and cabinet.

[1] Leitch, John. "Man to Man." The story of Industrial Democracy. New York, 1919, 249 pp.

The Government of the United States was designed
to promote deliberation and to prevent quick action.
Each house of legislation acts as a check upon the
other; each department of Government acts as a check
upon another department; so that our Government has
been characterized as a system of checks and balances.
Industry, on the other hand, must have action—prompt
action—and output. The question arises: Can a form
of government that "balances" authority and pro-
motes deliberation rather than action be appropriated
for industry with its need of prompt settlement of
disputed questions?

Leitch simply added a "legislative" to the already
existing "executive" phase of shop government. As
regards the popular branch of the organization, legislation becomes the major problem, the working out of
which involves two things: (a) Evolving a method
of legislation, and (b) creating a form of government
suited to that method.

The tense labor situation that began with the spring
of 1918 and held throughout 1919 brought to this shop
its critical period and forced a solution of these problems. There arose in acute form the questions of
wages and hours, of the form of government, of methods of adjusting grievances, besides a multitude of
grievances covering every imaginable phase of the
bonus question. The machinery for adjusting grievances was clumsy and at this time clogged up; for up
to this time grievances had to be acted upon by the
house, passed on to the senate, and then on to the cabinet before a settlement could be effected. If the senate refused to concur, there followed a delay while the
differences between the two houses were being ironed

out. It was a slow process at best, and this was a time that brooked no delays. Both sides recognized that "industrial democracy" had to be speeded up. When, therefore, a suggestion was made to the house, April 16, 1918, that a wage rate committee be selected and given full power to take up with the management directly complaints about wage and bonus payments and settle them, it found a ready response, and at a special meeting the next day the house agreed to create such a committee. A wage-rate committee, consisting of one member from each department, was then made one of the permanent committees of the house.

All the accumulated complaints were turned over to the new committee. For one whole year the committee busied itself investigating individual cases. The company was anxious to adjust these complaints satisfactorily to the employees and willingly coöperated to that end. But it proved a never-ending job, for while the committee was investigating and settling one case there was another case—sometimes two or three cases —added to the waiting list. The year's experience taught the committee that the way to handle a multitude of individual cases is to classify them and then make regulations for each class.

HIGH-COST-OF-LIVING BONUS CONVERTED INTO WAGE INCREASE

In January, 1918, the management introduced a high-cost-of-living bonus, which was intended to be the means of keeping wages in step with the cost of living. The amount of this bonus, which was to be varied from month to month on the basis of Bradstreet's index number, was put into a separate envelope so that employees would not confuse it with their regular wages. This seems to have complicated the bonus system. The production bonus was the successor of the old collective economy dividend, which was a group incentive plan. At this time there were four classes of production bonuses, based upon the per cent of the "standard time" used in completing the task. Thus, for example, employees who performed a given task in from 130 to 115 per cent of the standard time were put in class 1; from 115 to 100 per cent of standard time, in class 2; from 100 to 85 per cent, in class 3; 85 per cent and lower, in class 4. The house had voted its approval of the high-cost-of-living bonus, but it made the bonus system top heavy. The dissatisfaction which developed soon crystallized into a demand for converting the bonus into a wage increase.

On July 30, 1918, the wage-rate committee proposed to the management that a 12 per cent increase in wages be substituted for the high-cost-of-living bonus. At the following meeting of the house a representative of the company appeared to explain why this additional bonus had been granted instead of an increase in wages. The house took no action at this meeting, as it is the policy of each side to try first to come to an understanding with the other side before taking action, but at the next meeting a bill was passed providing for the wage increase. The house accompanied this bill with a statement of its intention to ask for wage increases from time to time to correspond to the rising cost of living. The senate and cabinet concurred in the action of the house.

RESULT OF ONE TEST OF INDUSTRIAL DEMOCRACY

During the summer of 1918 the International Ladies' Garment Workers established their union in many factories of the city. The union organizers look with no more favor upon Leitch's "industrial democracy" than upon the "Rockefeller plan." They tried to organize this factory along with the others. They engaged the employees in conversation and asked them all kinds of questions about their "industrial democracy," their bonuses, and their wages. When an employee mentioned his wage rates, the organizer would tell him about the rates in New York and would compare in dollars and cents the value to the worker of "industrial democracy" and the union. If an employee got tangled up in trying to explain his bonus system, the organizer "kidded" him about it, and wondered if he wouldn't like to have a system he could understand. The union won but very few sympathizers, but among these was a member of the house. There were a number of questions pending between the employees and the firm, and the union activity helped bring them to a focus. There had to be action, and a joint discussion of the situation took place before the house.

The spokesman for the employees reminded the management of the constantly rising cost of living and the hardships it was imposing upon the workers. The workers, he continued, not only had to support themselves and families but were also being constantly solicited for subscriptions to Liberty Bond issues and the many other voluntary war activities. Then, too, there was the higher wages in New York. Were they not worthy of as good wages as the garment workers in New York?

To this the spokesman for the management replied in substance: You should take the seasonal character of the industry in New York into consideration when comparing the wages paid in the two cities. This company by careful planning and with your coöperation has circumvented this seasonal character of our industry and can provide steady employment the year round. The New York firms, not having made these arrangements, are obliged to take orders when they come and shut down when the season ends. This means periods of unemployment for the workers there. If you compare your annual wages with the annual wages of the New York clothing workers, you will find that your wages average more than theirs. No doubt the employees in New York have increased their hourly and daily rates by resorting to strikes. But these very strikes bring chaos into the industry there, manufacturers are unable to avoid seasonal shutdowns, and what the employees gain by the strike they lose again during the long periods of unemployment. The situation in New York can be duplicated here if the employees will it, by substituting the method of the strike for the method of coöperation. The greater the stability of the firm the more prosperous it is and the better able to pay wages to its employees. When the clothing workers strike in New York, the firms there are at a disadvantage with the firms, not tied up, elsewhere. This firm has had the advantage over their New York competitors, has not had to shut down, and has been paying the greatest annual wage. If a strike comes, the situation will be reversed. The company will be at a disadvantage with competitors, will lose trade, will have all plans for stabilizing the industry upset, and will probably have to bow to the seasonal fluctuations. You are partners in the good or bad fortunes of the industry. You have your choice of alternatives.

After the close of the discussion the house refused any sanction to strike, and condemned the union for "threatening to call a strike without our approval." The wage-rate committee was instructed to hasten the two proposals which it was handling, namely, a revision of the rate schedules, and the transfer, which has already been described, of the high-cost-of-living bonus to the regular pay envelope.

The union called a strike. A few of the employees joined the strike in spite of the action of the house, but, so far as this firm was concerned, the strike was inconsequential. However, when the house found out that one of its members sympathized with the union it promptly expelled him. Later the company discharged this ex-member of the house and another employee. When the union leaders heard about these dismissals they had the company haled before the War Labor Board on charges of discrimination against trade-unionists. If the union had succeeded in establishing a case against the firm, it would have been ground for bringing the company under the award of the War Labor Board. This would have meant, practically, the adjournment of the "industrial democracy."

Neither the management nor the house desired to see this happen. The case was long drawn out and stubbornly fought, though the company did not make out a very strong case for itself. It had dismissed these employees for making trouble, but the union and dismissed employees replied that it was merely another case of malice toward trade-unionists. The company might have lost the case if a delegation from the house had not defended these dismissals before the War Labor Board upon the ground of disloyalty to the existing organization in the shop. They told the board that the employees had the kind of organization that the great majority of them wanted, and that they had the same right to expect loyalty to their organization that the union had to exact it from union members. They told the board, further, that they wished to continue to settle their affairs directly with the company, and protested vigorously against being brought under the award.

The company was not brought under the award, but there was a general feeling that it had had a narrow escape. The house discussed the matter and concluded that, since such controversies involve the house as well as the firm, the company should not take action of this kind in the future without first getting the approval of the house. The house concluded, also, that the handling of grievances should be speeded up, so it submitted two proposals to the senate and the cabinet, one providing for joint action in discharging employees, and the other providing that all grievances respecting wages, hours, and bonuses be handled by the wage-rate committee without previous reference to the employment department. Both proposals were concurred in by the senate and the cabinet.

The union had charged that the house was dominated by the company. The company executives had frequently participated in discussions before the house, as they are doing in other Leitch organizations. It is not affirmed that this accusation of the union had any influence on the subsequent action of the house, but, at any rate, a resolution was adopted soon afterwards that company representatives be permitted to be present only upon the invitation of the chairman of the house, and that they be required to retire immediately after their remarks. The aggressive temper of the house was shown again a little later by its dismissal of the betterment committee and the appointment of a new one because it was convinced that the old committee was not doing its duty.

REVISION OF THE CONSTITUTION

The annual elections took place about October 1, 1918. Sentiment was strong for a revision of the constitution and a simplification of the government. When the house reorganized on October 8 the president advocated larger powers for the house and its further separation from the management. He urged the house to have its own secretary and treasurer and pay them out of its own funds. Two weeks later a committee was appointed to revise the constitution.

The revised constitution was submitted to the house on November 26, 1918. It provided a house of representatives to deal directly with the management and abolished the senate. The factory organization had begun with one house—the senate. Six months later the house of representatives and the cabinet were added. But the senate had proved a failure as a legislative body, although it had served its purpose as a training school. Now the organization was again to be a one-house affair, but the employees' house. The new constitution was adopted by the house and approved by the senate and cabinet. The old system had not provided the expected direct contact of the management with the employees. The senate was always a buffer. The management now has a planning board of six members through which it deals with the house. This board meets twice a week and keeps in close touch with the house committees. By such consultation and coöperation it is possible for the house to know the management's position on proposals that are submitted to it by the committees.

REVISION OF WAGE RATES—PHYSICAL EXAMINATION OF WORKERS

While the house was busy with the revision of the constitution, the wage-rate committee was preparing a revision of the rates. The work of the committee had been hampered both by the previous method of revising rates, which was not abandoned until August, 1918, and by the uncertainty of the outcome of the controversy with the War Labor Board. If the company had been brought under the award, the employees would have been bound by the rates specified in the award, and the wage-rate committee would have been powerless until its expiration. As soon as assurances came that their desire to remain independent would be respected, the committee began preparing the new schedules.

For the purpose of this revision employees were classified according to the degree of difficulty of the operations they performed, e.g., (1) most difficult, (2) difficult, (3) medium, and (4) simple. After applying the classification in a few of the departments, the committee decided to have the foremen and superintendents do the rest of the classifying of employees, but reserved to itself the right to review individual classifications upon complaints by the operators. The committee and planning board reached an agreement also that any person who is changed to a different operation shall receive his old rates for three days after the change.

The wage-rate committee submitted the new rate schedules and agreements to the house, where they were adopted. The senate gave its last approval to a wage bill, and the rates and agreements then became effective.

The question of physical examinations for new employees came before the house and was approved in January, 1919. The fear that such examinations will become an economic hindrance to those found defective seems to pass away as employees feel themselves strong enough to prevent abuses. Nothing else of importance seems to have been done by the house during the winter.

THE 44-HOUR WEEK

The spring of 1919 opened with the 44-hour week as the major issue. The Amalgamated Garment Workers of Chicago and the International Ladies' Garment Workers of New York had won easy victories, and the drive for the shorter week was on everywhere. On April 8, 1919, the chairman of the house appointed a special committee to investigate the problems incident to introducing the shorter week in the shop. The committee was ready with its report the following week.

The report emphasized at the outset that reduction in hours should not be permitted to result in reduced production. Such a reduction, if it should occur through the whole range of industry, the committee argued, would inevitably be a factor in the further advancement of prices, the final outcome of which would mean a virtual reduction of income to the workers as the result of the shorter hours and curtailed production. Since the workers' aspirations for higher standards of living are connected with efficient production, and also with the prosperity of the industry, the report emphasized the mutual responsibility of management and employees for the improvement of processes and the reduction of costs. The most important of the recommendations of the committee may be summed up as follows:

(a) That hours be reduced from 48 to 44 without diminution in pay.

(b) That a 44-hour committee be appointed by the house to see that the rules governing the introduction of the 44-hour week be carried out and that employees coöperate in maintaining the previous standard of production.

(c) That there be no work on Saturdays; however, operators who fall below the permanent standards of production may be required to work on Saturdays at the regular rates.

(d) Regular overtime to all those who work on Saturdays, except those mentioned in (c).

The recommendations were adopted by the house and approved by the planning board.

The good results of the coöperation of the management and 44-hour committee in the introduction of the shorter week suggested the idea of having a subcommittee of the wage-rate committee meet with the heads of the standards department and note the methods of taking time studies and arriving at final standards, on which the bonus system is based. With this intimate contact the house is able to take more effective action on bonus questions that arise, while the management, as a result of this consultation and coöperation, is enabled to introduce its standards with more assurance of success.

REVISION OF BONUS RATES

In the meantime the union renewed its attack on the company and the "industrial democracy." The bonus system was denounced as a device on the part of the capitalist owners to speed up the employees for the sake of profits, and the employees were warned that such speeding up meant premature old age and shortened lives for them. The accusation of the union came in for considerable discussion at the next meeting and both the house and the company agreed that there should be an investigation to settle this controversy one way or the other. A physiologist from Johns Hopkins was engaged to come and make the investigation. Considerable interest was manifested in the shop over this investigation and the subsequent report. Certain measures, like extension of the medical and dental service and improved equipments, were recommended in the report, but the charge that the bonus system was working injury to health and shortening the lives of employees was not sustained.

The controversy helped to bring the bonus question again to the forefront. The union had struck at the psychological hour when the company was revising the wage and bonus rates to conform to the 44-hour agreement. In the hurried recalculations of all these rates it was inevitable that errors would be made. Complaints about the bonuses were numerous and of every description, but this time instead of taking up individual cases, the wage-rate committee went to the source of the trouble and collaborated with the planning board in devising a schedule that would be more satisfactory.

Under the agreement there was to be no reduction of any kind in weekly rates in the transition to the 44-hour week. None of the employees were willing to take a penny less. This temper the planning board did not seem to appreciate as keenly as it might at first, and so when it submitted the new bonus schedule providing increases for the first three classes but a reduction of 4 cents a week on the fourth-class bonus, the committee promptly returned the schedule with its disapproval. The planning board sent back word that the bonus rates would be "gone over again." Four proposals were submitted to the committee at its next meeting. In all four proposals the second and third class bonuses were the same amount. The alternatives lay with the first and fourth class bonuses. The first two proposals offered less than the existing weekly rate for the fourth-class bonus; the fourth proposal offered less for the first-class bonus. The committee chose the third proposal, which provided increases for the first, second, and third class bonuses, and the existing rate for the fourth class. Obviously, the committee acted upon the principle of the greatest good to the greatest number.

The old and new bonus rates stood as follows: Old bonus, 48-hour week: First class, $1.92; second class, $2.88; third class, $4.32; fourth class, $5.76; new bonus, 44-hour week: First class, $2.20; second class, $3.08; third class, $4.40; fourth class, $5.76.

This settled the production bonuses. But on the heels of this settlement the management came forward with another bonus proposal—a service bonus. It was to be based on the length of continuous service with the company. The wage-rate committee was asked to prepare the new schedule of rates. After two weeks' consideration the committee submitted the following schedule, which was approved by the management:

	Weekly bonus.
3 to 5 years of continuous service	$0.50
5 to 10 years of continuous service	1.00
10 to 15 years of continuous service	2.00
15 years and up of continuous service	3.00

When these new schedules had been approved by the house they were posted in the shop, as is the custom. The employees were then able to figure out to what their service and production bonuses would amount. Some of the workers who were certain that they were going to get service bonuses were disappointed and complained to the committee. The committee began an investigation and found out that the difficulty had its source in the strikes of 1911 and 1918. The company took the position that those who struck had terminated their service records at that point and that when they came back their period of service began anew.

The committee was made the arbiter of the case. The question was, Did these strikes interrupt the continuous-service records of the strikers? Each side presented its contentions. The committee's decision sustained the company. The committee then requested that the service records of all employees be put at its disposal for investigating further grievances that might arise under this bonus.

ADJUSTMENT OF MISCELLANEOUS COMPLAINTS

With the bonus question practically settled for the time, the committee turned to the numerous complaints that had accumulated respecting wage rates and time studies. Profiting by its experience, the committee decided to waive individual cases and have each department prepare a list of all its grievances. The opportunity seems to have appealed to several of the departments, as they submitted long bills of particulars. Some of the lists contained from 35 to 40 grievances. What appear to be the 10 leading grievances are noted:

1. Wages too low.
2. Standards too high; too few workers measure up to them, and consequently bonuses are difficult to earn.
3. Lack of uniformity in wages.
4. Bonuses are lost whenever new operators come in with changing styles.
5. Work not ready when workers call for it.
6. No time allowance for heavier garments.
7. Too long delays in attending to complaints.
8. Long delays at route boards.
9. Time allowances insufficient.
10. Losses in both wages and bonuses from transfers from one operation to another.

The committee then hit upon the idea of sending these bills of complaints to the management. This served to give the committee both sides of the controversy and, at the same time, to introduce the management to conditions and opinions in the departments. The management promptly replied with great detail. Many of the complaints were frankly acknowledged as valid and remediable, and promises were given that the causes for same would be removed and the existing grievances adjusted. Detailed explanation of the policies of the company smoothed out other grievances and showed that still others were unavoidable under the conditions and limitations of the industry. In the case of the long bill of grievances, the committee accepted in toto the management's response.

FURTHER REVISION OF WAGE RATES

With the situation thus clarified and simplified the committee began the task of revising the rates. The workers were classified on the basis of "operations in the departments." Four classes were formed, named in a descending scale of difficulty, A, B, C, and D.

On July 15, 1919, the revised schedule of rates for women and girls was submitted to the house and made known among the employees affected. Dissatisfaction developed and the committee reconsidered its action. The second schedule showed many revisions in favor of employees, ranging from a few cents to $1.50 per week. A comparison of this with the preceding October's schedule shows increases ranging from $3 to $4 per week.

At the conclusion of its session on July 15, 1919, the

committee notified the finishers, cutters, estimators, and sample tailors to have their representatives on hand the next day to present their cases. July 16 was a lively day. It was men's day. Representatives from all the departments invited were before the committee with their "kicks," with their "facts and figures," with "proofs" and "arguments" on their need of higher wages. There was competition among the departments for the higher rating and higher rates, and some evidences of jealousy. The cutters led off with the statement that they were getting the worst of it all round. One of their representatives said: "We have everything to lose and nothing to gain." The cutters were the most skilled and valuable workers in the shop, he said, but there was no recognition of it in the pay envelope. The representative of the estimators entirely disagreed with that. He wanted to know, if cutting was such a highly technical and skilled operation, why the cutters were always so anxious to get back to cutting again when they were transferred to the estimators' department? The estimators were the real people of the shop and deserved the higher rating, he concluded. Then came the representative of the sample tailors who affirmed that his department contained the real skill of the shop. The fact that the sample tailors had to make the whole garment and make it right proved that their work was the most exacting and the most valuable. See what losses the company would suffer if it were not for the great skill of the sample tailors. This was too much for the estimators whose representative interrupted to point out what great losses the firm would suffer if they should make miscalculations. And so it went back and forth that day, a striking picture of group struggle within the ranks of the proletariat itself.

After these representatives had presented the respective cases (and judgments), the committee excused them and called in representatives of the company to get the management's rating of these departments as to skill. The committee was in doubt about the comparative skill of cutters and estimators, and questioned very closely the company officials on this point. The conclusion reached by the committee was that cutters and estimators were equally skilled and rated them so. The committee was inclined to rate the pressers slightly lower than the cutters, but as the company had been paying the same rates for both, that rating was not disturbed.

The wage schedules and recommendations of the wage rate committee were submitted to the house of representatives, which approved them. The management then gave its approval, and the new wage rates went into effect on July 23, 1919.

ALLOWANCES FOR LEARNING TIME

There remained the question of "allowances for learning time." When new operations are introduced, the question arises as to who shall pay for the time necessary to learn the new operation and as to how much time shall be allowed. There was some dissatisfaction with the existing time allowances, so the wage rate committee set out to prepare a definite schedule of "learning time" for the various kinds of operations.

The committee developed a schedule through actual tests in one department, and then tried its schedule in the other departments. When the schedule had been proved by tests, the committee and management embodied it in the following agreement:

1. Three times standard operation for the first day, two times the second day, and one and one-half the third day, when an employee is given a new operation.

2. Twice the standard time is allowed when, after 10 days or more, an operator is transferred back to former operation.

3. Operators transferred to lower grade of work are to be given one day to come up to normal. Twice the standard time is allowed for this day.

4. No learning time is to be allowed when the new operation requires less work or is easier than the operation it displaces, nor when new styles require same operation as in vogue.

5. Operators able to perform, in standard time, those new operations for which learning time is allowed are to receive 5 cents an hour in lieu of learning time allowance.

This agreement was sanctioned by the house and by the planning board.

The records of the house show a great falling off in the number of complaints after these several schedules went into effect. The wage-rate committee had met the problems and, on the whole, satisfactorily disposed of them.

EMPLOYEES DESIRE A "HAND" AS WELL AS A "VOICE" IN MANAGEMENT

This shop organization was constructed upon the theory that what employees desire is a "voice" in their own affairs, a chance to "talk" and "air" their grievances. The house of representatives was designed particularly to serve this purpose. But a study of the records of these two years shows clearly that this group of employees desire a "hand" in their own affairs as well as a "voice."

Throughout the whole process of changes that have been passed in review there has been a progressively increasing participation by the employees in the making of policies and decisions that vitally concern them. The establishment of a wage-rate committee marked the triumph of collective bargaining over the earlier policy of a collective economy dividend. With the passing of the senate, the house of representatives completed its evolution from a house of suggestion to a house of legislation. To-day the president of the house is a member of the planning board. In noting this gradual increase in the power and responsibilities of the employees, it should be remarked that the management has welcomed and encouraged this development.

The growing power of the employees is revealed again in the matter of discharges. When the case before the War Labor Board was pending the company agreed with the house not to discharge employees thereafter without first consulting the latter. Since then the management and house have adopted a set of rules prescribing the offenses that justify discharges. Now when the company wishes to discharge an employee it must go before the betterment committee (a standing committee of the house) and prove that the employee is guilty of one of these offenses. This committee is the jury in the case and decides the facts. The company must drop the action for discharge if the committee decides that the case has not been proved. But if the company wins, the employee may appeal to the board of review, upon which the house and management have equal voting power.

The necessities for prompt action in this clothing shop soon demonstrated the cumbersomeness of the machinery and methods borrowed from our Federal Government. Yet it should be recalled that the Leitch plan, while having the form of the United States Government, does not embody all its principles of representation. The changes that have augmented the power of the employees have been, at the same time, in the direction of direct and continuous contact of management and people. The legislative policy is still adhered to, but joint conferences precede legislative action. Legislative action becomes more a matter of ratification under this arrangement, although the house has the right to proceed independently.

This method of shop direction is proving a great school of experience for the employees, and for the management also. There is no denying the fact that this organization has to its credit a record of substantial achievement and that it is entitled to distinction among those introducing popular government in industry.

APPENDIX

The following table gives the rates for male and female workers, effective July 23, 1919, the old rates, and the rates paid for similar work in the same city:

OLD AND NEW WAGE RATES COMPARED WITH RATES PAID FOR SIMILAR WORK IN SAME CITY UNDER WAR LABOR BOARD AWARD.

Operation.	Grade.	Old rate. Hour.	Old rate. Week.	New rate. Hour.	New rate. Week.	Weekly rates under War Labor Board award.
MALES						
Pressing and finishing	A	$0.73	$32.12	$0.85	$37.40	$35.00
	B	.71	31.24	.79½	34.98	34.00
	C	.65½	28.82	.73	32.12	31.00
Fore and machine	A	.65½	28.82	.73	32.12	30.00
	B	.60	26.40	.68	29.92	28.00
	C	.54½	23.98	.63	27.72	....
Operating:						
Full skilled	A	.65½	28.82	.82	36.08	36.00
	B	....	....	.77½	34.10	34.00
Semiskilled	A	....	....	.69	30.36	30.00
	B	....	....	.61½	27.06	27.00
Cutting	A	.73	32.12	.85	37.40	37.00
	B	....	....	....	....	35.00
						33.00
	C	....	....	....	...	29.00
						25.00
						23.00
Estimating	A	.79	34.76	*.91	*40.04	38.00
Pattern grading	A	.79	34.76	*.91	*40.04	38.00
Sample tailoring	A	.65½	28.82	.82	36.08	34.00
Minor operations	....	....	....	.57	25.08	25.00
FEMALES						
Machine operating	A	$0.48	$21.12	$0.57	$25.08	$25.00
Do	B	.42½	18.70	.51½	22.66	24.00
Do	C	.38½	16.94	.37½	20.90	20.00
Do	D	.35	15.40	.42	18.48	18.00
Hand work	A	.46	20.24	.55	24.20	23.00
Basting lining	A	.43½	19.14	.53	23.32	....
Do	B	.40½	17.82	.47½	20.90	20.00
Do	C	.37	16.28	.44	19.36	....
Felling lining	A	.35	15.40	.42	18.48	18.50
Do	B	.31	13.64	.38½	16.94	17.00
Tacking	A	.35	15.40	.42	18.48	18.50
Do	B	.31	13.64	.38½	16.94	17.00
Button sewing (machine)	A	.35	15.40	.42	18.48	18.50
Button sewing (hand)	....	.31	13.64	.38½	16.94	17.00
Cleaning	....	.27½	12.10	.32	14.08	....
Bench work (pin)	A	.29½	12.98	.35	15.40	....
Do	B	.27½	12.10	.32	14.08	....
Marking	A	.29½	12.98	.35	15.40	....
Do	B	.27½	12.10	.32	14.08	....
Cutting, assemblers' } Pin-ticketers fitters' }	....	.34½	15.18	.42	18.48	....
Pressing—parts	A	.41½	18.26	.57	25.08	23.00
Do	B	.49	21.56	.53	23.32	20.00
Do	C	.41½	18.26	.47½	20.90	....
MINIMA ON ALL OPERATIONS						
First three months	....	$0.27½	$12.10	$0.32	$14.08	$12.00
Second three months	....	.31	13.64	.35	15.40	14.00
Third three months	....	....	....	.38½	16.94	15.50
Fourth three months	....	.35	15.40	.42	18.48	17.00

* Includes 6 cents bonus.

X

A SHOP COMMITTEE THAT FAILED

In July, 1919, at the headquarters of local machinists' unions in many large cities was a conspicuous poster commanding machinists to stay away from a certain firm in a large city. The company was "unfair" to organized labor, and a strike was on for union recognition and standards.

This company had installed an employees' representation plan. It had every evidence of manifest good faith. Many of the plans embody reservations of authority in favor of the company. One plan enumerates over twenty such reservations. This firm made no reservations whatever. There were no high-sounding phrases. The purpose was stated in a sentence: "to give the employees a voice in the conditions under which they labor, and to provide an orderly procedure for adjustments of possible differences." The plan was simple, short, flexible. "Nominations and elections shall be conducted by the employees themselves." The elections were held frequently and employees had the right to recall an unsatisfactory representative. With respect to the freedom of the representative, "It is understood and agreed that each representative shall be free to discharge his duties in an independent manner without fear that his individual relations with the company may be affected in the least degree by any action taken by him in good faith in his representative capacity. To insure each representative his right to such independent action, he shall have the right to take the question of an alleged personal discrimination against him, on account of his acts in his representative capacity to any of the superior officers, to the General Joint Committee, and to the General Manager of the Company." Elsewhere the plan provides for arbitration when the General Manager and the General Joint Committee fail to agree.

The strike had followed soon after the introduction of the representation plan. What was the difficulty? Had this firm, with all its seeming good faith, really tried to "put one over" on the employees? And had the watchful unions caught it in the act? We were ushered into the office and introduced to the Industrial Representative. He made a few inquiries. He related the whole history of the representation plan. He was critical of himself, charitable toward the unions that had opposed and overthrown it. He had read a magazine article by John Leitch, the Industrial Evangelist. It put him to thinking. The more he thought about it, the more compelling became the logic of Industrial Democracy. He began agitating in the inner councils of the company and succeeded in "selling" the idea. He was appointed Industrial Representative to help create and deal with the democracy that was to come into this shop.

He informed the employees of the decision to introduce employees' representation. His business experience had made him a pragmatist, to whom a good thing is the thing that works well. He selected a committee to visit the several types of Committee plans and observe the success they were attaining. After this committee had concluded its itinerary it submitted its observations to the Industrial Representative, and was discharged. He now appointed a second committee to draft a plan for the works. This committee drafted such a plan as seemed best adapted to this shop, while, at the same time, squaring with the observations of the first committee respecting the successful experience elsewhere. On both of these committees the employees had their quota of members. The principles of "Justice" and "Coöperation" had been observed.

The plan worked out was democratic. All employees eighteen years of age and over who had been on the pay roll sixty days or longer were made eligible to vote. The factory was to be divided into voting precincts having from fifty to sixty workers each, and the workers in each of these precincts elected a committee to conduct the first election in the precinct. Subsequent elections were to be conducted by a general committee of five employee representatives, the Committee on Rules. This committee had power, also, to readjust the voting units. The employees were put in full control of their own elections.

An election was now held to approve or reject the plan. Ninety-six per cent of the employees participated, and a majority voted for adoption.

The election of representatives and the organization of the shop committees followed. American citizens twenty-one years of age and over with a year's service record were eligible for election. No company executive, however, from the rank of assistant foreman on up could be chosen to represent employees. The framers made sure that there would be no bosses representing the workers. Thirty-seven representatives were elected, one-half for the full term of one year, the other half for the intervening period until the next regular semi-annual election. After each such election the representatives for the employees were to meet and reorganize. This was intended to make the organization expressive of the popular will at all times.

This representative body did not function as a congress, but through various committees of its own choosing. Particular pains seems to have been taken to see to it that employee participation would not be limited to minor and inconsequential matters as regards the workers' interests. The roster of committees here copied from the plan shows the wide extent of their participation in shop affairs.

Wage Committee: Rates, Bonus, Piece Work, and Factory Working Hours.

Education Committee: Schools, Americanization, and Upgrading of Employees.

Employment Committee: Medical Relief, Insurance, Home Conditions, and Pensions.

Working Conditions: Sanitation, Safety, Factory Equipment, Plant Alteration, and Employees' Surroundings.

Production Methods: Improving Product, Improving Quality, Improving Design, and Reducing Scrap.

Recreation Committee: Athletics, Amusements, Commissary (including restaurant), and All Coöperative Activities.

General Committee: to consider all matters not falling within the scope of any other committees herein provided for.

Rules Committee: To direct elections.

The employee representatives chose five of their number for each of these committees. Each committee of employees held a regular meeting every two months. On alternate months each met with a like committee representing the company. The two committees were called a Joint Committee when meeting together.

By this arrangement the employee representatives were given an opportunity to have their own meetings and to decide upon their line of action before facing the company's representatives. Joint shop committee systems have been criticized for providing no adequate and effective means for independent action and for the rights of free speech and association on the part of the employee representatives. Employee committeemen have been deterred from taking the initiative in arranging meetings of their own when not provided for, so it has been charged, by the fear that some company "spotter" on the committee would report the proceedings to the officials, who in turn would "fire" the leaders. Not only did the plan throw safeguards about the free action of the employee representatives, but provision was made that no financial sacrifices were entailed in the discharge of committee functions. "For time necessarily occupied in actual attendance at regular meetings or at special meetings of conferences jointly approved (by Industrial Representative and Chairman of Employees' Representatives), representatives shall receive from the company payment commensurate with their average earnings."

There were already hundreds of union men in the plant and a move was in preparation to push the work of organization and secure recognition. No sooner had the company announced its new policy than the trade union leaders began observing closely the course of events. A "company union" is a red flag to the American Federation of Labor trade unionists. "The company is trying to Rockefellerize the works," declared the watchful unionist. Organized labor looks upon such moves on the part of employers as strategy in the game of economic warfare. To the local leaders this movement that the company saw the handwriting of Trade Unionism on the wall and was now paying hypocritical homage to the principle of collective bargaining by setting up a union of its own. It was all a scheme on the company's part to deceive the workers and put off the final triumph of the bona fide unions. It makes the organizer and agitator grit his teeth when he has to stand by and witness the birth of a bastard company union.

The company had neglected too long its labor policy. The trade unions were on the ground and were determined not to be brushed aside. A bitter struggle for the control of the labor force was inevitable.

The unions, evidently, thought that there was a possibility of their getting control of the committees, and planned to this end. But they elected only eleven out of the thirty-seven. They were thus in a minority, and considered that the company was in control and that the cards were stacked against them in the representative body.

When the shop committees were organized, the company, as an earnest of its good faith, voluntarily reduced the hours from fifty to forty-eight per week. There was a general sentiment for a revision of the wage rates and the Wage Rate Committee at once began the task. The investigation was carried to every department of the works, hearings for the workers were held, living costs were compared with former years, and a new schedule prepared. The committee then asked for a meeting with the Industrial Representative to present its demands. But in the meantime the Industrial Representative had conducted an investigation on the quiet and prepared a revised wage schedule which the company would be willing to accept.

The meeting was promptly arranged and the demands presented. The Industrial Representative waited until the committee had presented its demands in full and then he presented the schedule which had been prepared under his direction. The surprising thing about his schedule was that its rates were much in advance of what the committee had demanded. The committee was rather nonplussed, but soon recovered and voted to accept the company's proposition in preference to its own.

One would naturally infer that this incident would have strengthened the company with the employees and would have been convincing proof of its good faith. The result was just the contrary. The unionists pointed to it as proof that the company knew it was whipped and was falling over itself to make any kind of a peace that excluded union recognition; as proof, again, of their contention that committees under such a plan had more regard for the firm than for the workers they were supposed to represent. The wage-rate committee was thoroughly discredited.

While this was transpiring the worst agitator in the shop was caught mutilating his time card. Under the standing rules of the company such an offense was grounds for instant and unconditional discharge. No doubt it was intended as a direct challenge to the company "to start something." The agitator frankly admitted his guilt, but stated that many other workers were doing the same thing and that if the firm "canned" him he and his fellow trade unionists would have to consider such action as intentionally discriminatory.

In former days the agitator would have been fired without even ceremony. But the Management had just announced its conversion to the principles of Industrial Democracy, and to have fired this unionist would have given the unions just the club they wanted. The Industrial Representative, however, was anxious that there should be no occurrences that would in the least reflect on the good faith of the firm. He perceived at once that this was a very ticklish situation, to mishandle which would threaten the success of the plan from the very outstart. He had become aware of the strength of the unions in the shop, and he knew that to fire this man would, under the strained situation, appear to unionists as prima facie evidence of the hostility of the firm to them. So he merely suspended the agitator and turned the case over to a committee of employees' representatives. This committee was to learn whether the charges of the agitator were true that mutilation of time cards was a common occurrence.

Had the suspended agitator so desired, he could have appealed his case for adjustment. Under the plan adopted he, or his representative for him, could have gone to one of the superior officers of the company, and failing to get satisfaction there, could have appealed to the General Committee of Appeals. "The General Joint Committee on Appeals shall consider any such matter with reasonable promptness, at a regular or special meeting, and may adopt such means as are necessary to ascertain the facts and effect a settlement," read the plan. Failing to arrive at a settlement here, recourse to arbitration was finally provided for.

However crooked the agitator may have been in his dealing with the company, he was absolutely foursquare on his union principles. He refused to recognize the plan even to the extent of using its adjustment machinery. He made the management face the naked situation.

In the course of its investigation the committee found that the agitator's charges were true. There were numerous cases of mutilation that had been slipping through undetected. The company was strictly up against it. If the agitator was now discharged, consistency would compel the discharge of scores of employees. The management was caught between the horns of a dilemma, the Trade Unions on one side and shop discipline on the other side. The agitator was reinstated.

For these endeavors at liberality and fairness the company received no credit from the union leaders. The reinstatement of the agitator was to them but another sign of wavering and weakness in the councils of the management. They decided the time was ripe for a show-down. They informed the Industrial Representative that they could no longer recognize the representative body as bona fide and asked the company to annul the recent elections. The management replied that the present representative body was properly representative, that it had been duly elected in free elections controlled by the workers themselves, that the company felt itself obligated by the plan adopted by both sides and must insist that all questions requiring adjustment be submitted to the committees authorized to settle such matters.

When the company took this position the eleven union representatives promptly resigned.

Mass meetings for the union employees were held in the trade union halls, where about forty committeemen all told were elected to constitute the new Trade Union shop committee in this factory. At the same time an effort was being made in the shop to fill the vacancies made by the resignation of the eleven union representatives. Eight of the vacancies were filled, but in three departments the unions were solidly organized and refused to have any more elections in the shop. So there were three vacancies in the representative body.

The unions formally demanded the recognition of the all-union committee as the representative body of the employees. The management declined. A strike was called. Eighty per cent of the employees walked out.

Then followed one of the bitterest labor struggles in that city. Many of those who had walked out soon after returned, but there were many others, among them the best of the mechanics, who never returned. Both company and unions suffered heavily in this struggle.

When the strike was at its height, the Industrial Representative called into his office the remnant of the employees' representatives to tell them that the representation plan was at an end in this plant. The unions had killed it. Only four hundred workers had remained loyal. The strikers who returned, as well as the recruits, were new employees. The old government could not be reconstructed, for the plan required sixty days' service as a requisite for voting and one year's service for election as representative. The voting districts were without qualified voters, and many of them without qualified workers for representatives. There was nothing to do but to give up.

In the light of such an industrial tragedy—and this is but one among many that strew the course of recent years—what shall we say? The management beyond a peradventure attempted to do the right and fair thing by its employees. But every attempt on its part to be fair and to give the unions the benefit of the doubt was carried out at just the particular time that convinced the unions of the weakness of the company and not of its spirit of fairness. Every attempt at conciliation abetted the oncoming struggle. Instead of being credited with liberality and fairness, the management was accused of hypocrisy, deception, and cunning.

The management had chosen the wrong time to undertake any such adventure in shop democracy. It didn't understand the psychology of organized labor. It never dreamed that this brand of democracy is regarded by Trade Unions as a challenge to them for a trial of strength. All these things it had to learn in the mill of experience.

Employers who have neglected their labor policy until the unions are in the midst of a drive to organize them had better watch their step. Then above all times is the most treacherous time to begin a shop organization independent of union connection. The time for a company to make a move for a shop organization is when all is peaceful and no organizers are about. The employer must be ahead of the game if he expects to win. Let him put it off until the unions are on the ground and getting better entrenched every day, and he will have the fight of his life when he wakes up and tries to put across an organization that leaves the unions in cold storage.

This firm's experience demonstrates once again that good motives are not sufficient for a successful labor policy in modern industry. Labor must be better understood if the present organization of industry is to stand for any considerable length of time. The two primal forces of today, as of all ages past, are the force of numbers resident in the multitudes and the intellectual force possessed by the few. The few can lead and control only so long as they understand the multitudes they are leading as well as the job to be done. Capitalists know the job of production, but do they any longer understand the organized workers, the class conscious workers, who are developing programs and philosophies of their own? Understanding the human element in industry is the acid test of the competency of Capitalism today. Ignoring this great human problem and fumbling it add fuel to the fires of class conflict, and class conflict and production never go hand in hand. The leaders of industry must come to an understanding of the labor problem; they will have to get on the job with cool heads and be able to sit down and converse dispassionately with the trade unionist, the socialist, and the communist to learn what men think the wrongs of the present day are. The above account of the bitter and costly fight over this Shop Committee that Failed may well be concluded with the official statement of the American Federation, adopted at its convention in 1919.[1] The resolutions read:

"WHEREAS, Many steel corporations and other industrial institutions have instituted in their plants systems of collective bargaining akin to the Rockefeller plan; and

"WHEREAS, Extensive experience has shown that while the employers are busily carrying on propaganda lauding these company unions to the skies, as a great improvement over trade unions, they are at the same time just as actively enforcing a series of vicious practices that hamstring such organizations and render them useless to their employees. Of these practices the following are a few:

"1. Unfair Elections and Representation.

"The first essential for the proper working of a genuine collective bargaining committee is that it be composed entirely as the organized workers may elect and altogether free from the company's influence. Only then can it be truly representative of the men and responsive to their wishes. Upon such committees bosses, representing as they do the antagonistic interests of the company, are so much poison. Not only is it impossible for them personally to represent the men, but they also negate the influence of the real workers' delegates. Knowing this very well, the steel companies, through campaigns of intimidation and election fraud, load their company union committees with bosses, usually to the point of a majority. So baneful is this practice that, were the company unions otherwise perfect, it alone would suffice to entirely destroy their usefulness to the workers.

"2. No Democratic Organization Permitted.

"It is common knowledge that, in order for the workers to arrive at a uniform understanding through the systematization and formulation of their grievances and demands, it

[1] "Proceedings, Thirty-ninth Annual Convention, American Federation of Labor," p. 302. (1919.)

is necessary for them to enjoy and practice the rights of free speech, free assembly, and free association. They must conduct an elaborate series of meetings under their own control, and generally carry on their business in a democratic organized way. But with the company union system this is impossible. All independent organization and meetings are prohibited on pain of discharge. Consequently the workers are kept voiceless and destitute of a program. They are deliberately held down to the status of a mob. Under such circumstances, intelligent, aggressive action by them is out of the question.

"3. Intimidation of Committeemen.

"As part of the general plan to keep their company unions from being of any possible service to their employees, it is customary for the companies to summarily discharge committeemen who dare to make a stand in behalf of the workers. The records show a multitude of such cases. Being unorganized, the men are powerless to defend their representatives. The natural consequence is that the committee soon degenerate into groups of men supinely subservient to the wishes of the company and deaf to those of the workers.

"4. Expert Assistance Prohibited.

"When dealing with their employees in any manner, employers always thoroughly safeguard themselves by enlisting the aid of the very best brains procurable. The only way the workers can cope with this array of experts is to have the help of experienced labor leaders, but under the company union system this is impossible. All association with trade union officials is strictly prohibited. The company reserves to itself the right to expert assistance. As a result the green workers' committee, already weakened in a dozen ways, is left practically helpless before the experts upon the company's side.

"5. Company Union Lacks Power.

"In establishing wages, hours, and working conditions in their plants, employers habitually use their great economic power to enforce their will. Therefore to secure just treatment, the only recourse for the workers is to develop a power equally strong and to confront their employers with it. Unless they can do this, their case is hopeless. In this vital respect, the company union is a complete failure. With hardly a pretense of organization, unaffiliated with other groups of workers in the same industry, destitute of funds, and unfitted to use the strike weapon, it is totally unable to enforce its will, should it by a miracle have one favorable to the workers. Weak and helpless, all it can do is to submit to the dictation of the company. It can make no effective fight for the men.

"6. Company Diverts Aim.

"As though the foregoing practices were not enough to thoroughly cripple the company unions, the employers make assurance doubly sure by seeing to it that their committees ignore the vital needs of the workers and confine themselves to minor and extraneous matters, such as fake safety-first movements, problems of efficiency, handing bouquets to high company officials, etc. Discussions of wages, hours, and working conditions are taboo on pain of discharge for the committeeman who dares insist upon them. Thus the company unions complete their record of deceit and weakness by dodging the labor question altogether.

"WHEREAS, in view of the foregoing facts, it is evident that company unions are unqualified to represent the interests of the workers, and that they are a delusion and a snare set up by the companies for the express purpose of deluding the workers into the belief that they have some protection and thus have no need for trade union organization; therefore, be it

"RESOLVED, That we disapprove and condemn all such company unions and advise our membership to have nothing to do with them; and be it further

"RESOLVED, That we demand the right to bargain collectively through the only kind of organization fitted for this purpose, the trade union, and that we stand loyally together until this right is conceded us."

XI

TOWARDS GOVERNMENT BY EMPLOYEES

THE chairman of the shop committee was formerly the acting business agent of the shoe workers' union. After the disastrous strike of 1914 this was the only shoe factory that would hire him. Now he is the business agent of his "shop union." He is elected by the employees and paid by them the same wages that he had been earning at the bench. He has his private office, gives all his time to grievances and shop management, works under the direction of a shop committee also elected by the employees.

A foreman comes in with a discharge slip. A boy had poured a can of oil into a batch of cement. His discharge had been approved by the Joint Council, the highest authority in the shop, composed of four representatives of the company and four representatives of the employees. But the boy cannot be discharged unless that business agent of the employees O. K.'s the discharge slip. He hesitates, makes inquiries, flatly refuses. The foreman is surprised, chagrined, "beats it."

The facts were these. The boy had committed the offense two months before. The foreman had not discharged him then but had waited two months, until he did not need him. The business agent of the employees did not approve that style of discipline.

A new employee is hired by the company's employment department and put to work. He cannot continue at work unless he joins the shop union and pays the dues. But he cannot join the union unless the chairman and the employees approve. So he is sent to the chairman for an interview. The chairman usually knows whether he has been a "scab" or a professional trouble-maker. He has had experience with such. So he tells the new employee there is no chance for him in the factory. Or he tells him that he can go to work and explains to him the advantages of the shop union and why he should be a member and pay the dues.

Thus the business agent, along with the shop committee, has the last word in hiring and firing.

This government by employees did not drop down suddenly. It was not a brilliant thought of the Nunn, Bush & Weldon Shoe Company of the city of Milwaukee. It was not thrown at the employees without previous notice. It was not fought for and won by them to make the shop safe for democracy. It was not a struggle for power. It just growed, like Topsy and the British constitution. It has taken seven years to reach its present shape, but it keeps on growing—rapidly. You have to visit it at least once in three months, or else you will be talking about history instead of a live up-to-the-minute representative democracy.

Seven years ago Mr. H. L. Nunn, general manager of the company, did all of the hiring and firing. The firm was rapidly expanding. Superintendents and foremen got between him and the workers. It occurred to him that it would be a good thing to organize the older employees and give them a voice in affairs that concerned them. The older ones took to it. They organized the Nunn-Bush Coöperative Association. Membership was limited to those who had been with the company three years or longer. The "board of directors"—not of the corporation but of the Coöperative Association—was equally divided, three appointed by the company, three elected from the association by its members.

The general manager of the company turned over to this board the right to discharge any member of the association, as well as the settlement of all grievances affecting any member. If the board could not agree the case was to be settled by arbitration.

The board soon discovered that it was not big enough. There were twelve departments in the factory, but only three could find representation on the board. So a new board was created—a grievance committee. The board of directors of the association appointed this grievance committee of twelve members, one from each department. The grievance committee could only investigate and recommend. It investigated grievances, made findings of fact, then made its recommendations to the board of directors.

The next step in constitutional history was the extension of the suffrage. Only members of the Coöperative Association vote for the employee representatives on the Joint Council.

After a short experience the membership was enlarged by admitting employees after two years' service, instead of three. Then, after a little more experience, it was reduced to one year. Then, an attack from the outside convinced them that they must admit every regular employee to membership in the association.

The United Shoe Workers, a seceding union from the Boot and Shoe Workers of America, began organizing one of the departments. About a dozen of the forty employees in that department had signed up. They were the more recent employees not eligible to the association. The situation became acute. A meeting of that department was called. Each side presented its case. The decision was reached to remain with the association. So the suffrage was widened to admit all employees who might otherwise be admitted to the United Shoe Workers' Union.

It was before this trouble that Louis Karl, formerly the acting business agent of the union, found employment in the shop and membership in the Coöperative Association, although retaining his membership in the Shoe Workers' Union.

The extension of the suffrage was followed by a revision of the constitution. The old "board of directors" of six members now gave way to a "Joint Council" of eight members—four company appointees, four employee representatives, the latter elected by all the employees.

Much more important was the change in the grievance committee. The former committee was *appointed* by the board of directors. The new one was *elected* by the employees. Each of the twelve departments elects separately its representative on the grievance committee of twelve. The grievance committee now becomes a House of Representatives and its name is changed to shop committee.

The next step was evidently for this shop committee to take over power from the Joint Council. The shop committee represents solely the employees, elected by departments. The Joint Council is equally divided between employer and employees, the latter elected by the whole shop.

The shop committee began to grow in several directions. It added a chairman, nominated by itself, elected and paid by the employees. This is Louis Karl, the business agent. Karl presides at all meetings of the shop committee. He personally investigates all grievances in the factory, takes them up with the foreman or superintendent, and in this way settles 80 per cent of the grievances. He investigates wages and hours in other shops. The company gives him access to every part of the factory and all its records and books. He is a bureau of investigation and statistics for the shop committee and the employees.

But the shop committee finds itself too bulky to handle all the grievances. So the next step was to appoint an "investigating committee," composed of its chairman, the representative from the department where the trouble arises and three others from its own membership. Karl is chairman also of this investigating committee. He brings before it any of the troubles he has not been able to settle directly with the foreman, superintendent, or general manager. The committee notifies both sides to appear and present their respective sides of the controversy. Here the dissatisfied worker is not afraid to express himself. Karl tells him to forget his "grammar" and tell the committee just what his trouble is and what he thinks about it.

Seldom is a matter seriously contested. Before the investigating committee recently a small group of employees asked an increase in pay and submitted what they claimed were the "facts" to the committee. The

company took issue on these "facts." The committee
had previously gathered information which conflicted
with the statements of the complainants. It concluded
that here was a bald attempt to deceive them. It sent
back the reply: "If you want this committee to represent you, you must tell the truth."

The investigating committee completes its work on
Wednesday, reports its findings and recommendations
to the shop committee of twelve which meets on Thursday at 4 o'clock.

Here Karl again is chairman. The shop committee
may also take testimony if it wishes. One of the best
workmen had been transferred to a new job with the
understanding that he would receive the same pay by
the week. After several months he showed no improvement. The company, suspecting that he was taking advantage of the situation, appeared before the
shop committee and asked permission to substitute a
piece rate. The worker stated that he would have his
own price or quit. The committee decided against him
and he quit.

One of the representatives of the shop committee
reports that two workmen in his department wanted
"more money." The committee voted to investigate
this claim. The next Thursday the same representative reports two or three others in the same department
who had asked him to get them a "raise." This time
the committee decided to investigate the entire wage
scale in that department, and agreed that it was their
business to do justice, not merely for those who had
the "nerve to kick," but for everybody. So they instruct Karl and the investigating committee to find out
what the other shoe factories are paying for the same

kind of work. They reason that it would not be fair to ask the company to pay wages that would put it at a disadvantage with competitors. They instruct the chairman also to call a secret meeting of that department and report to that meeting the schedule of wages prepared by the investigating committee.

Departmental meetings have their place in this scheme of government. A department may, if it wishes, call a meeting and try to settle a question directly with the management. It is at these meetings also that new members are admitted to the association, for, at the present stage of development, any department can deny an employee's application, and this obliges the company to discharge that employee. The shop committee also calls departmental meetings as recited above to pass judgment on its proposals, before the committee presents them to the company.

Up to October, 1919, the shop committee was merely an investigating committee. It had no power to decide a dispute. It reported all cases to the Joint Council, which alone had power to decide. The Joint Council represents equally the company and the employees. The shop committee represents only the employees. But it was found that the Joint Council was actually approving every report and recommendation of the shop committee—with one exception. So the next step was taken. If the Joint Council nearly always approves, why not give the shop committee power to decide at once and let the Joint Council decide only when either side to a dispute appeals to the Joint Council?

This change was made. The Joint Council is now a court of appeals. The shop committee of employees is the body that makes final decision, unless there is an appeal.

Along with it, another change was made. The employee members of the Joint Council had been elected by direct vote of all employees. Now they are elected by the shop committee, and the chairman of the Joint Council must come from the employees' side. So far, the Joint Council has never failed to reach a unanimous decision, except once. If 't divides equally, then the case goes to arbitration, but this has not happened as yet.

The Joint Council is at times even more considerate of the individual employee than the shop committee. A girl was discharged and the discharge was approved by the chairman and the shop committee. The girl appealed to the Joint Council. The testimony showed that the foreman had given her a task that she was not performing according to directions. He ordered her to do what he told her or "get out." She got mad and balked. Dismissal followed. The girl admitted to the council that her actions were wrong, but insisted that the foreman had threatened her and was not a gentleman. Both sides argued the case. The council discussed it at length. It was a choice between insubordination and gentility. The council decided to reinstate the girl in her old position and to advise the foreman to be a gentleman.

We come to the last chapter up to date.

Karl has resigned his membership in the United Shoe Workers' Union. That is about what the trade unions and the American Federation of Labor have said would happen. The "shop employees' union," they say, is started to undermine and oust the trade union.

But the matter is more complex than that.

Five years ago Karl was the militant leader of the militant United Shoe Workers, a union which had seceded from the conservative Boot and Shoe Workers of the American Federation of Labor.   The Boot and Shoe Workers' Union always believed in arbitration. They had a union label.   The shoe business is highly competitive.   The union did not control all of the shops.   The universal rule in the business is piecework. Hence the conservative union did not try to force piece-rates above the rates paid by non-union shops.   What it offered to its members was practically the same piece-rates as in non-union shops, but with this advantage, that the union label and the arbitration agreement would give them steady employment.   They could increase their earnings for the year, although they were paid the same rates per piece as non-unionists.

This was partly why the militant union seceded from the conservative union.   It wanted to force up the piece-rates by direct action without the label and without arbitration.

Karl led them in the fight.   It failed.   Karl now is leading a "shop employees' union."   His fellow-workers trust him, for they know the sacrifices he has made in behalf of labor.

He frequently prevents a fellow-worker from taking hasty and ill-advised action.

In March, 1919, they reduced the hours to forty-six.

They have put in a little rest-period of ten minutes every forenoon.

They believe they are earning higher wages for shorter hours than employees in competing factories.

The shop union is becoming gradually an employees' union, with the consent of the company. Competition still continues to keep down the piece-rates, with the consent of the employees' union.

What ought Karl to do? Should he stick to the militant Shoe Workers' Union that seceded?

Should he join the conservative Boot and Shoe Workers' Union and get his company to adopt the label?

Should he stick to the Nunn, Bush & Weldon Co-operative Association and gradually take over government by employees as fast as they show themselves competent to govern?

CHAPTER XII

PROFIT-SHARING THAT FAILED

WHEN we visited the Wayne Knitting Mills, of Fort Wayne, Indiana, in August, 1919, Mr. Theodore F. Thieme, the founder, president, manager and idealist, was out of town. Practically all that we learned about the establishment we learned from employees. These employees were officers and members of "Knitters' Union No. 2," the local branch of the national trade union of Full-Fashioned Hosiery Workers. On the strength of their enthusiasm we placed the Wayne Knitting Mills at the top of our list, "Faith in Management." Sixteen months later, after prices had begun to tumble, these same employees were out on strike and the whole works was shut down. You never can say anything for sure about labor and management. You ought always to write history and never prophesy. Mankind has a distressful way of swinging from intoxication to the "day after." And it seems to follow the swing of prices from inflation to deflation.

Here is what the employees told us and showed us at the height of pecuniary intoxication. The business was started in 1891. Mr. Thieme had been educated in a Lutheran theological school. He taught school, then went into the drug store business at Fort Wayne, then sold out and went to Europe to see if he could find an industry that might be moved to America under the protection of the new McKinley Tariff. He hit upon the full-fashioned hosiery business, in which fifty or more stockings are knitted at once on a great machine tended by a highly skilled mechanic and three or four girl helpers. He organized a $30,000 corporation at Fort Wayne, brought over from Germany twenty-five experienced knitters and finishers, and started in a rented store room.

From this small beginning has grown the great business which now employs nineteen hundred people, with a capital stock of $1,200,000, not a dollar of which is water, according to the boast of its proud and confident employees. Six of the twenty-five employees who started with the original plant thirty years ago are with it today. About seventy employees have been with the company twenty-five years or more.

The Wayne Knitting Mills, as might be expected from its founder, president and manager, presents some unusual features. We have found university professors, of late, in demand as employment managers. We have found even labor leaders drafted into this service. The Wayne Knitting Mills added to the variety by bringing in a man who had been lawyer, judge, and political reformer—Mr. Ross F. Lockridge, fellow-worker with Mr. Thieme in the fight of the latter for better government in Indiana and Fort Wayne. For Mr. Thieme was a political reformer as well as an industrial reformer. He was founder of the Citizen League of Indiana, substantial supporter of the "New Constitution" movement for the state, as well as of local movements for public ownership of public utilities and of general political house-cleaning.

At the head of *The Citizen,* the official organ of his
Citizen League, edited by Mr. Thieme and Mr. Lockridge, had appeared Lowell's anti-slavery defiance:

> The time is ripe, and rotten ripe, for change;
> Then let it come; I have no dread of what
> Is called for by the instincts of mankind.
> Nor think I that the world would fall apart
> Because we tear a parchment more or less.

With a political reformer as president and a political
reformer in charge of employment and welfare activities, one is not surprised to find surprises. Here is
an immense club house, built by the company—really
more than an ordinary club house, for it is in fact and
name a "community center" for management and labor, for social, educational, political and union gath-
erings, as well as a home for young women workers
whose families do not live in Fort Wayne, and who
prefer to live together here rather than outside in the
boarding houses of the city.

The president and secretary of the union showed us
through the place; they fed us in the great dining-
room and told us of the goings-on in the place. They
showed us a pamphlet on public ownership that Mr.
Thieme handed them to read. They showed us copies
of *Rav-lings,* the shop paper, with a column or two
edited by "Knitters' Union No. 2," and its notices of
union elections and its comments on union affairs and
events. *Rav-lings* had a column of "Community Center Notes." Mr. Thieme had lectured on the present
system of city government and the issues at the coming municipal election; at another time on "The Political Machine"; at another time, after six months'
absence in recovering his health, on "World Poli-

tics"—each lecture followed by a free-for-all. He had also attended the union meetings, as well as the Community Center meetings and had spoken there on public questions, such as workmen's insurance, public ownership and the tariff. Colonel Foster, the foremost promoter of park improvements, had talked to the Community Center on "how to secure our most needed public improvements." The biggest crowd that attended the Community Center was the one that heard the debate on the liquor problem—described as "a roaring success." Another meeting was "a great suffragette demonstration."

The employees did not hesitate to follow the example of their employers. Here is a program offered by them in *Rav-lings*. "Every person, male and female, should be on an equality, both as to voting and power to hold office." "In order to get the form of government we want and to keep it most suited to our needs, we must have constitutional home rule." "We cannot, under the present two-per-cent limit, buy and operate the gas plant, street railway, or any other new business. This limitation must be raised."

Rav-lings tells us also of a talk by John A. Thieme, brother of the founder: "Even in our own good times," he said, "times of a great deal of frivolity and amusement, there are surely openings for reforms and changes, and we have many men and women who have ideas, ideals, convictions and fads, if you please, which they would like to bring before the public. This, then, is the place to come to air your ideas and get these reforms out of your system. The people will be glad to hear and take up these new ideas."

But political reform was not the only reform agi-

tated in this Community Center. Industrial Reform
was prominent. We were told of the Textile Industrial Club, composed of the management and upper
workmen, and of other clubs and committees discussing everything from street-car service to the best way
to handle orders in the finishing department. Here
were classes held on company time with teachers provided under the federal and state laws granting aid
for vocational education. These classes are adapted
to all levels of intelligence and need. The hundreds
of girls in the factory, looking like healthy school
girls, have improved themselves through these classes.
More pretentious are the courses for young employees
in Economics, Psychology, Public Speaking, Political
Science, taught in the evenings by university professors.

As a result of these industrial and educational clubs
and classes the place buzzes with plans for improving this or that condition, and with new problems constantly offered for solution as new conditions arise.
A woman's organization, the Waynew Club, was recently formed—of foreladies and inspectors, forty-two
in number—to promote coöperation among inspectors,
to improve inspection, to seek the principal causes for
defective work, to bring about "a general and uniform
adoption of remedies."

The union organization, too, was alive with public
questions as well as plans and efforts to increase production. The union originally included only the three
hundred men knitters on the full-fashion machines.
The men later opened the organization to their girl-
helpers—each man has three—and then they went the
whole way and threw open the door to every employee

in the factory down to the youngest girl. The girls were coming in slowly, it is true, but surely. They were not coming because of solicitation. The union did not want a lot of members whom they would find difficulty in holding. They wanted members who came because they wanted to come. They were coming in partly because the $50 a week of the men workers on the full-fashioned hosiery machines looked good to them. Their own wages were coming up rapidly. The minimum wage of $12 a week applied to young girls only. The girl workers averaged $18 or $20 a week, to which the profit-sharing bonus must be added.

That the union did not urge the girls to come in, did not mean, however, that the union was not interested in the welfare of non-members. Their shop committee frequently took up with Mr. Thieme matters of concern to the entire plant; and Mr. Thieme in turn referred to the committee of the union matters concerning the whole plant in which he wanted the cooperation of this force. The union, according to the men, was actually a convenience to the company. It was a body through which changes could be presented to all the people, and its power was sometimes exercised in a most salutary way, where disciplinary force was needed.

There was no doubt of it. The organized workers were sincerely interested in efficient production. They had no fear of being placed at a disadvantage because of high wages for efficiency, and were confident in the good faith of the management. They told us how they were always able to present their case to the company officials and to receive satisfaction; how the company kept their employees on during the period of

shortage of dyes in 1914-15, and continued to manufacture as before and to take the risk of piling up
large stocks; how, nevertheless, large profits were un-
expectedly made when a tremendous demand set in,
so that a policy fair to employees proved to be profitable to the firm; how this had always been the policy
of the company, so that, in the last twenty-four years,
the employees had not lost a single day on account of
lack of work. This was due to the large surplus
which the company accumulated to take them over
periods of depression. They told us there had never
been any water in the stock, and, in the periods of
highest profits, the stockholders had never been paid
more than twelve per cent.

Along with it all they told us of their own interest
in efficient production and of items which they had
contributed towards greater economies, such as the
raveling out of spoiled articles and use of the thread
later in weaving; the salvage of the thread at the bottom of the spool which used to be thrown away; the
saving of steps by a change in the position of the box
holding the spools, and similar economies.

These skilled workmen had a pride in their work.
Their job requires real workmanship. They were
proud to be treated like men. They think and study.

But we were surprised to find a trade union along
with all these welfare and educational activities, this
profit-sharing which adds twenty-five per cent to the
already high wages, this club house, community center,
textile club, and other harmonizing agencies. Yet here
it was—a real union, with spirit, with prospects, and
most of all, with confident praise of the management.
The union officers noted our surprise and explained

how the union came into existence. "Mr. Thieme was away for a long time. He was reported to be very sick. Things were going bad. So we organized. Then he came back. Things began to go all right again. But we keep up the union partly because we are afraid he might die."

The company described their relation with the union in a pamphlet shown to us by the union officers: "We recognize the union, and the union recognizes the management. Annually, with the election of new officers, the union appoints a factory committee of from twelve to fifteen men, who meet with the management upon a call from either side, when mutual plans, suggestions, grievances, recommendations, etc., are discussed and acted upon. These meetings are attended by the general manager, superintendent and other assistants as well as such shop foremen as are interested in the subjects under consideration. Through this close contact of officials and working people, a better understanding of each other's wants and viewpoints is created. Naturally, it took some years before sufficient confidence and mutual respect were inspired to get results and convince both sides of fairness. It is not entirely a one-sided proposition, for while labor presents its grievances to the management, on the other hand the management brings its problems and grievances, affecting such questions as production, quality and labor supply, before the committee. In other words, the management uses the union quite as freely as the union uses the management. It goes without saying that while the management has obtained an ideal situation with regard to labor, quality of work, etc., the employees have also obtained a maximum of wages and bonuses, as well as a fifty-fifty share in the profits. Yet we are not averse to saying that from the time that this arrangement became truly operative the stockholders' profits went up every year. In other words, it has proven up to this time a profitable investment for both capital and labor."

This was Mr. Thieme's ideal. "We have no more important function today in the Wayne Knitting Mills," he said, "than the development of our welfare work. This we are doing in part through certain aids such as old age pensions, special assistance to sick and needy, sick and accident insurance, group insurance and health department, which do much to alleviate misfortune. Important as these are, they are secondary in my judgment to our more constructive welfare work through profit sharing, club house culture and recreation, which organize and promote efficiency, good fortune, good feeling, community well being and satisfaction, individual success and leadership. It is this kind of welfare work that must be vastly increased through manufacturing institutions in the immediate future. But this welfare work must not operate to keep the payroll down."

Thus it was in August, 1919. In October, 1920, the financial intoxication began to pass off. Payrolls had previously been adjusted to meet the high cost of living, until in June, 1920, the last advance had been made, after the profit-sharing checks for twenty-five per cent on wages, out of the preceding year's earnings, had been issued to all the workers. Everything looked rosy. Then the union committee demanded that the twenty-five per cent profit-sharing bonus should be put thereafter into the weekly pay envelope instead of paying it at the end of the year. The company got at once a rude glimpse of the workers' psychology. To the workers, profit-sharing in cash is but deferred wages. It was here, as always, wage-psychology against profit-psychology. But the glimpse in June was not rude enough—the intoxication was on the company also. Business was rosy. The company agreed to take its chances, make everybody happy and assure ideal working conditions for the season. But they hesitated enough to agree only to the committee's program for a period of six months, ending December 1st. Thus for six months, unearned profits became current wages. Profit-psychology yielded to wage-psychology, notwithstanding wages proper had already kept up with the cost of living.

In October the company found itself with $2,000,-000 inventory depreciated approximately forty per cent. Mr. Thieme called in the committee. He proposed to take off the last advance in wages proper, made in June, and to pay profits as before, only when earned, at the end of the year. He met the committee often. He wrote a long statement which was read at the union meeting. He implored them to accept his statements and to have confidence in his judgment and integrity. He appealed to individuals and presented facts and figures of every kind.

But wage-psychology could not think in terms of profit-psychology. Wages are paid now, but profits are paid a year, maybe ten years from now. They require different kinds of imagination. The committee of the union went to headquarters at Philadelphia. They came back confirmed in what they started with. "No wage reductions is the motto of our union."

On December 1st the 1,900 employees walked out.

It was nuts for the company. Raw material had been going down in price since October—twenty-five per cent in November, then fifty per cent in December. The price made on hosiery in October was already too high in November, and November prices much too high in December. Even had the union accepted the company's offer the company claimed it would have been losing money, although it would have been following its twenty-five-year policy of not laying off the workers, even at a loss, but making up the loss out of its unemployment reserve. The union laid itself off, and the reserve was not called upon.

On the worker's side, the union members felt that Mr. Thieme had fallen under the influence of other stockholders, who objected to the too high wages with their bad effects on the labor-market of Fort Wayne.

But Mr. Thieme himself believes that he has not changed his mind. He is only adjusting himself to new conditions. He warned the union what would happen. He used all his personal influence and prestige. A strike would be a slap at him personally. It would say that they did not trust him, that he was not straight. If so, he would not continue to do business with those who repudiated him after these many years of confidence.

So his new program, when the strike shall end and the men come back, is the Open Shop—no discrimination between union and non-union labor, but no recognition of the union through committees or otherwise. Instead, there will be a plan of organization which will put factory operations in control of the workers, by the workers, excluding officers of the company. All of the other features will not only be continued, but expanded. Profit-sharing again will be the leading feature, and with it, life, accident, sickness and unemployment insurance, old-age pensions, club house, community center, vocational education, efficiency through committees, and so on.

Was it profit-sharing or unionism that fell down?

XIII

FROM WELFARE TO DEMOCRACY

The management took the initiative, in 1912, and incorporated the Employees' Mutual Benefit Association of The Milwaukee Electric Railway and Light Company. After the details were worked out the proposal was submitted to a mass meeting of employees. They voted to adopt it. Membership would be voluntary, would be open to all, but after a lapse of four months new members must pass a physical examination and be within twenty and twenty-five years of age. About one-half of the employees were enrolled. The initiation fee is $1, monthly dues fifty cents, and the company contributes the running expenses and a sum equal to the total contributions of employees.

The benefits would be $1 per day of sickness for the first 100 days, then fifty cents per day for the next 100 days. Life insurance would be $300. The Association would be governed by a Board of Directors, the employees electing twelve, the company selecting an equal number. The company side elects the president and he appoints an executive committee of three from the employees and two from the company.

While this Association was being formed the company placed its social policies, other than those entrusted to the Association, under the control of a general director. He was made Secretary of the Association, paid by the company. The Secretary, Mr. Bert Hall, previously a popular social worker in the town, began by arranging definite and regular days off for trainmen, so that they could make and keep appointments instead of being called back at will of the management if there happened to be a shortage of trainmen.

A large number of the men were in debt, and garnishments were coming in at the rate of twenty or twenty-five every pay-day. The Secretary circularized practically all of the attorneys, collection agencies, installment houses, asking them to send the bills to him and keep the cases out of court. The company was induced to start a loan office, confidential conferences were held with men in debt, no interest was charged on loans, and now there are almost no garnishment actions. The Secretary is, in fact, a legal aid society. Threatened divorce suits are averted. Wives bring to him their grievances about sharing their husband's wages. Even neighborhood quarrels get into his office. The point is, the men are better workers when not worried by debts, courts and domestic troubles.

Two years passed. Additional life insurance, up to $2,000, was then offered to members at cost. Accident insurance while on duty is cared for by the state compensation law, and does not come under the Association. But sickness and accidents off duty were now provided with benefits additional to those mentioned above, at the actual additional cost of the risk, up to $120 per month, as the member might wish. Even accidents on duty may be insured by a member at cost, in addition to what the state requires the company to pay. Medical and hospital services for sickness and accidents off duty are provided free out of the funds of the Association.

Another change was made in the articles of incorporation. The employees were given thirteen and the company eleven members on the Board of Directors, each with one vote on amendments to the by-laws and other matters, except the benefits. A change in benefits requires a two-thirds vote, and, in order to give the employees control of the "additional" benefits which they alone pay for, the vote of each company director counts only 59/100 of a vote. But, on the "regular" benefits, to which the company contributes one-half, it is one-member-one-vote.

The free medical service was not getting the results hoped for. It had been installed on the assumption that employees would go to the doctor at the central building. But many did not. The average loss of working time on account of sickness was nine or ten days per year per employee. But while they forgot to consult the doctor they did not forget the sick benefits. Thousands of dollars were being paid. The question was, How to *prevent* sickness and how to get prompt attention when not prevented.

The Board of Directors experimented, tried various plans, discussed the matter at great length. Finally they evolved this: A doctor's office is opened at every place where the 4,000 employees go to work, including the cities of Racine, Kenosha, Waukesha and Watertown, where the company's lines extend. Assistant doctors are stationed there. A man cannot go to work without passing the doctor. Superintendents and foremen are instructed to watch for men who seem to be under the weather. A man with a cold, or a headache, or a touch of rheumatism, does not put off going to the doctor. If he does not show up and reports himself sick—which report is his claim for benefits—he is visited at once by some one from the Secretary's office. He is asked, "Do you want the Association physician?" If he does, the physician comes. If not, he gets another. An Association nurse, and medical supplies, are sent if needed. There is a complete X-Ray outfit at the central office.

At the end of the first year the time lost on account of sickness was reduced 35.8 per cent, and the average is now only four or five days instead of nine or ten. It can easily be estimated how much more money is earned by 4,000 men who increase their working days four or five a year. It is much more than their dues of $6 a year. During 1919 there were 15,542 of these office calls, 2,167 house visits, and 96 surgical operations for members.

The close attention to prevention of sickness of employees revealed the fact that sickness in the family was a cause of absenteeism, of inefficient work, of accidents. Moreover, the savings effected by preventing sickness showed themselves in a big surplus in the Association treasury. Evidently free medical attendance should be extended to the wives and children of employees. This was done in 1916. Additional nurses were added. The doctor and nurse at the house enable the man to be at work. In 1919 there were 2,156 office calls of wives and dependents, 6,240 home visits for them and 181 surgical operations. The value of the services rendered to families was $41,218. And the dues remain where they were—$6 a year. Naturally the wives of employees have formed the Women's Auxiliary of the E. M. B. A.

A conductor on the street car told us what he thought of the E. M. B. A. It saved him $50 week before last. At another time his little girl had adenoids. The Association surgeon removed them, and "it didn't cost me a penny." His boy needed an operation. He had arranged for it the next week. "The free medical service will save me $100 this year."

From the standpoint of the doctor this development of social insurance with industrial medicine and surgery has brought a decided change of front. Dr. C. H. Lemon, the Chief Surgeon of the company, has commented on it. It is a change from Individual to Group Medicine, and from Cure to Prevention.

If the relation between the physician and the family becomes unsatisfactory, in ordinary practice, the relation is easily terminated. Another patient comes to the doctor, and the former relation is perfectly balanced without prejudice to either. But both the family and the association of families within the corporation are a group. If the relation between physician and patient now becomes unsatisfactory, the entire group becomes an interested party. The man higher up must be dealt with, and he is the General Manager, who is personally interested in the welfare of *all* his employees. The doctor must make good to all and not expect to advance with some patients if he fails with others.

"From the standpoint of health," says Dr. Lemon, "the group plan has many advantages. A service which can be had for the asking, will be used effectively. Men are curious to know what ails them, and this curiosity can be satisfied if no extra expense is incurred

in the investigation.   And why should not this be so?
If medicine is of any use whatever, its greatest usefulness should be the seeking out of blind disorders
and remedying them before they have become dangerous factors in a man's life.   Preventive medicine,
therefore, finds its highest application in the group
form of medical service."

In 1915 the company established a profit-sharing,
or rather, efficiency-sharing plan.   The employees elect
a bonus committee for each department.   The employee, dissatisfied with his bonus, gets his bonus committee to ask for a review and adjustment.

Take the transportation department.   From its
records for several years the company determined a
set of operating cost standards.   If the employees keep
the actual costs below this standard, they share one-
half the saving with the company.   There are five factors in the bonus.

1.   Injuries and damages are expressed in per cent
of operating revenues.   This percentage had been fairly
constant, and was taken as the standard.   If the men
keep the amount of damages below that standard, the
difference is profits to be shared.

2.   The speed factor is expressed in trainmen-wages
per car-mile.   If the trainmen keep up their schedules,
which are fixed below the standard of speed, they get
a corresponding profit in terms of cents per car-mile.

3.   Maintenance of equipment factor is based on a
standard cost for wrecks, fare-box and glass maintenance in so far as directly controlled by the men,
expressed in cents per car-mile.

4.   Operating-revenue factor is expressed in cents
per car-mile excess over a standard revenue.   The cents

per car-mile gained above the standard multiplied by the actual car-miles per month gives the gross profit for the month.

5. Power-coasting: the skilled motorman who shuts off power when he can coast saves electrical energy. There are seventeen different standards, of which seven apply to recording meters and ten to coasting clocks. The meters give the kilowatt-hours and the coasting clocks the time for coasting. The saving is computed in terms of gross profits.

With these standards established, the trainman begins each month with a credit of 1,000 merit points. Schedules of demerits have been arranged. The total demerits for the month are subtracted from 1,000. An employee is disqualified for profits if his demerits for the month are 250 or more. At the end of the month the grade points of those with 751 or more points are added, the employee's share of the gross profits is divided by this sum, and the unit thus obtained, multiplied by the individual's points, gives his share.

For November and December, 1918, ninety-nine per cent of the trainmen shared the bonus. The average bonus for 1918 was $11.18 per month. The maximum was equivalent to 4.2 cents per hour, the minimum 3.15 cents.

The company then introduced old-age pensions. An employee sixty years of age, in the service of the company fifteen years or longer is permitted to retire on pension for the rest of his life. At the age of seventy, with continuous service fifteen years or longer, the company retires him. If, by misfortune, an employee is incapacitated just preceding the time for his retirement, he is granted a pension for fourteen years. One and one-half per cent of the annual average wage for the past ten years multiplied by the number of years of continuous service of the employee, gives the amount of the annual pension. No pension falls below a minimum of $240 nor exceeds a maximum of $750. In July, 1919, the administration of this pension was turned over to the E. M. B. A. The company has obligated itself to the Association to continue its financial support up to an amount equal to one-fourth of one per cent of the total operating revenues per annum.

We now come to the Labor Agreement of April, 1918, by which the company granted the right of collective bargaining and gave the E. M. B. A. supervision over employment and the employment bureau. The company agreed to employ thereafter only persons who "indicate their willingness to become members of the Association." The employment manager is hired by the company. Prior to this agreement the membership ranged from 2,500 to 2,900. Now it is over 4,000.

Under the direction of the E. M. B. A. the Employment Bureau has prepared trade tests, by which a man's fitness for a job is determined before sending him on to the foreman. Such careful selection will reduce turnover. This is quite a considerable task here, since there are 179 different trades. Another task, that of finding the causes of "quits" and discharges, is investigated. What is going on here is a centralization of power in the Employment Office. Employees demand security of employment. They have no business agent, like the trade unions, to look after their interests in this vital matter, but they have the Employment Bureau.

The influence of the Association shows itself again in the work to combat the high cost of living. Thousands of dollars' worth of food and clothing have been bought and sold to members at wholesale prices. The Women's Auxiliary handles the sales. A building and loan association is another feature.

Finally "collective bargaining." It came about in this way—not the usual kind, but an Industrial Triangle—the E. M. B. A., the company and the state of Wisconsin.

In April, 1918, the E. M. B. A. began a demand for more wages. The company acknowledged it but plead financial inability until the state Railroad Commission should increase its revenues by raising the street car fares. The employees sent their committee to the State Commission. It declined to fix wages, having no legal power to do so, and sent the committee back to the company. Before the matter was cleared up, the Governor of the state, the Legislature, the Socialist administration of Milwaukee, and a one-day strike came into the mêlée.

The company, in April, 1918, in granting to the employees control over the Employment Bureau, granted them the right to bargain collectively through committees of their own choosing. This added a Labor Adjustment Committee to each of the thirteen departments of the company, composed of two employees elected for the purpose and the employee Director from that department. The Labor Adjustment Committee of the Transportation Department demanded the eight-hour day and fifteen cents an hour increase. Motormen and conductors were getting twenty-five to thirty-two cents per hour. The Railroad Commission told the employees in May, 1918, that it would not fix wages but would provide for a reasonable increase in wages when it fixed the street car fares. Finally in June the decision came, granting fares estimated to bring $800,000 increased revenues to the company. This took care of a ten per cent increase in wages.

In July the employees were clamoring for more wages. The company replied as before. Men were leaving for war industries, but the majority hesitated. The Association member who left sacrificed his sickness insurance, his free medical service, his life insurance, his old-age pension, and his rights to purchase benefits, commodities and homes at cost. Yet enough left to seriously embarrass the street car service. Two more meetings were held with the State Commission. The Commission granted increases in rates on electricity and heating furnished by the company, but not on transportation. The E. M. B. A. engaged accountants to go over the books of the company. A state commissioner intimated to the committee that the company was dodging the increase in wages. Then the E. M. B. A. demanded an increase of eight cents per hour and gave the company nine days to reply. Meanwhile, their accountants reported the company financially unable to pay. The report was submitted to the State Commission at two more conferences. The Commission replied as before. It was a rate-fixing body and not a managerial or wage-bargaining body. The Governor was brought in and tried to arrange another meeting with the Commission. The Commission declined.

Then the E. M. B. A. resolved to strike. The demand was changed from eight cents to four cents an hour. The strike lasted one day. The Secretary of the E. M. B. A. "struck" with the members. The company granted the four cents increase.

Then came the legislative investigation. The legislature created an Arbitration Board for public utility disputes. The Board is a kind of annex to the Railroad Commission. It submits its award to the Commission for approval, and within forty-five days the Commission must render its decision on increased revenues. In August, 1919, the Board awarded forty-eight cents per hour to trainmen, up to fifty-five cents for those with five or more years' service, and a working day of nine hours. The Railroad Commission approved and car-riders in Milwaukee began paying six cents instead of five cents.

XIV

FROM SCIENTIFIC MANAGEMENT TO UNIONISM

"THE Plimpton Press now deals with the union organizations and no essential difference exists between them; and the unions are anxious to assist the management of the Plimpton Press in developing the greatest productivity based on the fundamental principle that the health and well-being of the employees in their joint relation to the Plimpton Press and the unions is the largest single factor in the solvency of the concern."

The idea of good-will in an industry has seldom been put more strongly than in this statement from the agreement between the Plimpton Press and the four great international unions whose members it employs.

The Plimpton Press, of Norwood, Mass., is one of the few concerns in the country which can offer an answer to three questions which are of great interest to the public and to industry. Can scientific management operate to advantage in a union shop? What effect does scientific management have upon union employees? What effect do unions have upon scientific management?

For convenience let us answer the third question first. The Taylor system was in operation at the

Plimpton Press when that concern became a preferential union shop. The attack of the International unions was concentrated on one feature—the task and bonus system of wage payment, with its accompanying feature, the time study. In spite of the fact that those union representatives who were actually employed under this system voted in favor of its retention, and that the only Plimpton Press employees who voted to abolish it were themselves piece workers and not affected by the change, the Internationals succeeded in carrying their point. The task and bonus gave way to a straight day wage.

When the task and bonus system was in use, each job ticket issued by the Planning Room showed the standard or bonus time, and the additional amount which would be earned by the worker if the job were completed in that time. Since the abolition of the bonus, the ticket which goes to the worker does not show this standard time, but the duplicate ticket kept in the Planning Room still shows it. Although the company and the unions agreed on doing away with the setting of a time and the payment of a bonus for meeting the time, the company keeps records of individual performance, paying the union rate as a minimum and adding a premium rate to those whose previous records show an output which warrants it. A considerable number of the employees at the Plimpton Press are receiving premium rates—that is, more than the union scale. If a normally skillful and intelligent worker is not able to bring up his grade to the normal performance, he is tried out upon other work. Usually he can be shifted to some department where he can bring up his production.

The company still finds the time study essential in making estimates for contracts, in planning the work, in establishing a basis for grading employees and in fixing certain piece rates which will be discussed later.

Employees on certain work are very doubtful about the value of the time study for any of these purposes, so far as their own work is concerned.

"How in the world," they say, "can you make a time study for a proofreader or a printer? Here is an author whose manuscript is a mess of typewriting, handwriting and hieroglyphics of all kinds. Here is another who sends in pages so neat and clear that it is a joy to go through them. One chap keeps sending in changes and causing all kinds of trouble. Then there is a book with pages and pages of tables, and another with just as many, but entirely different kinds of tables. The only way you can make a time study of these things is to do all the work. And when you have it done you have a record of performance, but nothing to go by for the future. How can there be any sense or reason in making a time study when you aren't going to have any more objects like the one measured? Even if you have an industry where the raw material and the product are standardized, the time study still is inaccurate. You cannot standardize the weather, domestic troubles or the health of the worker."

On the other hand, even those employees who see little value in the time study agree with the company that there is considerable merit in the system of grading on the basis of production. "It is all right to pay more to those who show steadily high production over a considerable period of time. That is not the same as holding the hope of a bonus over the head of the worker, constantly tempting him to strain himself to the breaking point every minute of the day, and creating a nervous tension which results in the long run in a shortened period of productivity."

The straight hourly rate has been adopted in all except one department—the book bindery. Here the straight piece rate remains on three of the thirty-odd operations. The policy of the International Brotherhood of Bookbinders is opposed to piece work, but the binders themselves seem loath to part with it. Individual workers in the shop may be opposed to it, but the existence of piece work here, or in any New England shop, is due to the fact that the local binders themselves are overwhelmingly in favor of it. The Internationals are trying to educate their members away from the piece work system, but it seems to be a long, slow process.

There is no complaint here of decreasing productivity of employees. Apparently neither the company nor the people are consciously trying to decrease or to increase output. "No one can tell me that workers in general are shirks," said a member of one of the planning departments. "They are not. If the work is ready for them, they do it. Much of the blame laid by uninformed people on the workers does not belong there. The trouble in many factories is that the worker sometimes has to wait too long for his work, or he has to go all over the place to find his work and tools, or he may even have to go home for lack of work. Sometimes a piece of work may have been given to too high priced a workman. Sometimes the estimate and the contract may have been too low."

But none of this occurs at the Plimpton Press.
Scientific management saves the Plimpton Press from
all such causes of low productivity. The aim here is
to avoid all delay by having everything ready for the
worker and by bringing it to him at the right time.
The work is laid out for him two weeks ahead of time.
It is all laid out in the three planning departments—the
one for the composing room, the one for the press
room, and the one for the bindery. Instead of a
"group boss" or straw boss, there are production instructors over every group of ten or twelve persons.
There are practically no foremen of the old type.
Over the production instructors are the production
clerks of the planning department. The salesmen are
brought into the routine of the planning department.
Whenever they want rush orders, the planning department makes them take the responsibility for going
over all the orders and making arrangements to put
off certain ones in favor of the orders being rushed.

"It is perfectly natural," said one of the managerial
force, "that the worker should slacken up in rush times
and try to make the job last. We have to expect that
in industry until unemployment is abolished. Our
industry used to be highly seasonal, but we are gradually making it more regular. Our salesmen are trying through the publishers to influence schools to adopt
their text-books before Christmas for the next year
so as to avoid the rush in the late summer and early
fall. With the consent of the unions, we use high
school girls and boys to take up some of the rush work
during the summer vacation. Occasional rushes during the year we meet partially by having former women
employees come for part-time work."

This part-time work, according to certain representatives of the company, is not necessarily disadvantageous. The person who comes in fresh for a few hours of work, which is a change from the routine of housework, often does better work after a little practice than the person who stays all day. Shorter hours in general are desirable. On certain kinds of work, employees should certainly not be left all day. People who may be able to endure a few hours each day at certain kinds of heavy or monotonous work with no ill effects may be permanently injured by keeping at it continually. The change in work may not suit the worker at first, and over a period of a few months a loss in efficiency may occur, but over a long period of years, the results will be better from both points of view.

The printing business offers many varieties and grades of work. There is apparently, so far as preparation and training go, a vast stretch between the girl who folds the pages in the bindery department and the cultured proofreader of Greek and Hebrew. But both have the real trade union fighting spirit, as their wages attest. Experienced women piece workers claim that they can easily make $25 to $27 a week. They have secured large increases during the past year and are working energetically to raise the scale for women to a point that will bring their wage up to that of the men.

Among the skilled employees, both men and women —the same employees who are looking out most actively for their own interests—are many who show a great interest in their work itself. They have a gratifying sense of their own value to the industry. They believe that if the company saw fit to utilize fully their information and ability they could render greater contributions than they now do. They could give good advice, for example, when contracts are being let— advice more dependable, they think, than time studies. As a matter of fact, they do offer their suggestions through an elected production committee which discusses various matters with the management.

We started with three questions. We think that we have practically answered them all. Scientific management and the unions can and do exist together here. To be sure the task and bonus have gone and this, according to the ideas of some people, spells the end of scientific management at the Plimpton Press. But we do not think so. Neither does the management of the Plimpton Press. Neither, it appeared to us, do the employees.

The scientific management which exists and is developing at the Plimpton Press is the scientific management of coöperation between two groups of partners who have practically equal power and consequently equal interest in production. If this were the only union plant which we had visited, we might be inclined to conclude that it is the careful planning—a scientific management feature which has survived the coming of the unions—and the grading system of wage payment, which have kept up production, and have won over the employees to an interest in production. But the fact is that we have found production keeping up in the union shops where no formal system of scientific management has ever been installed. Perhaps, then, some credit needs to be given to the union itself.

The unions involved here are a part of one of the

most complete developments of industrial government in this country. The four great international craft unions of the Printing and Publishing business—the Typographical, the Pressmen, the Stereotypers and Electrotypers—and the Bookbinders, while each reserving complete autonomy within the craft, have been organized into the International Allied Printing Trades Association. The local unions of each international are likewise federated into local Allied Printing Trades Councils. The employers likewise have a national and local organization, known as the Typothetæ.

It is the Allied Printing Trades Council of Greater Boston with which the local unions represented in the Plimpton Press are affiliated. The Plimpton Press makes its agreement as to hours of work and conditions with the Boston Allied Printing Trades Council, and its wage agreement with each one of the local unions. As the members of the scale committee are elected from the locals and not from the shops themselves, the Plimpton Press may not be represented strongly, if at all, on the scale committee. The scale is submitted, however, to the local unions, and voted on by them.

Questions arising at the Plimpton Press concerning the agreement or concerning working conditions, may be settled, and often are, by negotiation between the labor manager and the individual concerned, or by the labor manager and the business agent of the union, or by the labor manager and a shop committee selected for the purpose. If this method fails, the dispute goes to Boston, fifteen miles away, to the Joint Board of Employers and the Allied Printing Trades. If they fail to reach an agreement, the parties resort to arbitration. The union chooses one member, the company chooses one, and the two members select a third member of a board of arbitration, the decision of which is binding on both parties.

Only one of the unions has a permanent shop committee in the factory. Among the employees numerous temporary committees are elected as occasion arises to present to the management whatever any group desires to bring up. Each committee is elected for a special purpose and when it has served that purpose its life ends. There is no local assembly and no court.

Is the production morale in the Plimpton Press kept up in the last analysis, then, by the existence of an efficient planning department? Or is it the knowledge of every worker that back of him are powerful organizations ready to support him in every move to retain or to secure his fair share of the product? Or is it due partly to the recognition by the company that it is the right of their employees to satisfy their elementary desires for safe hours, American wages, steady employment and treatment in keeping with their dignity and self-respect? Is it due to the strong personalities in the management—among whom are found one of the Joint Chairmen of the International Joint Conference Council of the Allied Printing Trades and the Typothetæ—a man who is known in Boston and among employers throughout the country as a friend of the workers in their orderly progress toward democracy and prosperity? To what extent is it due to the very unusual type of labor manager—a woman who combines a thorough knowledge of the industry with a sympathetic understanding of the employees and a love for efficiency and democracy?

All of these things must undoubtedly have their influence. Just how much credit should be attributed to each factor is something we cannot measure. Certain it is, however, that a fundamental experiment is being worked out here. Orderly industrial government and efficient production exist here not as a result of overwhelming authority on one side, but as the result of balanced power, of reason and knowledge on both sides. The same scientific spirit which prompts the Allied Printing Trades and the Typothetæ to the joint employment of research workers to present unbiased facts for consideration in negotiations is shown here in the relation between employers and employees of the Plimpton Press.

Have we not here in process of development a scientific management broader and more fundamental than the older form of wage system which has been abolished? When we find employer and employee *together* gathering facts for their negotiations, when we find both recognizing that tremendous possibilities may exist in the capacity of employees to interest themselves in the problems of production, when we find both sides going along steadily and patiently, willing to give new things a trial and yet not trying to force premature developments and experiments; then we feel that surely this is truly scientific management—scientific management based upon a democracy as sober, as dignified, and as solid as New England tradition.

XV

STANDARDIZATION AND STABILIZATION

THE INTERNATIONAL JOINT CONFERENCE COUNCIL

THE book and job printing industry, like other industries, faced a serious labor crisis during the period following the war. Business was good but it was impossible to get production. Scarcity of workers and apprentices resulted in a high labor turnover. Local unions broke their contracts and forced up wages by "direct action," thus demoralizing competition. The ranks of both employers and employees were disorganized. Stealing of labor was in common practice. In the large centers conservative trade unionists had lost control and were supplanted by radical leaders who flouted the disciplinary powers of the internationals. Some employers went far ahead of the game and met the problem by tempting labor with better wages and better conditions than employees had anticipated. But the printing industry had something that the other industries did not have. It had four national strongly organized groups of closed shop employers who were accustomed to deal with labor along constitutional lines and it had five intelligent American trade unions, organized to act together in the International Allied Printing Trade Association.

Almost simultaneously, these two groups recognized

that the situation had got beyond their control and that coöperation was necessary if either group was to reap the benefits of the possible increase in business. In February, 1919, members of the employers' associations met with the Board of Governors of the International Allied Printing Trades Association to discuss the situation and to find a means, if possible, of stabilizing the printing industry.

Other meetings followed in Cincinnati and Chicago, in which it was decided to effect a permanent organization. And in April the draft for an International Joint Conference Council was agreed upon, the first national industrial government in the United States. Its purpose, expressed in the Preamble, is as follows:

"Only through joint conference in the spirit of mutual helpfulness between employers and employees can the foundation be laid for stable and prosperous conditions within the Printing Industry. To promote the spirit of coöperation and to deal with the problems of the industry in a way to insure the protection of the interests of all concerned, the establishment of the International Joint Conference Council is considered essential."

The Council is a representative body of twelve members, four trade unionists and eight employers.[1] Each

[1] Membership of the International Joint Conference Council.
Employers' Associations:
Closed Shop Branch of the United Typothetæ of America (2)
Printers' League of America (2)
International Association of Employing Electrotypers and Stereotypers (2)
Employing Bookbinders of America (2) (not yet jointly affiliated)
International Unions:
International Typographical Union (1)
International Printing Pressmen's and Assistants' Union (1)
International Stereotypers' and Electrotypers' Union (1)
International Brotherhood of Bookbinders (1)

union representative has two votes. This division was
made because the unions felt that they could not afford
to send more than one member to the meetings, while
the employers, on the other hand, needed a larger number of representatives on account of diverse local conditions. There are two joint chairmen who sit side
by side at the head of the table, a trade union president
and an employer. Meetings are held usually once in
two months in different printing centers.

Though the chief function of the Council is legislative, its law-making power is limited. All resolutions
not only have to be passed unanimously by the Council,
but they must be ratified by all of the organizations.
Once accepted, however, they become the law of the
trade for the United States and Canada. In this way
the machinery has been set up to develop a body of
law for the printing trades which will be representative
of the will of the electorate, the employers and employees. The power of enforcement lies in the disciplinary control of the different organizations over
their members. In prosperous times it is the trade
union radical whom it is hard to curb and in periods
of falling prices and an overstocked labor market, it is
the employer with open shop tendencies, the man who
wants "to run his own business."

Judicial authority, also, has been left in the hands
of the separate organizations, but their practice has
been standardized by an arbitration code which the
council has drafted to be used by all members. Unless
some such provision was made, the Council realized
that it would be required to pass upon cases involving
its own recommendations. If the experience of the
Whitley Councils in England can be considered a

parallel example, the decision was a wise one, for recent reports indicate that the functions of those councils have been subordinated to the judicial and that they have become in many instances merely courts for the settlement of disputes rather than progressive legislative bodies.

In spite of the governmental activities of the Council there has been no real power delegated to it. Any organization can block any resolution either in the Council or by referendum vote so that in no sense has individual automony been sacrificed. No action can be taken on international union laws and it has little or no power of enforcement. The constitution is without an "Article Ten." Age-long craft jealousy and independent spirit of the locals would have made a stronger association impossible. Its real force lies rather in good-will and the intangible elements of moral power which have grown out of the mutual trust created by the frank "man to man" relationship in the Council. Too much credit cannot be given to the first small group of pioneers who cast prejudices aside and united in a common cause, the welfare of the industry.

Right of contract and joint counsel on problems of management are the two principles on which the Council is based. These have been incorporated into a scheme or organization which makes no change or redistribution of the balance of power. In this sense it is not a government but rather a Council where opposing groups can meet to present important questions and to plan constructively for the future of the industry. It has assumed no obligations, but as it vindicates its existence and inspires confidence there is every expectation that its powers will increase. As one

enthusiastic trade union president put it, "It is in fact
an evolutionary instrument that provides the gradual
promotion of a relationship that will be stable and
lasting."

There are many who fear an element of danger in
this form of organization. When labor and capital
get together, there is a strong possibility that the public
will be "held up." The force which keeps labor and
capital apart is the antagonism between wages and
profits. When an increase in wages cannot be passed
on to the consumer in the form of higher prices, because of competition, it must come out of profits. If,
however, through joint councils, an agreement can be
reached which will apply to all employers and employees, the public pays the bill. Such a situation has, in
fact, arisen in the photo-engraving industry which is
almost completely organized. But there is little danger
of it in the book and job printing industry since over
half the employers run open shops. The United
Typothetæ of America, which is by far the largest
employers' association in the printing trades, is composed of both closed shop and open shop employers.
They hold joint meetings on all questions involving
"educational policies," such as costfinding systems,
credit, and apprenticeship. For determining matters
of labor policy the members are divided into two divisions, the Closed Shop Division and the Open Shop
Division, which function as two separate organizations.
When labor is scarce the influence of the open shops
is not so strong, since they have to provide even more
attractive wages and conditions to maintain their
working force. At such times labor is dictator. When
the supply of labor is normal, however, the open shops

are a powerful restraining factor, capable of under-
bidding in the highly competitive market. Thus they
act as a balance wheel. The power of the courts to
dissolve price-fixing combinations and to curb activities in restraint of trade checks any obvious and formal
attempts to conspire against the public.[1] Another
means of offsetting the dangerous effects of such trade
alliances is to have the public represented on the councils. In the Whitley Councils the government has
representatives. In New York the publishers of books
and periodicals, though not as emissaries of the public
yet as customers of the printers, have been asked to
send a representative to the New York Printers
Council.

But there is too much of good to be gained from this
form of government to repudiate it on account of the
possibility of future monopolistic control. Inefficiency,
loss of time through strikes and lockouts, industrial
unrest, duplication of effort, business failures are just
as disastrous to public welfare and react on prosperity.
If the danger becomes imminent, some different form
of control must be created which should, however, pre-
clude the possibility of return to the former "big stick"
method of industrial relations. Meanwhile the International Joint Conference Council has been justifying
its existence.

THE WORK OF THE COUNCIL

From the outset, the Council was no paper organization. It immediately set to work to find some
practical solution of the problems of reconstruction

[1] See below, pp. 180 and 181.

facing the industry. It was a time when there were no standards. Each group had adopted a policy of expediency and made what gains it could for its own ends. Consequently, local as well as national industrial relations were in a chaotic state. What was needed was a crystallization of a labor policy into fundamental principles, capable of immediate and general application which would provide common methods and common standards in wage negotiations and in the settlement of disputes. The Council adopted for its slogan "stabilization and standardization," and as the first step in its program, formulated Five Cardinal Points of a Labor Policy to be used in all wage negotiations:

1. That the industry frankly recognize the cost of living, as compared to 1914, as the basic principle in wage adjustment.

2. That the industry pay at least a reasonable living wage; scales below this to be adjusted in frank recognition of the basic principle involved.

3. That, when not in conflict with the existing laws of the constituent body, local contracts be for a period of not less than three years, and include a clause providing for annual readjustments of wages based upon the cost of living, as determined by authorities jointly agreed upon, and upon the economic conditions of the industry at the time of the readjustments.

4. That a uniform standard system of cost-keeping is considered fundamental to insure stability, permanence, and prosperity to the industry, and to provide a basis for securing a greater degree of uniformity in conditions throughout the country; a clause to be included in local agreements providing that such a standard system as is recognized by the organizations represented in the International Joint Conference Council be required.

5. That controversies over wages, hours, and working conditions between employers and employees can and should be settled without resorting to lockouts or strikes, through voluntary agreements to refer disputes, where unable to settle through conciliation, to joint boards of arbitration composed of equal representation of employers and employees, provision being made for an impartial arbitrator if necessary.

The failure of the employers to increase wages to meet the rising cost of living had been an aggravating factor back of the "direct action" movement. At the outbreak of the war many local unions were under long-term wage contracts which contained no clauses providing for readjustment. When prices rose, the workers asked for higher money wages and were invariably refused on the ground of the sacredness of contracts. In some cases they resorted to "direct action" and won out. To mitigate this situation the Council drafted the first three points, recommending a reasonable living wage and its maintenance by means of an automatic readjustment clause to operate on the basis of the changes in the cost of living. By this means flexibility has been secured for the long-term contract which is desirable for stability in the industry.

The first application of these principles was made in Chicago in August, 1919. At the reopening of the wage negotiations both sides produced statistics. According to the union's figures, which were based on wholesale prices of a wide variety of products, the cost of living had increased 102 per cent since 1914. The employers' figures, obtained from the U. S. Bureau of Labor Statistics, showed that *retail* prices of all articles in the family budget had risen only 74.47 per cent. The employers' figures were finally accepted as pertinent to wages and the wages were increased 74.47 per cent above the 1914 scale. In the new supplemental contract provision was made for an automatic readjustment of the scales every six months according to the cost of living figures of the Bureau of Labor Statistics.

Since then the principle has had wide application in nearly all of the big printing centers. In instances where the 1914 scale was obviously below a reasonable wage the base was revised. One employer reported as follows:

"I got the cylinder feeders to appoint a statistician to check me up on cost of living figures and after a series of conferences between employers and employees, in which not a heated word was spoken, by the use of facts, reason, and a square deal, we arrived at the first peaceful settlement of a wage controversy in this local printing industry since 1917. I am sure if the employers continue in the policy they are now adopting, they can eliminate direct action."

The aim of such a clause is to substitute the use of facts for the gambling method of determining wages in which both sides refuse to display their cards. In wage negotiations it has been customary for the unions to ask for six dollars when they expect to get three dollars, and for the employers to use similar tactics. But there is still another factor. "Family budgets and family bread bills" are only one element in the wage which in the ultimate analysis should rest upon the prosperity of the business. There is no labor group today which has not before it the vision of a higher standard of comfort. Whether they can attain it, is dependent upon two factors: the earning capacity of the business and their bargaining power. Again and again labor has been told that the industry could not stand a wage increase and yet such demands have been met not once but many times, until labor has lost sight of the "economic conditions of the industry" as a limiting factor. According to the Third Cardinal Point, however, it must be included.

This is a more difficult theory to apply concretely, for it is composed of many unknowns. What is the "economic condition of the industry" and what items does it include? To reduce this element to a factual basis the Council recommended that economic surveys be undertaken in the various printing centers. The first was inaugurated in Chicago under the direction of Dr. Horace Secrist of Northwestern University and was based on the following analysis:

"1. Production Facts—Factory Analysis.
"Under this head such topics as production methods, specialization, sources and prices of materials, purchasing methods, handling of stocks and inventories, character and amount of output, etc., should be investigated.

"2. Labor Facts—Industrial Survey.
"Under this head, employees should be fully classified by types, duration of service, and wage rates; and hours of labor, turnover, sources of labor supply, welfare and working conditions and industrial discontent, etc., should be measured where possible. Moreover a study should be made of apprenticeship relations and the bearing of these upon the labor market. It is not intended here to include a complete list of facts to which attention should be given, but only those which seem to be of primary significance.

"3. Financial Analysis.

"Under this heading, inquiry should be addressed to such matters as the following: types and amount of investment, earnings, resources, equipment, accounting methods and control, cost analysis, etc.

"4. Trade Facts and Analysis.

"In relation to this topic, the significant facts having to do with local and regional competition and coöperation, as well as to the concentration of the industry in Chicago should be considered."

Another interesting case occurred during wage arbitration proceedings in New York in the winter of 1920.[1] In arguing the case of the union, President A. G. Hayes of the New York Paper Handlers' Union, No. 1, maintained that the union was greatly handicapped in the presentation of its case and that the arbitrators could not render an intelligent decision because of lack of complete information as to capitalization, assets, liabilities, earnings, dividend payments, and surplus of the printing firms, covering the past five years. Both the arbitrator and the employers agreed that the "economic condition of the industry" could not be determined without the facts. Though the employers refused to make their books available to the union, they assented to a joint survey by expert accountants on a broad, comprehensive basis, if a feasible plan could be determined upon.

But there is one point upon which the Council did not touch. When the economic condition of the industry has been ascertained, upon what basis is the division between wages and profits to be made? This after all is the crux of the problem and upon it the Council is

[1] Under consideration, January, 1920.

silent. Since the unit of measure has not been discovered, the share of each factor will still depend upon bargaining power, swinging between the limits of the bare cost of living for the workers and the minimum of profits necessary to keep the business alive. The real service of such an investigation is the publication of the facts upon which to justify demands. In the past bargaining power has been blind, and ignorance of conditions has been a cause of hostile feeling and suspicion. With the facts thus ascertained and weighed, collective bargaining ought to enter into a new era. Everything will depend upon the method used and the willingness of the employers to open their books, for there are many trade facts which competitors necessarily wish to keep from each other.

Statistics require accurate and uniform cost-keeping and this is the Fourth Cardinal Point. Cost-keeping will serve as a business barometer. The progressive printing employers have favored it for many years because it eliminates competition from cut-prices due to ignorance, the bugbear of the printing industry. It is only recently that it has been considered an element in the labor policy. With the adoption of arbitration, and the principles which have just been considered, the settlement of disputes depends upon facts. Usually there is no coöperation in the collection and assembling of statistics and often the labor group does not understand the employers' figures. The adoption of a uniform standard cost-keeping system through joint action of unions and employers would eliminate the misunderstanding arising from the use of facts in wage negotiations and in arbitration proceedings. It would also serve as an agency for standardization.

In the customary clause adopting the principle, the unions agree not to work for employers who do not operate their business under the Standard Cost-finding Clause and the employers agree to employ only union labor. In this sort of an agreement there is an element of danger as illustrated in the photo-engraving industry, where the unions have carried the development further and have set even the minimum selling base for photo-engraving. Union members will not work for employers who charge lower prices on the theory that they would react unfavorably on the conditions surrounding the industry. The publishers of trade papers and newspapers brought suit against this combination in the New York Court under the Donnelley Act for conspiring arbitrarily and unlawfully to raise and fix prices of engravings. They lost their case on the ground that photo-engravings are not commodities within the meaning of the laws in restraint of trade but a process or act, the result of which is not merchantable. They are considered in the light of a contract between buyers and sellers of labor or services rather than salable commodities. As a result of this decision of Judge Mulqueen's,[1] labor not only can fix the prices of its services with employers, but also the price the customer must pay for these services.

The photo-engravers are not members of the International Joint Conference Council. The printers, who are members, are not in a favorable situation for two reasons: they produce commodities instead of services and standardization of prices is difficult since the unit of measurement is variable and not the square inch of

[1] Not reported. See *American Photo-Engravers*, March, 1915, p. 183.

photo-engraving. Realizing the possibility of an adverse court decision, the Council has been very cautious in adopting even a standard cost-finding clause and has sought legal advice from the consulting lawyers of the different organizations represented. Their opinion has been practically unanimous that a simple cost-finding clause, such as the one mentioned above, is legal, and that, since the courts have upheld the right of any man to refuse to work for an employer unless he employs union men, the same rule would apply in regard to refusal to work for an employer unless he adopts a cost-finding system. One lawyer included a note of warning: "The serious situation, however, is whether it is a conspiracy to fix prices. That would depend a good deal on how it (the clause) operated. So long as each individual employer maintains his own cost-finding system and ascertains the actual bona fide cost of his individual plant, there cannot be any charge of price fixing. However, if a group of employers under such a contract get together and average the cost by which they make a fictitious cost instead of an actual bona fide cost, then I am inclined to think it would be a conspiracy to fix prices." Only last year the United Typothetæ of America was investigated by the Federal Trade Commission because of their campaign to install a standard cost-finding system. They were exonerated, however, because there was no evidence of restraint of trade. Rightly interpreted, therefore, the application of such a clause will make for business stability and an enlightened labor policy. And, as previously stated, as long as there is an active and strong open shop organization in the book and job printing industry, as there is not in the photo-engraving industry, there will be no actual danger of a price conspiracy.

Since the adoption of this principle by the Council, it has met with unexpected opposition both from the radical labor group and a conservative element among the closed shop employers. The left wing of labor is against its application on the ground that it is not the proper function of labor to run the employer's business, but to exact as high a recompense as possible and to take advantage of conditions as they arise. In other words, theirs is a militant philosophy which contains no element of coöperation. Some of the employers, on the other hand, are afraid of it because they fear that it will open the way for the unions to demand an investigation of the employers' books and to secure a hold on the industry similar to that of the union of photo-engravers. As one employer forcefully said, "I for one will never consent to unions investigating my company's books, *never*. It is none of their business." Cost-finding systems are fine apparently when they are in the control of employers, but they represent advantages which cannot be shared.

There is little that need be said concerning the last Cardinal Point which deals with arbitration, a corollary of all real collective bargaining. To put it into immediate effect, the Council drew up a standard national arbitration agreement to be used by the separate international unions and employers' associations. As it is to some extent an experiment, a duration clause of only three years was included. It contains an international agreement between the two national organizations affected with a detailed code of procedure and a standard form of individual arbitration contract to be used by the locals with an appeal to the international board. It can be considered the "last word" in arbitration agreements. With both the employers and the unions urging its adoption by all their members, it will do much to standardize the method of dealing with industrial disputes and will give the strongest possible security of industrial peace. If the leaders of both sides can control their local constituencies, such an agreement practically guarantees the elimination of all strikes and lockouts, except in cases of extremity, for as one union president said, "these national boards are boards of exhaustion."

THE 44-HOUR WEEK AND "DIRECT ACTION"

Another immediate problem facing the Council was the question of the forty-four hour week. The issue was not a new one, but the position of added strength of the unions, following the war, forced the demand in the more radical centers. Indeed, it was partly the realization of this situation which made many employers eager to organize the Council, for unless the forty-four-hour week were a universal proposition, it would be difficult for the forty-four-hour shops to compete with the forty-eight-hour shops. It was a critical time for the Council. The New York unions included it in their demands for October 1st; the photo-engravers secured it for January 1, 1920, and withdrew from the Council after the second meeting because of its conservatism on this issue; other demands were in the offing. The union presidents were animated by two desires: to secure its universal adoption at the earliest possible moment and to avoid another such conflict as the fight for the eight-hour day in 1906 which cost them $11,000,000. The employers, on the other hand, felt that the industry could not stand a sudden transition. After considering all factors, May 1, 1921, was set as the date for its inauguration, and the action was duly ratified by all organizations. The four international unions have since passed a resolution stating that, "a moral obligation rests upon their members to stimulate production so that the introduction of the forty-four-hour week shall carry with it as small a decrease of output as possible," with hope of forestalling wage decreases.

The New York strike-vacation-lockout in the fall was the "direct-actionists'" answer to the Council. As it forced the Council to take a stand on several other issues as well, it is worth while to review the case.

Since the eight-hour strike of 1906, there had been no serious industrial disturbances in New York. Both the Closed Shop employers, who do about seventy-five per cent of the business in New York, and the unions were well organized and accustomed to deal with each other through arbitration agreements. "Big 6," the local union of the International Typographical Union, was working under a contract dated from January 1, 1916, to September 30, 1919, and No. 51 of the International Printing Pressmen's and Assistants' Union under a contract dated from December 1, 1915, to September 30, 1919. No. 23, the Press Feeders' Local, was also under a long-term contract. By 1917 the cost of living had increased thirty per cent over 1915 and the feeders, whose wages have always been notoriously low, felt the pinch first. When they asked for a revision of the wage scales in April, 1917, they were refused on the grounds that such a change would affect the stability of contracts which meant business confidence. The unions, including No. 51, had no thought of breaking contracts but wanted to arbitrate the question of wage increases. Demands were made again in October. At length the employers offered a small increase, but their offer was refused. It was too late. No. 23 quit work to wait for a four-dollar raise. Since it was during the rush season, the employers were forced to capitulate and to grant increases to the other unions as well. Thus, after six months of talk, direct action forced the issue in three days and the unions discovered a dangerous weapon.

Cost of living continued to mount and in 1918 new requests were made. This time the War Labor Board was summoned to the rescue by the employers who feared another strike. This action angered the unions, who considered it a violation of the arbitration agreement. Adjustments were made finally and an agreement signed to reopen the scales again in May, 1919. By that time the New York unions had learned the value of coöperation among themselves and had united their forces. Three issues were involved:

1. Wage increases to meet the cost of living.
2. The adoption of the forty-four hour week on October 1, 1919.
3. The adoption of the photo-engravers' plan of fixing prices.

As a result of negotiations, wage increases were postponed, the employers agreed to work for the national acceptance of the forty-four-hour week in the Council and to abide by its decision, and to accept the third proposition if legal. Meanwhile the Council passed the forty-four-hour week resolution to take effect in May, 1921.

When negotiations began in August the temper of the New York unions was militant. They had taken for their slogan "44-50 or fight." All other considerations, including arbitration which had been adopted as the Fifth Cardinal Point by the Council, were flatly refused. The situation became further complicated by the fact that both No. 23 and No. 51 were suspended from the International Printing Pressmen's and Assistants' Union for non-payment of dues. They belonged to a group of locals who were trying to impeach their president, George L. Berry.

It was, it will be remembered, the time of the illegal strike of the Railroad Shop Men. Secession and radicalism were in the air. The balance of power, for the time being, had been destroyed in favor of the workers. The international union presidents realized that the issue was a national one and that united effort was needed to fight the "orgy of radicalism." Their first step was to join forces with the employers. The International Printing Pressmen's and Assistants' Union set up new local unions in New York for old line trade unionists. The photo-engravers and the electrotypers, who had gotten what they wanted through their national unions, shut off plates and engravings from firms employing recalcitrant members. The American Federation of Labor threatened to revoke the charter of the Central Federated Union of New York if that body continued friendly relations with the outlaws. But the deciding factor was the mandate issued by the President of the International Typographical Union ordering the vacationists back to work and to arbitrate. Expulsion from the International Typographical Union would have serious financial consequences. Consequently, not only did the compositors return to work but the pressmen and feeders affiliated themselves with the new locals. Combined action had succeeded in holding the weaker employers from yielding to the "direct actionists," and in breaking the power of the radical leaders.

The strike was over and "direct action" was defeated. The influence of the Council had been intangible, but it was, nevertheless, very real. It had defined the issues on which the employers and international unions had taken their stand,—cost of living in wage adjustments, arbitration, the national inauguration of the forty-four-hour week, and the underwriting of local agreements by officers of the international unions. But most of all it was important because it provided the machinery for open discussion of the strike, its causes, the principles involved, and the tactics to be employed, and made possible combined action without which neither group could have won single handed. It is significant, however, that the president of the International Typographical Union was defeated for reëlection in 1920, and a New York "direct actionist" was placed at the head of the national union. Also, in their convention in September, 1920, the Open Shop Division of the United Typothetæ of America passed a resolution opposing the introduction of the forty-four-hour week.

APPRENTICESHIP

Among the more fundamentally constructive plans, which the Council has initiated, is their treatment of the apprentice problem, a cause of much friction in the past. Since the life of the trade is dependent on skilled workers, the necessity of a long period of training has placed demand and supply on an artificial basis. On one side the employers have been desirous of increasing the numbers to keep down wages, whereas the unions have fought for a limitation of supply in order to maintain and to raise industrial standards. As a result of the lack of coöperation there has been duplication of effort and a really chaotic condition has been created in regard to numbers and training. The twenty-five per cent increase in business since 1914 made the situation acute and the Council immediately tackled the problem, on the ground that it was a question of joint responsibility.

As the first step, the following questionnaire was sent out by all the unions to their locals and by all the employers' organizations to their locals:

"1. How many apprentices in proportion to the number of Journeymen in the book and job offices are permitted under your local contract?

"2. How many apprentices are there actually employed in the book and job offices in your city?

"3. What is the total number of apprentice vacancies in book and job offices in your city which could be filled?

"4. What wages are paid during apprenticeship?"

Startling conditions were disclosed: apprenticeship vacancies varying from ten to fifty-four per cent at a time when employers were asking for a favorable change in ratios; differences in ratios varying from one apprentice to four journeymen, to one apprentice to ten journeymen; instances where wages were considerably lower than those of untrained messenger boys. When the returns are all in the Council will analyze and publish the facts in order to present the situation to the industry as a whole, and to stimulate local committees to act on the basis of their recommendations. These include a definite plan for the organization of local joint apprenticeship committees, a scale based on a specified ratio of the journeymen's scale, a definition of the proper work for an apprentice and provision for local contracts in regard to registration and training. If the Council realizes its ambition, there is every possibility that this factor in the industry will be both standardized and stabilized.

STANDARD CONTRACTS

As a further means of standardization, the Council has drafted several standard clauses to be included in local contracts on cost of living, arbitration and the organization of joint apprenticeship committees and has under consideration a cost-finding clause. Now, contracts are all different and often incomplete and crude. They have grown up like local common law. Custom, rather than well defined principles, has been the guide in drafting. The dissimilarity which results causes great unevenness in local conditions and makes a comparison of contracts impossible without complete rearrangement. Standard clauses defining the major issues will partly remedy this situation. But what is needed is a recommended standard form of contract drafted on scientific and legal lines, adaptable to the different crafts and diverse local conditions. For instance, one model which has been suggested is divided into four parts: I. Identification, Duration, Ar-

bitration.   II. Wages.   III. Working   Conditions.
IV. Execution, Ratification, Underwriting, with appropriate headings under each section and suggested standard clauses.   If such a form were in universal use, comparison would be easy and much of the burden which rests on scale committees would be lightened. There would be less opportunity to confuse issues. This is one of the problems scheduled for the future deliberation of the Council.

Another and perhaps the most valuable function of the Council is intangible in its nature.   The spirit of mutual trust and confidence which has been engendered between the members who "lay all their cards on the table" has made possible the consideration of many delicate problems.   Difficult local situations are openly discussed and analyzed, contemplated changes in policy, such as the question of abolition of piece rates in the binderies now under discussion by the International Brotherhood of Bookbinders, and difficulties arising out of the application of union laws and regulations. Though it is not within the province of the Council to act in many of these cases or even to recommend as a Council, the new light which is thrown on many questions by getting the point of view of the other side in such a meeting is of considerable influence.   One ardent Council member has gone even so far as to express his belief that the Council "can come pretty near settling all the problems that concern the printing industry."

DISTRICT COUNCILS

Though no agreement has been reached on any definite plan, the Council has under consideration the establishment of district joint conference councils. Many questions, such as wages and certain working conditions are local in their nature and lack of uniformity affects district rather than national competition. The need for some form of organization has long been recognized and in several districts temporary local councils have been formed to meet critical situations. Other districts have asked the Council for a constitution. But the complexity of the problem has delayed the adoption of any policy. The size of the districts, classification of cities, representation, jurisdiction and the relation to the International Joint Conference Council are difficult questions requiring careful treatment. The inauguration of district councils, however, will do much to insure the existence and influence of the national Council which at the present time is government superimposed from above. Local organization is, after all, the germ or cell of democratic government, and unless it finds an outlet for expression is unlikely to take a friendly interest in the national Council or to submit to its authority. The Whitley Councils in England and the national councils in Belgium have recognized this principle and built upon it. If some plan of decentralization can be worked out for the book and job printing industry, there will be greater assurance of the permanence of the national industrial government.

The Council may look back with pardonable pride to the record of its first year of probation in which it took no small part in returning the industry to a peace basis. The legislative and judicial machinery which it set up, worked. The principles laid down in the Five Cardinal Points have been widely and successfully applied; immediate demands such as the forty-four-hour week and "direct action" have been met as they arose and plans have been put into operation to remedy some of the more fundamental problems which have been undermining the industry. Through joint effort, the first scientific and comprehensive statistics covering the field of apprenticeship have been gathered and point to the possibility of building up within the craft a joint statistical service. Scientific collective bargaining has been demonstrated. Under the slogan of "standardization and stabilization" there is much that can be accomplished in the future for a business which has been the victim of competition and extreme individualism. Radical trade unionists and radical open shop employers will fight the Council. Its success will depend upon the maintenance of the balance of power and the realization by both employers and unions that their ultimate welfare is dependent on the prosperity of the industry. It has still to meet other tests in an era of falling prices and unemployment. During the period when labor had the upper hand, the rank and file of the employers were willing to accept the benefits secured for them by the Council, but whether or not they will continue to put into practice its ideal in their new position of power is still a problem of the future. Also, labor has still to prove its willingness to accept wage reductions in proportion to the decrease in the cost of living.

XVI

DUE PROCESS OF LAW

PROCEDURE

In a small, rectangular room on the second floor of their central factory, Hart, Schaffner & Marx and their employees hold court. A window opens on the commerce of Monroe Street; through the often open door the conversation of the halls and offices comes in. At the head of a plain table sits a big man with a VanDyke beard, a strong voice and a strong, understanding face, Mr. Mullenbach, chairman of the Trade Board. Mr. Mullenbach is umpire, paid equally by union and company. His position is that of a judge in a court of original jurisdiction. All day he adjusts the rival claims of company and "people"; keeping industrial warfare from becoming anything more than verbal conflict; turning out good-will for firm and people.

On the six floors above and in three other buildings in the city, the republic of eight thousand people, for whom this court dispenses justice, carries on its work. On the top floor the cloth is stored. On the floor below men are at work examining it and shrinking it, as it is unrolled, and then hanging it in long, movable frames, set next to a high ceiling to dry. In a high, well-lighted relatively quiet room, the cutters lay out their patterns in such a way as to waste no cloth, chalk around them, and cut their "lays," either with a hand tool or an electric machine. They are the aristocrats of the industry. Before the time of the Amalgamated Clothing Workers of America they would have scorned to ally themselves with the less skilled stitchers and pressers, spongers, buttonhole makers and helpers, who, with seventy other subdivisions of workers, make up the members of the union. In another room· women are stitching at long rows of clattering machines; on piece work, their hands flying so fast that the eye cannot follow them.

For all these workers and their fellows, and for their employers, the court below is the protector of rights and the enforcer of duties in those matters which affect their welfare most vitally, matters of the daily job. Under the agreement which is the constitution of the republic, the Trade Board is the first agency to determine the conditions under which a man is entitled to possess his job, and the wages and conditions of work which he may claim under the contract.

A case occurred in which a minor union official was brought to trial, charged with being a "trouble maker." He held two positions in the plant. For the union he was a "shop chairman." He earned his living by working for Hart, Schaffner & Marx, as a tailor. His position with the union involved taking up grievances of workers in his shop with their foremen. If questions are not settled in this way, they are taken to union deputies, paid officials of the union, not necessarily in the company's employ. These men try to settle matters by conference with the representatives of the company—"company deputies." Failing settlement by any of these methods, a cause of action comes before the Trade Board. A's position is that of the famous "shop steward" in England. He is also the man whom the open shop employers have in mind when they say they will deal only with representatives of their own employees.

In this case the company had lodged complaint against A with the Trade Board. The action petitioned for was his removal from his position as shop chairman. Under the agreement, a shop chairman may not be discharged by the company, nor may he lose his union position except after trial by the Trade Board.

A was charged with being a "trouble maker." A squat, square-headed, white-faced, phlegmatic Jew, he sat and listened to his trial. Next to him at the table sat two tailors from his shop, picked at random, the only members of the Trade Board of eleven, as originally constituted, besides the chairman, whom either side had found it worth while to have present. They were there to answer questions and watch proceedings. The Trade Board was originally organized as a body composed of five union representatives, five company representatives and an impartial chairman, but it no longer functions as a joint council. Both sides are interested only in Mr. Mullenbach's decision and their Trade Board representatives have ceased to meet. Next to the tailors sat the two union deputies who were conducting the case for A, one a soft-eyed man with a sharp tongue and a refined, peculiarly oriental face; the other a Russian bulldog. At the end of the table Mr. Mullenbach presided. On his left the dark, keen deputy for the company carried on the prosecution.

The first witness, a fiery Jew, foreman in the defendant's shop, testified that A had refused him "any satisfaction" in the case of a stitcher who was doing bad work; and that when the witness insisted on taking the matter up with the superintendent, A had said "I'm through with you," hinting at trouble ahead among the foremen's workers. The foreman gave testimony also to convict A of lying in order to gain recruits for the union. In a cross examination of the witness by the union deputies, an instance of bad language used by him within hearing of women came to light, and, lawyer-like, the union deputies pounced on the item to discredit the character of the witness. Examinations of witnesses occupied the better part of two mornings and eight or ten men and women gave full testimony as to the activities and character of the accused. The types examined ranged from the Irish "forelady" who "always cried when she got mad," "but always apologized when she told a girl to shut up," knowing it to be unladylike, to the stolid next neighbor, who didn't know anything to A's discredit. In the course of proceedings the people in A's shop asked for a postponement of the hearing and during the interval they disposed of the case by deposing A and electing a substitute.

The case described is typical of the great number of actions that come before the Trade Board, in that most of them relate to discipline. No one can be discharged by foreman or superintendent directly. The labor department, directed by Professor Earl Dean Howard, formerly of the economics department in Northwestern University, must give its consent to a dismissal. But after dismissal the worker may appeal to the Trade Board for reinstatement, and many such appeals are made.

This case got no further than the Trade Board. The union deputies might, however, have had it appealed had it gone against them, to a higher tribunal. This tribunal is the Board of Arbitration, composed theoretically of the company's lawyer, the union's lawyer, and Mr. Tufts, Professor of Philosophy in the University of Chicago, but practically of Mr. Tufts.[1] Mr. Tufts acts also as a supreme court for the other men's clothing houses in Chicago which have installed a similar system.[2] The board is therefore a court of appeals for 35,000 workers. Its members, like the members of the Trade Board and the company and union officials, may act further on administrative commissions for Hart, Schaffner & Marx to determine interpretations of the agreement or to legislate on doubtful issues between company and people.

[1] Owing to the resignation of Mr. Tufts, Professor H. A. Millis, of the Economics Department of the University of Chicago has been elected to fill his place.

[2] Mr. Williams, the first professional arbitrator, was a universally honored father of the republic. He is spoken of by a member of the business as "the wisest man I ever knew." Born in Wales, he emigrated to Streator, Illinois, at the age of eleven. He worked in a coal mine near Streator until he was twenty-six years old. As a laborer he gave himself something of an education. Among other activities he organized a reading class, in which he first became acquainted with the work of J. S. Mill. At twenty-six he left the mines, and became successively newspaper reporter, insurance agent, theatrical manager and composer, a vice-president of the Drama League of America, and a leader in the Unitarian Church. In 1909 he secured compensation for the Cherry Mine sufferers from the C. M. & St. P. Ry. From 1910 until 1914 he was arbitrator for the United Mine Workers of Illinois and the operators. From 1914 until his death, in the early part of January, 1918, he was arbitrator for Hart, Schaffner & Marx. Mr. Williams was a philosopher and a judge; a believer in trade unionism; and in the application of reason to the discovery of means to serve the common social interests of workers and employers.

In the afternoon following the first part of A's trial, the "court room" was occupied by a meeting of the Board of Arbitration. On this particular afternoon Mr. Tufts represented, as usual, the board. The board "met" as a commission, the "trimmers' commission," rather than as a court; primarily to argue the knotty question of what constitutes a fair day's work. Four union representatives were present, three regular workmen, led by the bulldog who had defended A in the morning. Three men represented the company. The two who led the discussion were the company's prosecutor of the morning, and a clear-headed, clear-faced young accountant, a law student of the University of Chicago.

Before the discussion of the fair day's work question, the meeting had been considerably warmed up by a short argument on another issue pending before the board, the issue of the number of workmen Hart, Schaffner & Marx ought to take on to supply a demand for clothes, which, as the company agreed, was temporarily inflated. Mr. Strauss, the head of the production department, a member of the Board of Directors, had testified. The "people's" delegates had insisted that some assurance should be given that the lay-off, expected to follow the boom, would not involve all of the usual unmitigated hardships of unemployment for the men turned out. No conclusion was reached, and in the heat of the argument there was visible a final source of disagreement and dissension between the parties. Each was determined that its view should be accepted. Several times the chairman, Mr. Tufts, a nervous, rugged man, brought quiet out of the confusion of shouting disputants with a request for order or by a sensible suggestion.

The question of what constitutes a fair day's work arose particularly in connection with the "trimmers" who do various types of work auxiliary to that of the cutters. The company claimed that the trimmers were not giving a fair day's work for what was admittedly a fair day's wage. The union deputies insisted on the exclusion from the discussion of the question of a rigidly set fair day's work as determined by time studies. Banging his hand on the table for emphasis, the bulldog deputy shouted that whatever might be determined in the meeting, his people would not stand for the settlement of a standard by any such means. The afternoon was spent largely in the presentation of figures by the company's accountant tending to show a falling off in production in the trimming rooms, and the detailed criticism of these figures by the union deputies and Mr. Tufts.

DISCIPLINE

This account of the operation of the agreement during a typical day at the Hart, Schaffner & Marx factory will serve as a description of procedure, and a background to the discussion of the elements of industrial law here and elsewhere. It is to be noted that many schemes of "industrial democracy" involve no such provision for judicial government as is here described, and that practitioners and proponents of these schemes believe them more efficient than a system based on litigation. Safety committees illustrate one extreme of non-litigious industrial government. Such plans for constructive and forward-looking planning as that of the closed shop Building Trades Parliament of England, and the open shop White Motor Company, of Cleveland, illustrate the other extreme. But in such industrial governments as those conforming roughly to the Leitch plan, those of the joint council type, and those providing frankly for arbitration as the main agency of regulation, whether under governmental or private control—in these American types it is believed that the rulings of governmental agencies may conveniently be grouped under two heads—discipline and the wage contract. The development under the Hart, Schaffner & Marx constitution of rules relating to these subjects may, within these limits, be taken as illustrative of the growth of industrial law.

The rule with regard to discipline and discharge is thus stated in the Agreement or "Constitution": "The full power of discharge and discipline rests with the company and its agents, but it is understood that this power should be exercised with justice and with due regard to the reasonable rights of the employee, and, if an employee feels that he has been unjustly discharged, he may appeal to the Trade Board, which shall have the power to review the case." All discharges, whether appealed or not, must be passed on by Mr. Howard, the employment manager. The judicial interpretation of the general ruling of the Agreement has led to the employment of the greatest possible leniency in dealing with cases of discharge. Thus, in a case which reached the Board of Arbitration involving the discharge of a cutter for inefficiency, Mr. Williams ruled that the burden of proof is on the company to show such a falling off in work as to warrant a discharge. In the case in question the company was held not to have sustained the burden and the cutter was reinstated. In another case the Trade Board decision refers to the fact that the ruling of the Agreement that any worker who strikes or incites others to strike during working hours "shall be subject to suspension, discharge or fine" has been generally disregarded by judgments of the boards; and in this case the Trade Board ordered the reinstatement of some armhole basters who had participated in a stoppage.

To compensate it for the employment of this rule of leniency, which is, of course, carried to no ridiculously logical extreme, the company enjoys the full cooperation of the union in maintaining discipline and restoring order after stoppages. Thus in the case of a serious stoppage in the cutting and trimming departments in May of 1917, as well as in a similar more recent case, a condemnation of the action of the highly skilled workers involved, and an appeal to the union leaders, who in turn effectively appealed to the workers, proved in the hands of the Board of Arbitration a sufficient remedy. In the small stoppages which occasionally occur in the various plants, the results of minor disputes, the intervention of an every ready union deputy or two restores order.

The strength of the union is thus recognized throughout the agreement as a foundation for the strength of the shop government. Further, the agreement recognizes the importance of maintaining union discipline. "The Trade Board and Board of Arbitration are authorized to hear complaints from the union concerning the discipline of its members and to take any action necessary to conserve the interests of the agreement."

Accordingly, it was ruled in one case that girls, members of the union, must pay their union assessments under penalty of discharge. In another case, involving a question of strengthening the union position, it was ruled that the jurisdiction of the union should be extended to include the inspectors in a certain department. The company's interest in efficient and independent executives was to be protected by special favor in cases involving the application of the preferential shop principle to these inspectors. That is, the company was not to be unduly restricted from the hiring and retention of good non-union inspectors.

The "government" also claims an interest in union regulations. The agreement says: "The provisions for preference made herein require that the door of the union be kept open for the reception of non-union workers. Initiation fee and dues must be maintained at a reasonable rate, and any applicant must be admitted who is not an offender against the union and who is eligible for membership under its rules. Provided, that if any rules be passed that impose an unreasonable hardship, or that operate to bar desirable persons, the matter may be brought before the Trade Board of Arbitration for such remedy as it may deem advisable." Accordingly, it was successfully contended by the company in one case that the imposition of an initiation fee of $100 for an individual, whom the union claimed to be disciplining for past offences against the union, violated the provision of the agreement; and the plea of the union that the fee as imposed was ninety-five per cent penalty and five per cent initiation charges was disallowed. Similarly, the Trade Board has held that collections may be made in the shop only with the consent of the two chief union deputies. The ruling is intended to prevent the practice of oppressive and extortionate charity in favor of popular men, as well as the illicit accumulation of strike funds.

The discipline of workers is further regulated by the ruling, laid down in the agreement and enforced in the decisions, that the company and company officials are subject to supervision by the two courts in matters affecting their relations with the workers, and subject to discipline in the same way as the workers. "The company's officials are subject to the law as are the workers, and equally responsible for loyalty in word and deed, and are subject to discipline if found guilty of violation. Any complaints against them must be made and adjudicated in the regular manner. They are to respect the workers and be respected by them in their position, and supported in the proper discharge of their duties." Accordingly, when the "people" petitioned for the penalization of the company for the use of a blackboard to designate off-pressers who fell off in production, the petition was denied not on the ground that such a measure as the one complained of was justifiable and ought not to be punished, but on the ground that it had been met by a stoppage of the off-pressers which, as a breach of the agreement on their part, ought to be punished by a denial of redress from the company. It is expressly provided: "If any foreman, superintendent or agent of the company shall wilfully violate the spirit of this agreement and especially if he fails to observe and carry out any decision of the Trade Board or Board of Arbitration, he shall, if charge is proved, be subject to a fine of not less than

$10 or more than $100 for each offense, at the discretion of the chairman of the Trade Board." In one case a fine, imposed by the Trade Board on a superintendent for failure to carry out certain minor arrangements in his shop to which he had agreed with a union deputy, was removed on appeal by the Board of Arbitration, on the ground that it was not shown that there had been any "wilfull and intentional" violation. The superintendent was let off with a reprimand for his negligence.

The principle of the preferential shop, a device characteristic of the clothing trade, designed to give the workers the maximum security consistent with the maximum labor market for the employer, and to strengthen the union power without unduly weakening the company, is thus stated: "Preference shall be applied in hiring and discharge. Whenever the employer needs additional workers he shall first make application to the union, specifying the number and kind of workers needed. The union shall be given a reasonable time to supply the specified help, and if it is unable, or for any reason fails to furnish the required people, the employer shall be at liberty to secure them in the open market as best he can. In like manner, the principle of preference shall be applied in case of discharge. Should it at any time become necessary to reduce the force in conformity with the provisions of this agreement the first ones to be dismissed shall be those who are not members of the union in good and regular standing."

It has been held that in the case of a shutdown of an entire factory, the preferential principle is to be applied as requiring the transfer of union men to the operating factories at the expense of the non-union men employed there. It has also been held that where changes in the volume of production necessitate the making of transfers at such disadvantageous terms as to produce quitting and to amount, in fact, to a lay-off, the preferential principle is to apply.

The seniority principle is thus recognized and applied. "If in order to properly balance a section, a reduction of force be required greater than can be secured by the laying off of non-union workers, as provided for herein, then there may be laid off those who are members of the union in the order of their seniority who have been in the employ of the company for a period of six months or less, provided that any exceptionally efficient worker, or any especially valuable member of the union, may be exempted from the rule of seniority. Provided, also, the company shall give notice to the chief deputy of its intention to discharge under this clause, and if he fails to agree, the matter shall be referred to the Trade Board." It has been held, also, in accordance with the contention of the people before the Trade Board, that where the quality of work done by two men is shown to be equal, the man older in service is to be given preference in promotion.

The provisions with regard to seniority and the preferential shop affect discipline in two ways. They prevent, to a large extent, arbitrary discrimination, and they strengthen the union, both as a coöperating and as a contesting agent.

The policy adopted by the government of Hart, Schaffner & Marx in dealing with that special class of discipline cases involving union officials has already been indicated. Shop chairmen, unlike the workers, may not be discharged except after trial and reduction from office by the Trade Board. Transfers of shop chairmen for purposes of discipline are also discouraged. Little trouble is recorded in dealing with the deputies, the extra factory officials of the union. These men are in constant opposition to the company deputies in presenting the claims of their clients and constituencies before the courts. Yet the interests of union and company in the success of their joint government have been so unified by the development of its constitution that union officials and company representatives alike exert themselves to the limit to keep the machinery running smoothly.

The great majority of the cases which arise in the factories are cases involving routine matters of discipline. These take the form of appeals from discharges or suspensions by the employment department, or with regard to any of the possible punishments imposed for breach of duty. These penalties comprise fines, suspensions, the disallowance of back pay between the time suspended and the time reinstated, transfers, loss of lay-off credit, and extra lay-offs at dull times.

Sufficient grounds for discharge are: poor work, disobedience, taking part in a stoppage, cheating, absence without excuse, and violent conduct or language. Under its general rule of giving the workers the maximum security consistent with the maintenance of production, the Trade Board, wherever possible, reinstates discharged workers who appeal. But it does not hesitate to impose lesser penalties nor to confirm discharges ordered on sufficient provocation. Thus, on petition of the people, a man who had been discharged for a refusal to cut with a machine, or "operate a machine lay" as it is called, was in one case reinstated without penalty. He said the machine made him nervous, and as there was plenty of hand work to go around, the Trade Board held there was no reason to require his employment at a machine. Had the case involved an effort to restrict output, the decision would undoubtedly have been different. On the other hand, a man who had refused to report for an interview with the superintendent of his shop without the protection of an accompanying shop chairman, and had consequently been discharged for insubordination was ordered reinstated, but without back pay for the time lost. And in another case, reinstatement was refused to a baster, who had been discharged for starting a stoppage during a time of suspension imposed for insubordination.

Transfers are used in the regular way to enforce discipline. A man may be transferred from week to piece work if his production is unsatisfactory. But such transfers are subject to court review, and it has been held by the Board of Arbitration that where a "youth has been transferred without adequate reason to his own injury" he may be reinstated by the Trade Board.

The courts further take a hand in settling minor quarrels and disputes in the shop. One worker was recently ordered by the Trade Board to apologize to another for calling him a liar. It was remarked that it is "to the interest of the people to have squabbles settled in public."

Thus, in a rough way, justice is done without too keen philosophical inquiries, and with more regard to equity than precedent. It is accepted that an able investigator, supported by company and worker, will devise means for serving the interests of both. The elimination of friction and the injustices of insecurity is designed to assure to the company coöperation in production; and to the workers stability of life and opportunity to progress.

THE WAGE CONTRACT

In the development of industrial law, an interesting set of cases arises over the various traditional union policies of interfering with production. These policies had their justification in the attempt to make the workers secure in the tenure of their jobs and guard them against the gradual change of standards expressed and implied in trade agreements. They involved an effort to standardize conditions of work through the limitation of output, the elimination of piece work and differential rates, the regulation of practices connected with the introduction of new machinery, and the limitation of apprenticeship. The conflicts of interest presented by these policies have been dealt with by agreement and decision under the government of Hart, Schaffner & Marx, and satisfactory compromises developed.

Thus it is agreed on both sides that the company is entitled to a "fair day's work for a fair day's wage." Three men were fined $5 each for organizing a conspiracy to restrict output in the back-making department, in order to get an increase in the piece rates in force there. They were not discharged because the union officials acted "courageously and intelligently" in helping to bring them to trial.

The union, on the other hand, contends—and thus far successfully—that a "fair day's work" cannot be construed, under the agreement, to call for greater production in any department than was being secured at the time the agreement was entered into. Any attempt to hold workers up to a standard above this point as determined, for instance, by time studies, would be regarded by them as an infraction of the agreement. The argument is that the amount of work that may be demanded under the contract is determined, in the absence of specific stipulations, by the trade custom at the time when the contract was entered into.

Within these limits, the determination of controversies involving questions of reduced output is left to a system of commissions. The difficulty of dealing with the problem without such a system is recognized in the following decision of Mr. Williams.

"On these questions of measurement of work I feel that the company takes the soundest attitude. It is anxious to agree with the union on some plan of judging work that will remove doubt and enable them to make a fair estimate of output. The union has thus far shown no disposition to cooperate in agreeing on such a plan. The present state of suspicion, of charges of slacking on the one side and of speeding on the other, is the inevitable result of such a planless situation. The burden of the situation falls with greatest weight on the company, for it is driven to try to secure an adequate output through the rather difficult and uncertain mechanism of trial boards. With the best of intention an arbitrator finds himself hampered in doing justice on the question of output, because he cannot grasp the inner facts with any accuracy, and is obliged to depend largely on the assertion of interested parties all keenly keyed up in a verbal combat and eager for victory. If the judicial method of settling disputes about output is to survive and be efficient. I feel very sure we will need to develop a rational plan or method for enabling us to form a correct judgment of work done; otherwise the award will be a guess, based on assertion, expediency, sympathy, authority—anything except enlightened judgment.

"It may be granted that this is a difficult task to impose on the employer, and it is possible that it may prove to be the weak spot in the attempt to secure efficiency by arbitration, unless some satisfactory method of measuring output can be adopted. But as at present conducted under the agreement it is the requirement the arbitrator must impose on the company. It must present definite evidence that a man's deficiency in output has been caused by some delinquency of his own. In the present instance the company has not been able to present such a clear and convincing body of evidence to the arbitrator, however much it may have convinced itself of the delinquency."

The first step in the development of the commission system was the establishment of the Cutters' Commission in 1914. This Commission is composed of "one member of the cutters' union, one cutting room official of the company, and one independent outside member, who shall act only when the other two fail to agree." It is appointed by the Trade Board, and Mr. Mullenbach is the outside member. In the decision by which this institution was added to the organization, it was said:

"The appointment of a cutter and a cutting room official is made because technical and practical knowledge is essential to their work, and not because it is desired that opposite interests shall be represented. The commission owes its allegiance primarily to the Board, and is expected to act fairly and impartially in the spirit of the Board, and not as representing partisan and opposing interests. In order that the commission may receive the support and cooperation of the parties in interest, the company and union are invited to express their approval or disapproval of the Board's appointees, the former to pass on the cutting room official, and the latter on the cutter appointed."

The functions of the commission are thus described in the agreement:

"The company shall not reduce the wages of any cutter. The company shall report to the commission all failures of cutters to produce their quota of work when in its judgment the delinquency is not caused by the condition of the work. The commission shall investigate the matter and advise with the cutter concerning it. At the end of a period sufficiently long to determine the merits of the case, the cutter's commission shall, if it deems necessary, find measures to discipline cutters to conform to their production. In judging the merits in such instances, the commission shall use the principle of comparative efficiency."

An example of the activity of this commission and an elaboration of its functions are contained in a decision of Mr. Williams rendered in May of 1917.

"1. A decision of the Cutters' Commission reducing the salaries of cutters having been appealed to the Board, a difference of understanding as to the meaning of the present agreement has been revealed which requires of this Board a very fundamental decision covering the disputed points.

"2. The company may make whatever changes in the records of the cutter's efficiency they find most accurate. Whenever the company has a complaint that a cutter is using too much time in cutting a ticket, it shall notify the floor committee of the Cutters' Commission, who shall agree, if possible, on the proper time for cutting such a ticket. If they are unable to agree, the case shall be referred to the chairman of the Cutters' Commission on the next day, at a regular appointed time, for final decision.

"3. Whenever the company has complaint against any cutter for laxity in cutting, the record of cutting, including ticket passed upon by floor committees, shall be presented to the Cutters' Commission. As heretofore, the Cutters' Commission shall be responsible for discipline of cutters for laxity, in whatever form and degree it may deem necessary to reduce such laxity in the cutting room to a minimum. The commission may reduce or discharge cutters, may impose suspension, immediate or deferred, or use such other penalties or remedies as in its judgment may be necessary to discipline and correct cutters with respect to their production.

"4. The Cutters' Commission shall appoint two persons on each cutting floor to act as floor committees, one selected from among the cutters and one selected from among the representatives of the company on the floor. Their duty shall be to pass judgment on the proper cutting time on tickets which have been complained of by the company. These floor committees shall be under the jurisdiction of the Cutters' Commission.

"With respect to the appeal of the union against the reduction of cutters which is presented to this Board, the Board is of the opinion that the case against the offenders would not be altered if tried by either of the interpretations put forward by the contending parties. The decision of the Trade Board is accordingly affirmed and the reductions are declared to stand as ordered by that Board."

A board similar, in theory, to the Cutters' Commission was established, in 1919, for the trimming room "to regulate shop practice, heights of lays, etc." The Cutters' and the Trimmers' Commissions have accordingly charge of production in the two most important week-work departments. An occasion on which the latter commission met, under the presidency of Mr. Tufts, has been described. The difficulties into which an attempt to "use the principle of comparative efficiency" led, have been suggested. The company, at this particular meeting, held in the summer of 1919, presented figures to show that the ratio of cutters to trimmers had fallen from 2.8 :1 in 1918 to 2 :1 in 1919, and relied on these figures to show a falling off in production in the trimming rooms. The union countered with the contention that this change was the natural result of the introduction of new machinery in the cutting department, and of the increased number of fancy cuts following the close of the war, and necessitating slower work on the part of the trimmers. It is by the slow sifting of such evidence that the commissions accomplish their results.

Both union and company agree that the commission system has increased production. But there is an important difference of opinion as to how much room is left for improvement by standardizing output. This difference of opinion is given particular significance by three events. A decision made by the Board of Arbitration in December of 1919 giving the cutters a $43 weekly minimum wage provides that the award shall not interfere with the development of standards of production in the various shops over which the Board has jurisdiction. Accordingly, on March 2, 1920, the Board made a further award granting the cutters a $45 minimum whenever such standards are set. In the third place, the last convention of the Amalgamated Clothing Workers went on record as favoring the setting of production standards.

It thus became important to know what constitutes a standard. The Cutters' Commission of the Hart, Schaffner & Marx factories has a system of allowances by means of which it judges of a cutter's efficiency.

Certain of the basic allowances for instance are thus listed:

"Scale for cuts including machine work"

Heights	1	2	3	4 Under 15 oz. 70 15 oz. and over	5	6	7	8	9	10	11	12
Allowances in minutes	60	60	75	100	110	120	130	140	150	160	170	180

Such basic allowances are accepted theoretically by union and company members of the commission alike. On the other hand, there are certain minor allowances, like three minutes for an all-around belt, which are not officially accepted by the commission, because of the objection of the union. These objections are based on the many opportunities for variation in such operations, and the alleged impossibility of setting fair and accurate standards.

On the basis of the minimum wage, a classification of cutters has made it possible theoretically to give different grades of cutters different weekly wages. The method by which standards of production were for a time enforced was by the reduction of slacking cutters from one wage group to another. This method developed considerable friction, and a scheme of extra lay-off, at dull times for the cutters whose production fell off, was substituted. Such a plan has obvious defects in a busy period.

At present [1] the union contends that standards have been set at Hart, Schaffner & Marx, and are administered by the Cutters' Commission. They hold that the problem of their enforcement is a separate matter. In short, they claim the $2 weekly increase granted in March, but refuse to permit a change in production methods.

The company claims, on the other hand, that both major and minor allowances must be definitely agreed on for the use of the commission before standards can be said to have been set. And, in the second place, the labor department contends that standards have not been installed, within the meaning of the decision of March 2nd, until an effectual means for enforcing them has been agreed upon. Mr. Howard believes that "this whole matter can be adjusted fairly only on an honest and simple basis, namely: the delivery of an exact amount of work for an exact amount of wages." Provision could theoretically be made for such an arrangement under the differential week-rate system, which would have neither the irritating and fictitious exactness of the bonus system nor the laxity of the time system. Under the latter system, the company feels that while the consideration moving to the workers, their wage, is fixed exactly by the terms of the agreement, the consideration moving from them, their work, is not clearly settled.

Thus far, the committee working on the problem has been unable to reach a satisfactory conclusion. It has made no report, and the Board of Arbitration can decide the matter only on the presentation of a report. The Board has ruled, however, that the problem of

[1] September 1, 1920.

standardization is a separate problem from that of enforcement.

The objections of union labor to piece work are based on the fear of speeding up, and its effects on health, earnings, and rate-cutting. These objections have been overcome in the piece-work departments at the Hart, Schaffner & Marx factories by the institution of a third commission designed to give each side a voice in the setting of piece rates.

"Responsibility for making piece work rates is lodged primarily in the Trade Board. For expediency, the responsibility, however, has been turned over by the Trade Board to a committee, known as the Rate Committee, and composed of three members, one representing the company, one representing the people, and the chairman of the Trade Board. As a matter of practice, the work of rate making is carried on almost exclusively by the two members representing the company and the people. While some cases are brought before the full committee, these cases are exceptional when compared to the number settled by the two members.

"The agreement provides that in fixing rates the Board is restricted to the following rules: Changed prices must correspond to the changed work and new prices must be based on the old prices where possible.

"Whenever a question of piece work rate arises, it is taken up in the first instance by the two members of the committee and an attempt is made to reach an agreement. If an agreement is reached, a specification of the work to be performed and the rate to be paid is prepared and signed by both representatives without any further action. If, however, the two parties are unable to reach an agreement, the case is taken up with the full committee and an agreemen reached, or a decision made fixing the rate and specifications. If this decision is unsatisfactory to either party, the decision may be appealed to the Board of Arbitration.

"New rates are always provisional and temporary and are subject to review after sufficient period of trial to determine their merit. The Committee seeks to make the temporary rate as nearly equitable as possible, both for its effect on the people and to save a repetition of the negotiation.

"After the specification and rate have been authorized by the Rate Committee, there can be no alteration of the terms either by the company or the people without permission from the Rate Committee."

The agreement further provides that, "In the event a piece worker is required to change his mode of operation so that it causes him to lose time in learning, his case may be brought to the Rate Committee for its disposition."

The loss of time resulting from waiting for work has developed considerable friction in connection with the piece-work system. Thus far the only attempt to deal with the problem is contained in a sentence of the agreement providing for coöperation between deputies and company in the attempt to abolish waiting. The Board of Arbitration has refused to sanction the adoption of any scheme of paying for waiting "until a plan is devised that will eliminate the dangers and safeguard against its possible abuses."

The problem of holding work for inspection has arisen in connection with the effect of piece rates on quality. Quality foremen in the shops may complain of a man's work. The question then arises as to how many pieces the worker may hold to confute the claims of the quality man. The rule now reads:

"That the shop chairmen must take the responsibility of deciding whether more than one garment is needed for representation. As a check upon abuse of this responsibility, it (the Board of Arbitration) suggests that if any superintendent has reason to believe that a shop chairman is either incompetent to judge whether several garments are needed for the investigation or is wilfully aiding in holding work beyond what is necessary, he may file complaint against such chairman with the Trade Board. In such a case the records of the work held for investigation by the chairman for a period of time may properly be considered."

The problem of union opposition to the introduction of labor-saving machinery and improved methods has occupied the courts in several cases. The rule laid down is that protests of the union will not avail to prevent the introduction of improved production methods, and that the company is at liberty to make any improvements it sees fit. This right of the company is subject to three limitations. In the first place, men employed under the new conditions are not to have their wages reduced. This principle was developed by the Board of Arbitration from the provision in the agreement that "change of prices must correspond to the change of work and new prices must be based on old prices where possible." In the second place, as a matter of practice the company is expected to provide work for any men whose jobs are eliminated through improvements, at as nearly the old rates and conditions as possible. In the third place, the coöperation and approval of union deputies is to be secured before changes are introduced. Mr. Williams' opinion was:

"Whenever a change needs to be introduced which is likely to give rise to objection or dispute, the foreman should take steps to have it authorized by the representative of the workers, who should at the same time see that their interests in the matter are safeguarded. The union mem-

ber of the price committee should be notified and he should
attend the call as promptly as practicable. After hearing
the nature of the change proposed, he should, if consistent
with justice and the just claims of the worker, direct the
section to proceed with the work pending the formal disposition of the matter by the price committee."

In accordance with these principles, it was held in
one case that the introduction of vest-pressing machines did not involve the creation of a new trade,
but constituted simply the introduction of new methods in an old trade, and so should be followed by no
changes in earnings resulting from revised piece rates.
In another case the union protested against the action
of the company in giving knife sharpening in the cutting rooms to one man. The protest was based on
the claim that such action would deprive the men of
skill in an operation which they might have to perform
in other shops. The Board of Arbitration allowed the
union's claim, evidently recognizing that the opportunity of one party to a contract to perform his part of
the contract may be regarded as a condition of the
obligation.[1]

With regard to apprenticeship, a definite ratio has
been established for the cutting room (10 per cent of
the permanent cutters may be apprentices) ; and in case
of any large increase of apprentices, the matter may
be brought by the union deputies before the Board
of Arbitration. The Board has hesitated to restrict
the right of the company to increase its force at will.
The union, on the other hand, hopes to reduce the evils

[1] Cf. Turner v. Sawdon & Co. [1901] 2 Kings Bench, 653;
Cooper v. Stronge & Warner Co., 111 Minn. 177.

attendant on temporary increases of force by its projected scheme of unemployment insurance.[1]

Another set of cases involving interpretation of the wage contract has to do with the equal distribution of work and the equalization of earnings. This requires equal treatment for all in the division of overtime and lay-off. Thus, in one case, "The cutters and trimmers complain that insufficient notice is given when overtime is required to be worked, and that it results in giving an undue share of the overtime work to those who do not need to make prearrangement at home. The company states that the need for overtime is often not known until late in the day and it is not always possible to foresee the exigency. In view of this situation, the chairman [of the Board of Arbitration] will not issue any rule, but will recommend to those in charge of issuing orders for overtime that they keep the need of the men in mind, and that they make every reasonable effort to inform them of expected overtime as far in advance as possible, so that the matters complained of may be avoided."

With regard to the equalization of lay-offs, the rule is as follows: "No union member who is a permanent worker shall be laid off in the tailor shops except for cause, whether in the slack or busy season, except as provided herein. . . . During the slack season the work shall be divided as near as is practicable among all hands." Thus, in one case in which a system of two-day rotation had been devised to keep all union hands at work during a slack period, the union objected to the arrangement on the ground that some days were

[1] See Hillman and the Amalgamated. William Hard, 23 New Republic 15 (June 2, 1920).

better for work than others. Mr. Williams accordingly ruled that the company should institute a scheme to allow all the men who came to the shops in the morning to have the day's work divided among them. A two weeks' notice before any lay-offs are made must be given by the company to the workers in question.

In the same connection the following rule was laid down by Mr. Williams.

"This is an appeal from a Trade Board decision which raised the question of whether a foreman may, during the slack season, perform labor that would otherwise be performed by union workers.

"The chairman feels that to permit the foreman to take the work which the workers feel they are entitled to under the agreement will cause more dissatisfaction than would be compensated by the saving.

"He recommends, however, that the union be not technical in its objection to the foreman performing such labors as do not run counter to union interests in a tangible way, and that they be encouraged to be useful in such ways as may be possible without raising greater difficulties than can be compensated."

The rule with regard to "overcrowding" in a section, consequent on seasonal fluctuations, is thus stated in the agreement:

"Overcrowding of sections is important in this agreement as the point at which the provision for the preference becomes operative. It is agreed that when there are too many workers in a section to permit of reasonably steady employment, a complaint may be lodged by the union, and if proved, the non-union members of the section, or as many of them as may be required to give the needed relief, shall be dismissed."

Increases in force are commonly made by the company with the consent of the union, but this is a matter of choice with the company which is governed only by its own interests in following the rule. Thus a decision of Mr. Williams' of March, 1918, gave the company the right to add not more than twelve cutters to the permanent force. It was said that there was no provision in the agreement requiring the consent of the cutters to the making of additions; and that, while coöperation in this matter had proved valuable in reducing friction over a delicate matter, the smallness of the claim in question and the absence of any constitutional right on the part of the union made the arbitrator unwilling to abridge the rights of the company. He said, however, that "the successful working of the agreement has been aided by joint selection."

As has been pointed out, the Amalgamated Clothing Workers of America expect to do away with this problem of irregular employment and reduced earnings by the maintenance of an unemployment insurance fund for the benefit of its members. The scheme has been advocated in the union for some time, and was approved at their last convention. A possible method of securing this fund would be by forcing the employers to contribute amounts proportionate to their respective turnover figures. The effect would be to lay a discouraging tax on irregularity of operation and employment, and to provide benefits for those to whom such irregularity of employment as remains is a menace. The matter, however, will probably be managed by the union alone. An increase in wages will be asked for to enable its members to support the fund.

Shop safety and sanitation are evidently sufficiently

provided for by the labor department and the Illinois Compensation Law, as no controversies on these subjects have been reported since the early days of the agreement. An interesting ruling on general conditions of work was made in February of 1920 by the Board of Arbitration. The Board then ruled that the sending out of work to be finished at home, practiced on a very small scale in some of the shops, should be discontinued as soon as possible. The Board commented on the danger to standards involved in such a policy, and appointed a joint committee to determine how soon the award could be carried out. The practice is now discontinued.

The hours of work in the men's clothing industry are forty-four a week. Fifteen dollars a week is the minimum wage for apprentices; $16 for apprentice cutters. The minimum for journeymen cutters is $43 a week. Time and a half for overtime is given week-workers and fifty per cent extra for overtime is allowed to those on piece work. On this basis, a series of differential rates for different classes of work has been constructed. The scales are the result of negotiations in the various departments, cutting, trimming, vest-making, tailoring, off-pressing, inspecting. Mr. Williams said in one case:

"There seems to be no uniform rule by which the wages of week-workers are fixed. The more common ground for basing week wages appears to be efficiency and length of service, and the lack of uniformity is naturally due to the variation in those factors. The practice is to deal with week wages as related to individual workers.

"The spirit of the agreement, however, is to maintain wages wherever equivalence of service is maintained, and it does not contemplate a reduction of earnings unless effort is correspondingly reduced. If, therefore, an individual week-worker is reduced, it is up to the company to show some cause why the reduction is made."

The union has accepted this system of differential rates, opposed apparently to all union traditions, because of the confidence it has in the justice of the labor policy of the company, and its support by the system of commissions and courts to which its members may appeal. A fourth commission, appointed on December 22, 1919, has worked out a new classification of week-workers.

This appointment was made in a decision rendered by Mr. Tufts which explains and illustrates perhaps better than any other decision the spirit of this industrial government and the considerations which influence its officials in dealing with its problems. Wage determinations have commonly been left to the triennial conferences of union and company representatives which draw up the labor agreements. The Trade Board and Board of Arbitration are ordinarily called upon only to interpret these agreements and apply their terms to individual cases. Examples of such interpretations have been given in other connections. There is, however, a clause in the agreement under which the Board of Arbitration may be required to perform the function of determining wage scales. The provision reads as follows: "If there shall be a general change in wages or hours in the clothing industry, which shall be sufficiently permanent to warrant the belief that the change is not temporary, then the Board shall have power to determine whether such change is of so extraordinary a nature as to justify a consideration of the question of making a change in the present agreement, and, if so, then the Board shall have power to make such changes in wages or hours as in its judgment shall be proper." Four wage adjustments had been made at various times under this provision. On December 9, 1919, an appeal for a fifth application was made, and in granting this appeal, Mr. Tufts wrote the decision in question.

It is in the field of legislative arbitration to which this decision belongs that conspicuous examples of government regulation are to be found, and that regulative principles are particularly scarce and desirable. Mr. Wilson Compton, in the *American Economic Review*,[1] pointed out that the Australasian arbitration boards have given predominant weight to considerations of the standard of life of the workers concerned and of what wages the industry will bear. They have also shown a disposition to make deductions, on general principles, from the claims of each party, and they have recognized that the wages which they set must be regarded as a standard, below which sub-standard workers must be allowed to fall. Two additional considerations have been introduced by Mr. Tufts in the disposal of the case under discussion. Granting at the same time that wage increases in the factories have kept up with the cost of living, and that the company can afford an increase, the arbitrator makes the reasonableness of the increase for which he provides turn on the bargaining power of clothing workers and the fact that the increase will not be passed on to the public to any serious extent. The introduction of the latter consideration into the discussion is important in

[1] "Wage Theories in Industrial Arbitration," Vol. VI, p. 324.

view of the accusation of profiteering which has been directed against the combination of Hart, Schaffner & Marx and the Amalgamated Clothing Workers of America.

In discussing the question of bargaining power Mr. Tufts said:

"The general question as to the propriety of any increase turns therefore on this: Shall a group of workers be permitted under this agreement to avail itself of market conditions of supply and demand to improve its standard of living beyond the general level of advancing rates in cost of living, or is it the duty of this Board to refuse such a demand on the grounds of public policy?

"In answering this question, the Board believes that it must be governed largely, although not exclusively, by the prevailing principles and policies of the country as embodied in its institutions. In endeavoring to give a just decision, the Board does not feel warranted in setting up a standard too widely at variance with our present social and economic order.

"The principles and policies of the United States are, with certain qualifications, those of individualism, or the competitive system. This means that prices, wages, and profits are fixed by bargaining under the forces of supply and demand. This general principle is qualified and limited in the case of 'property affected with a public interest,' such as railways. In private, as distinguished from public or semi-public business and industry, there is a moral disapproval on the one hand for such extremely low wages as make a decent standard of living impossible, and on the other hand, for extreme increases in the prices of necessaries of life, but there is no general disapproval of the general principle of profiting by market conditions. In time of national emergency, we used the word 'profiteer' to condemn taking advantage of the country's need for an unreasonable private gain. But in ordinary time, there is as yet no recognized standard for the fairness of prices of various goods, or for relative wages in different industries, other than what the bargainers agree upon. This method may often fail to give justice as measured by various other standards of merit or desert. But for the most part, labor has had to bargain for its wages, and it cannot be expected to forego entirely the advantages which market conditions now afford.

"Coming then to the specific concrete situation which confronts us, we have the outstanding fact that very substantial increases to clothing workers have been granted in all the other principal markets in this country and Canada, and in many less important centers. These increases have usually been five or six dollars a week; in some cases, they have been more. In these days when both employers and workers know of such increases and plan accordingly, it is not practicable to treat the Chicago market as an entirely distinct situation to be judged on its own merits, without reference to what is going on elsewhere in the country."

Thus far, considerations of social welfare have been replaced by those of economic struggle. There follows an extension of the field of inquiry with regard to public purpose, and the fourth consideration (if the first three be included under the questions of standard of life, resources of the industry, and bargaining power) is introduced.

In this connection four points are made. First, if the public interest in low prices is to be invoked to keep down wages, a similar justification would require a similar regulation of profits and efficiency in production. The argument is not carried to its final conclusion: that the failure of the public to exercise such regulation is exactly one of the factors which makes higher wages necessary. The arbitrator has already recognized that wages have increased with the cost of living, and carrying the argument to its conclusion would not advance his case. He leaves it, therefore, in the rather inconclusive state where the failure of society to do one desirable thing is taken to justify or require its failure to do another thing which is not shown to be in itself less desirable.

In the second place, Mr. Tufts makes the point, which is one primarily of standard of living, that in seasonal or periodically fluctuating industries high wages and profits ought to be permitted at the peak of production to compensate for losses from unemployment and idleness which are to follow.

The third point is the really significant one in this connection.

"Undoubtedly there is a limit, even if there is no scientific method for setting it, to what even individualism will or ought to approve. Prices of clothing have advanced and are certain to be further advanced whatever may be the decision of this case. In fact, retailers had to place orders for their light-weight clothing before this case was heard and inasmuch as general increases were asked for in September and granted in other markets in November, it may be presumed that such possibilities were in mind when prices were set for the light-weight consumer. The Board has carefully considered the effect to the consumer of the increase asked for. The fact is that making of clothes under modern methods has come to be an efficient process. A part of the increase in earnings which have come about in the industry has been accompanied by improvement in production. Thus part of the increased earnings, shown particularly in piece-work production, does not necessarily involve any increase in cost of clothing to the public. The increase involved in this award means a relatively small increase in the cost of clothing."

The fourth consideration of general public importance used to justify the award is the consideration of the interest of the public in "continuous production and a peaceful and orderly method of conducting industry." The assumption underlying the discussion of this point is that any failure to grant an increase would endanger the peace and order of the industry. The discussion has returned to the force of bargaining power, which is, after all, the motivating force of the decision.

THE POWER OF THE WORKERS

It should be clear from the preceding discussion that the possession of this bargaining power on the part of the workers has been of paramount importance in the development of industrial law. It must indeed be conceded that labor leaders, members of the business, and arbitrators have been very largely animated by ideals of public welfare in working for security and improved standards of living for the workers. But the manner in which these ideals have been put into practice has been as much dependent on the relative economic strength of the parties, as was the form of Magna Charta on the strength of the barons, or that of the Petition of Right on the strength of the bourgeoisie of England.

It has been indicated sufficiently that in the fields over which the government of Hart, Schaffner & Marx exercise control, the workers are assured of possessing equal power with the management. Their representatives are equal in each case to those of the management and they share in paying the impartial judges who administer the law. It may also have appeared that the workers have some advantage from the strength which their organization gives them, in securing favorable awards.   This may well be a permanent aspect of this industrial government, inasmuch as an element of its "public policy" must always be the keeping of peace.

On the other hand the field over which this judicial government exercises its jurisdiction is a narrow one. The courts are confined to the interpretation of the agreement as to wages, hours, and conditions of work, and the maintenance of discipline.   The only direction in which the workers show signs of extending their power and interests is that of technical production. They are not interested, as yet, in the financial, sales, or purchasing aspects of the business, and they make no demands for profit sharing or other welfare policies.

An account has already been given of the agreements which have been reached and the policies which have been mapped out with regard to the questions of production in which the workers are interested.   The union has been quite as conscious as the company of the importance of reaching compromises which would in no way cripple the latter, on the problem of regulation of output and the introduction of new machinery. The action of the national convention in the recent meeting at Boston in favoring the scientific development of standards of work and wages is a sufficient indication of the quality of statesmanship represented by the leaders of the Amalgamated Clothing Workers of America.   They recognize clearly that order and production in their industry are necessary conditions of the general as well as of their own prosperity.

The account of the law relating to a legislative as-

sembly of union and company representatives, meeting
every three years; an executive department composed
of labor, production, and quality executives of the
company; a judicial system of courts and commissions,
representing union and company; an account of the
way in which the law, with respect to these agencies, has
developed, to secure the coöperation of workers and
the owners of capital in turning out clothes, would be
incomplete without the quotation of statements of purposes and ideals which have inspired some of the pioneers of industrial law who have worked at this problem in these shops. These statements will help to
clarify the conception of the proper relation between
company and workers which has governed the development of the Hart, Schaffner & Marx constitution.

Professor Howard's statement of principles is as
follows:

"Industrial peace will never come so long as either employer or employee believe that they are deprived of rights
honestly belonging to them. Our experience has taught
that the business man in authority is a trustee of various
interests, including his own, and if he administers his business so as to conserve and harmonize these interests to
the best of his ability, he is most likely building an endur-
ing success.

"Arbitration and conciliation should be applied to all departments of a business wherever there is a conflict of
interest. If nothing more, it insures exhaustive discussion
of every matter of importance, gives everybody an opportunity to express his opinions, frequently brings to light
valuable suggestions, and makes possible a higher degree
of coöperation and team-work. It is a method to be employed continuously to secure harmony and satisfaction.
Patience and self-control are essential in administering a
business on this basis. It is human nature to resent inter-

ference and to desire unrestricted liberty of action, but these conditions are not necessary and are often inimical to true success. Few men can use unlimited power wisely and no wise man will dispense with checks which tend to keep him in the right path; certainly, he will approve of checks calculated to restrain his agents from arbitrary and unjust acts toward fellow employees.

"If the employer voluntarily limits his own authority and agrees to conduct his business according to the rule of reason and even-handed justice as interpreted by an outside authority, such as an arbitration board, he must insist that the organized employees submit to the same limitation, otherwise his sacrifice will be futile and his submission to injustice cowardly.

"Unions should be recognized and favored in the same proportion as they manifest a genuine desire to govern themselves efficiently. All agreements should be so drawn as to release the employer from his obligations whenever the unions fail to observe theirs. Arbitration boards, officials in charge of labor matters, and union leaders should direct their operations and make their decisions with the one purpose always in mind, namely, to make it profitable and easy for all parties to acquiesce in the rule of reason and justice, and dangerous and difficult for them to attempt to get unjust advantage.

"We regard it as an essential element in maintaining industrial peace to centralize the administration of discipline in one official having no interest except to maintain the efficiency of the shops without disturbing the harmony and good-will of the people."

Mr. Williams' famous preamble to the agreement may conclude this phase of the discussion.

"On the part of the employer it is the intention and expectation that this compact of peace will result in the establishment and maintenance of a high order of discipline and efficiency by the willing coöperation of union and workers rather than by the old method of surveillance and coercion; that by the exercise of this discipline all stoppages and interruptions of work, and all wilful violations of rules will cease; that good standards of workmanship and conduct will be maintained and a proper quantity, quality and cost of production will be assured; and that out of its operation will issue such coöperation and goodwill between employers, foremen, union and workers as will prevent misunderstanding and friction and make for good team work, good business, mutual advantage and mutual respect.

"On the part of the union it is the intention and expectation that this compact will, with the coöperation of the employer, operate in such a way as to maintain, strengthen, and solidify its organization, so that it may be made strong enough, and efficient enough, to coöperate as contemplated in the preceding paragraph; and also that it may be strong enough to command the respect of the employer without being forced to resort to militant or unfriendly measures.

"On the part of the workers it is the intention and expectation that they pass from the status of wage servants, with no claim on the employer save his economic need, to that of self-respecting parties to an agreement which they have had an equal part with him in making; that this status gives them an assurance of fair and just treatment and protects them against injustice or oppression of those who may have been placed in authority over them; that they will have recourse to a court, in the creation of which their votes were equally potent with that of the employer, in which all their grievances may be heard, and all their claims adjudicated; that all changes during the life of the pact shall be subject to the approval of an impartial tribunal, and that wages and working conditions shall not fall below the level provided for in the agreement.

"The parties to this pact realize that the interests sought to be reconciled herein will tend to pull apart, but they enter it in the faith that by the exercise of the coöperative and constructive spirit it will be possible to bring and keep them together. This will involve as an indispensable prerequisite the total suppression of the militant spirit by both parties and the development of reason instead of force as the rule of action. It will require also mutual consideration and concession, a willingness on the part of each party to regard and serve the interests of the other, so far as it can be done without too great a sacrifice of principle or interest. With this attitude assured it is believed no differences can arise which the joint tribunal cannot mediate and resolves in the interest of coöperation and harmony."

XVII

LOCAL REPRESENTATIVE GOVERNMENT

ABOUT twenty years ago the clothing manufacturers of Rochester, New York, formed among themselves a trade association. Since then the association has developed into a definite organization of the employers of the market—The Clothiers' Exchange—chiefly with the purpose of collective action in dealing with Labor. The word "market" as used in the clothing industry means a clothing manufacturing center of considerable size. The Rochester market comprises eighteen houses, including all the chief clothing manufacturers except one. The executive body is the Labor Committee, composed of five employers, who have a decision in matters affecting the market as a whole. Questions of policy are referred to this committee by the individual houses.

The Clothiers' Exchange maintains an office with an executive director, a secretary, and a statistician. Records are kept, correspondence is undertaken with other markets, research studies are made. The office serves as headquarters for employers and labor managers.

In April, 1919, the Clothiers' Exchange met the Rochester Joint Board of the Amalgamated Clothing Workers of America to form a Labor Adjustment Board, which should rule in all matters affecting Labor in the local clothing industry. At first the constitution of this government rested on a "gentlemen's agreement" between the president of the Clothiers' Exchange and the president of the Union. But the renewal of the Agreement, in the summer of 1920, for a period of two years, was signed by representatives of the two parties only after it had been ratified by a referendum vote in which every individual worker and every individual employer took part. The new agreement differs from the old only in its clearer statement of aims and in certain definite reforms to be accomplished and principles to be realized.

The first principle established is that of collective bargaining. The Agreement specifically recognizes the right of employees to organize, and the duty of employers to deal with their workers, through the agency of the Union, in all matters affecting wages and working conditions. There is to be no more changing of orders at the whim of superintendent or foreman; each separate executive decision must be in harmony with the Agreement. Nor is the whim of the workers to tie up production. It is definitely set forth in the Agreement that there shall be no strikes, lock-outs, or stoppages of work in the industry. Each plant has its house organization for adjusting the complaints of employees. When a difference arises that cannot be settled in this way, there is further machinery in the market for handling it. In brief, the policy is one of mutual and constant adjustment between the employer and the employee, in the individual shop and in the market as a whole.

The Agreement recognizes a modified "open union shop" policy. The power of hiring is to remain with the employer, but the fact of membership in the Union must not be a cause for discrimination against an applicant for employment. The Impartial Chairman is given the right to review the policy of any house which appears to have been guilty of such discrimination. In case of discharge, also, the employee has the right of appeal through the Union to the Impartial Chairman; if the Chairman finds that the discharge was not for sufficient cause, the employee is reinstated with pay for time lost. There are to be no lay-offs; instead the principle of equal division of work among all employees is accepted. This principle is being applied during the present slack season. Permanent reductions in force are permitted—but they must be proved to be permanent. This is perhaps the greatest gain to the Union under the new Agreement.

The right of the employer to manage his own shop is admitted, as is his right to introduce what changes in manufacturing methods he sees fit. But if such changes result in loss to the employees, the matter may be brought before the Impartial Chairman. Changes in the general wage levels or in hours of work may be considered, upon petition of either side, if the Labor Adjustment Board judges that changes in the clothing industry or industrial changes generally make such new arrangements advisable. In case of a disagreement on this as on other points, decision rests with the Impartial Chairman. Readjustments of wages of individuals or of sections may be considered, upon petition of either party, on the ground that such readjustment is necessary "to remove serious and unjust inequalities in pay"; but this matter may be considered by the Impartial Chairman only when he is specially so authorized by the Labor Adjustment Board.

Other articles in the Agreement provide for a minimum wage for beginners, fix the working week at forty-four hours, with pay at the rate of time and a half for overtime, authorize the Labor Adjustment Board to exercise sanitary control in the shops, and urge the abolition of home work.

The representative of the employer in Labor matters in each shop is the Labor Manager, an expert in adjustment, trained not in any apprenticeship to the trade, but in the school of liberal arts, by a culture of mind and soul which develops a broad sympathy with humanity. And he should be something of the sociologist, of the philosopher, of the poet in that he is the firm's representative who must see first the *man* in the employee, and so be able to guess at the human motives for the attitude he takes toward his work and his life. This new kind of labor manager has brought into the industry something vital which before had been missing.

The atmosphere of his office is hardly that of the factory; it bears rather the marks of the professor's study. The bookcases are well filled, the periodicals on the side table are of the literature which would interpret life; significant in the work-room of the human relations man. More often than not the Labor Manager is to be addressed as "Doctor"; the title is most carefully and reverentially applied, as if industry were not only proud but also a little awed by its new acquisition.

Not that this Labor Manager is essentially a theoretical person, but that he has brought to the study of actual facts and conditions a background of unimpassioned survey of general truths, and the critical attitude of the scholar who has learned to resist the enthusiasms of either side of a controversy. He has not come into business to bring academic rules of conduct, but to contribute to the consideration of what these business men and workers see as an *impasse,* a mind which has been sharpened to cut through problems.

And the employees who knock at the door of his office are received in a manner very different from that which they once met at the "employees' entrance." The professor—pardon!—the Labor Manager is first of all a gentleman. His habit is to bow courteously to a visitor and to offer a chair—a leather-cushioned chair. And really, it is not a bad plan; a man cannot fight in a comfortable chair as he can when he is standing in the cold. No more can he fight a sympathetic listener. The Labor Manager is there to listen to grievances, to judge them with reference to the Agreement and with reference to the causes behind them. His training disposes him to look for more than one possible cause for every phemonenon. His contribution to an understanding of the Labor Problem ought to be valuable.

The seven Labor Managers in the Rochester clothing market meet each week together as a Board to co-operate in the preparation of cases to come before the Impartial Chairman where the decision will affect the market as a whole, or to draw up policies for concerted action. They have meetings, for instance, relative to the Union's demand for a minimum wage for learners. They have been trained to research: they collect data on the minimum wage laws of different states, on wage levels in the other industries of Rochester, on wages in the clothing industry in other centers. They try to classify the blind-alley jobs in the clothing industry, and they study the possibilities for learners in the continuation schools. The Board of Labor Managers looks ahead and plans harmonious action in meeting changes which it foresees in the industry.

Again, the Labor Managers meet with a committee of the Joint Board of the Union. This meeting together constitutes the Labor Adjustment Board. This board is the legislative body in the local industrial government. On the Board each side has one collective vote: the Impartial Chairman presides and casts the deciding vote. All disputes or differences over questions arising under the Agreement which the parties to the Agreement are unable to adjust among themselves are referred to the Board for adjustment or arbitration. The Board has full and final jurisdiction over all such questions and its decisions are conclusive, unless otherwise provided by the parties to the Agreement. Except when the Board itself shall otherwise determine, the chairman of the Board—the "Impartial Chairman"—is authorized to take original jurisdiction of all cases and controversies arising under the Agreement and to adjust or decide them in accordance with the rules of practice and procedure established by the Board. Decisions of the Chairman are binding on both parties.

Technically the judicial power of the government, together with the legislative and the executive, resides in the Labor Adjustment Board. But as it is the Impartial Chairman who there casts the deciding vote, such power actually devolves upon his person. He is chosen by mutual agreement of the Clothiers' Exchange and the Amalgamated Clothing Workers of America. The expenses of his office are borne equally by the two parties.

Not only in the case of a grievance, but also for the building up of a general market policy Labor Managers and Union officials meet in conference. For the attempt is being made to establish government where anarchy has reigned. It is still the exception in industry for the representatives of the employers in a market to meet weekly for discussions leading to a common plan of management; it is perhaps more unexpected to find Union officials meeting with this group to coöperate in the development of such a plan. So all along the line, from a petty shop difficulty to a major market policy, the two sides come together to effect an adjustment. And when the two sides cannot agree, they go together to the Impartial Chairman, and whatever his decision may be, they accept it. This marks the beginning of a new stage in the development of industrial government in the men's clothing industry—that of an organized market. Establishment government came in with the Hart, Schaffner and Marx agreement in 1910. The Rochester Agreement applies the same principle to a larger sphere.

The Agreement provides a definite procedure for the handling of grievances. The employees from each shop hold "shop meetings" in the Union hall. Here they elect shop Chairmen and Section Chairmen. Thereafter any worker who has a grievance reports it to his Shop Chairman, who then takes it up with the Labor Manager of the house. If the Labor Manager and the Shop Chairman cannot arrive at a satisfactory settlement, they call in a Union representative.

If then no solution can be reached, the matter is brought before the Impartial Chairman. The procedure is similar where it is the foreman who brings complaint.

For some time after the adoption of the original Agreement, in the spring of 1919, there was no Impartial Chairman. It was necessary that the Labor Manager and Union official should agree. And as both were courteous, both interested in the accomplishment of order in industry, both eager to act according to the ethics involved, mutual agreements were usual. And when the Impartial Chairman assumed his rôle, he aimed at interpretation of joint interest rather than arbitration. He brought representatives of the two sides together, and watched them adjust their differences; he did not hand down a decision in the spirit of a judge. But personal convictions are in danger of being lost in positions; each side pushed its representative for an advantageous decision. The representative had to be an advocate, perhaps at times even an instructed delegate. And he who stood for the losing side was glad to shift the responsibility of the decision on to a judge. More and more the spirit of the lawyer is emerging in the court room.

The attempt is made to keep the hearing free from a legalistic atmosphere. The Impartial Chairman— Dr. William M. Leiserson—sits at a long table. Opposite him there are rather comfortable chairs. The procedure is for the Labor Manager and the Union official each in turn to examine the witnesses. Smoking is permitted. Although the object is informality, the dramatic possibilities of the situation are often too great a temptation to the agents, who take delight in introducing the formal language of the court room. This is perhaps less true of the year 1920 than of 1919, now that the novelty has worn off.

The "judge" enjoys his pipe. He allows eloquence to have its way for a while; he smiles appreciation at the good stories which lighten the day's business. But at length it becomes necessary to call the court back to the main line of argument, and to warn a side which has been weak in the presentation of its case: "Now this is impressing me, and unless you can answer it, it is going to influence me when I form my conclusions." For the "judge" is an *impartial chairman*.

Dr. Leiserson insists that his position is less that of an arbitrator between opposing parties than of an interpreter of the law inaugurated by agreement between these two parties, and of an agent responsible for the application of this law to specific cases. Whenever questions come before him which do not seem to be covered by the provisions of the Agreement, he calls for a discussion at the next meeting of the Labor Adjustment Board. He gets the two sides to tell him what they believe the law should be: he aims to avoid judge-made law. He tries to get both sides to agree on the principle involved. The principle established, it then forms the basis of precedent. While the Chairman does not wish to be bound by precedent, he feels that only by determining such principles and definite rules of procedure can a body of law be built up to which each side may know how to conform.

The normal business of the "court" is four cases a week. The first year there were two hundred cases. The subjects varied; the majority had to do with wages or discipline.

Some workers have been impatient and unwilling to wait for the machinery to take care of their grievances. Sometimes a group walks out, but only to be ordered back by a Union official so that the grievance may follow due process of law. Dr. Leiserson always refuses to hear a case while the men are out or until they have paid the penalty applied in such cases, which is to work off the time lost in overtime, but at straight time rate of pay. In several cases of flagrant defiance the time to be worked off has been doubled. The object of the Agreement is that the machinery is to carry off the friction without interrupting the smooth course of production.

The Union must discipline its own members. This is not always an easy task. Human nature will crop out. It has even been known to happen that while the Union was making a strong appeal for the preferential shop, individuals members have urged on a Labor Manager the employment of sister or cousin whom the Union had not recommended.

But the Union spirit is growing stronger. Where not long ago Union leaders held together masses of men and women by force of personality, today initiative is coming from the ranks of the workers themselves. Today a "class-conscious" Union is pushing ahead, while the leaders bear down on the brakes because they feel that the time has not come for presenting many of the demands which have been voiced. The radical element would like to take over the industry and run it: their leaders know that they have not the ability nor the experience for such a project. Nor are these radicals the most numerous, although possibly the most vociferous, of the thirteen thousand Union members in Rochester.

APPRENTICESHIP

A real problem just now is presented to both sides in the question of giving training to new employees, and to those who, already in the industry, remain unskilled. In 1919 because of the acute shortage of skilled labor, it was felt to be necessary to establish training departments for beginners. Formerly the tailor learned his trade in the sweat-shop as "helper" to a home-worker: if we abolish the sweat-shop we must provide some other gateway to the industry. Formerly America let Europe train her cutters for her, but this is hardly a satisfactory solution of the problem of trade education. Rosenberg Brothers took the lead among Rochester plants by opening at Fashion Park a vestibule school in a small cottage on the grounds. Unskilled employees are put through a course of training in essentials here before being passed on to the main factory. The employment executive frequently visits the school to encourage the pupils whom she has sent there.

The recent establishment of a minimum wage is making the education of apprentices imperative. The manufacturer can no longer tolerate the semi-skilled "helper" on his pay roll. Moreover, Dr. Leiserson is holding manufacturers responsible for bringing up the production of individual workers to a level with that of better workers in the same class. When a man is doing his best, and his low production record is due to poor training, the Impartial Chairman refuses to permit that he be paid at a lower rate than the better workers. The Chairman also refuses to permit his discharge, if he has been retained beyond the period of probation. In specific cases the Chairman has ruled that industrial training is a responsibility of the management and not of the men. The Agreement is at stake, for industrial democracy is impossible with unfit workers.

CONTRACTORS

Another problem which must be met is that of the contractors. There are at least eighty contract shops in Rochester; all but one are organized by the Union. Workers in them enjoy the benefits of the Agreement. In case of grievances in the contractors' shops, the contractor is represented by the Labor Manager of the house which has given out the contract. Lately the local Board of the Union has put forward a plan for a coöperative vest shop, to be operated by the Union, as a contract shop, receiving work from the manufacturers. The workers would then control their own production, but would be relieved from the cares of purchasing, cutting to style, and marketing. It has been suggested that in time such Union contract shops might take over the making of the whole suit, leaving to the manufacturer only the rôle of merchant-middleman.

FEDERATION

It is often asked: to what do the workers look forward? In the summer of 1920, Joseph Schlossberg, national secretary of the Amalgamated Clothing Workers of America, attended the international congress of clothing workers at Copenhagen. He reported its purpose "to bring about one all-inclusive organization, nationally and internationally, of all branches of the men's and women's wearing apparel." Collective bargaining on a world-wide scale? One Big Union of overwhelming proportions? At present the American clothing workers possess far greater advantages than the clothing workers of other countries, and the immediate aims of the organization are to bring to European workers some of these advantages. Nor only for altruistic reasons: if the European workers were more content at home, they would not come to flood the American market with cheap labor.

The employers also have been preparing for collective bargaining on more than a local scale. The Rochester Agreement was a step in advance. It was followed, in May, 1919, by the organization of the Chicago market. Labor Managers and Impartial Chairmen began to function in Baltimore and in New York, in Boston and in the Canadian markets of Montreal and Toronto. But this was perhaps not the final step in the organization of industrial government in the clothing industry. An unprecedented demand for their product led to rivalry between markets to attract labor at any price. The result was steadily increasing labor costs which were becoming more and more embarrassing to the industry as a whole. The markets saw that they were working at cross purposes: they were ready to consider coöperation. The result has been a federation of the exchanges and boards of employers in the different markets which now include all but three or four of the important firms in the country. The executive board of the national federation was made up of one manufacturer and one labor manager from the Rochester, New York, Chicago, and Baltimore markets. Final and complete coöperation in labor matters was hoped for from a joint labor council consisting of the manufacturers on the one hand, represented by officers of the national federation and of a committee of the Union on the other.

The national board was hailed by both sides as the logical outcome of collective bargaining, as an expression of democracy in industry. One year later we find less enthusiasm. How permanent this national federation of clothing manufacturers will be it is at present not possible to predict. Existing chaos in the New York and Boston markets, February, 1921, has caused many to doubt the continuance of any sort of government in the industry. However that may be, a development of greater promise than the federation is the coöperation between the Impartial Chairmen of the different markets, and their attempt to standardize the body of the law.

Unshaken by disappointments in the New York and Boston markets, the Rochester Agreement continues to hold the respect of both parties. The test will come this year or next, with the price-cutting and the hard times. Last year in the labor market the workers had the upper hand: it was to the employer's advantage that they held to the Agreement. At times they chafed under the law, and thought, perhaps with regret, of the days when to the strongest of the lawless belonged the spoils. This year, with depression in the market, the workers benefit—especially by reason of the rules prohibiting lay-offs and arbitrary reductions of wages. Now it is possible that the employer chafes. It is well that each side has had its turn: each side has experienced the benefits of law and order, and each side has been disciplined. A crisis was passed last summer (1920) when the Agreement was renewed without wage increases, although with substantial gains to the union in other particulars.

On the whole, both manufacturers and union have been satisfied with the results of the Agreement. Sidney Hillman, president of the Amalgamated Clothing Workers of America, rejoiced in the 1919 Agreement with the words: "Collective bargaining is past; instead we have the beginning of joint control in industry." Employers expressed the hope that the new plan would "substitute natural adjustment for constant friction." Today each side might claim realization of these hopes. Certainly a distinct "spirit" has been developed in the Rochester market, if not fully a spirit of brotherly love, at least one of absence of hostility. The visitor senses it. It may, after all, be nothing more than a forming habit of law-abidingness, now that there is a growing law, whose clear object is justice.

That attitude is becoming not unusual which was expressed by Dr. Leiserson in a talk which he gave in one of the other markets last winter: "It is just as foolish for an employer of human beings to think that he should be allowed to run 'his business' as he 'sees fit' as it was for the medieval king to claim the divine right. . . . It is just as erroneous for employees to think that they should take over a business and operate it according to their own ideas as it has always proved for anarchists to destroy the elements of government. . . . Labor management means control, discipline, an industrial organization held together by rules, orders, and authority, reaching down from an executive head at the top. Collective bargaining implies a questioning of that authority. . . . It says that there must be no rules or orders affecting the lives and welfare of the wage-earners without the consent of those who must obey them. . . . It joins the members of the industrial organization into a Union and forms a democratic legislative body for the purpose of giving to those who have to obey the laws of industry a voice in determining what those laws shall be."

XVIII

THE UNION IN CONTROL

THE past few years have been stormy and disappointing to capitalists in the Brewery business. But there was one circumstance for which they, at least, should be thankful; they had until the very end of the struggle the loyal support of the organized workers whom they employed. They had recognized labor years ago, and this was their reward.

The labor situation at the Huebner Brewing Company, Toledo, Ohio, is especially interesting since this is the state that has had the most fiercely and persistently contested prohibition struggle of any commonwealth in North America. The wets and drys have been fighting for twenty years at the ballot box. These local option elections, and later state-wide referendums, have been veritable Swords of Damocles for Ohio breweries. It has, therefore, been unsafe for them to challenge organized labor and go to the industrial mat for a knock-out. They have had to depend upon the votes and good-will of labor, for a militant Anti-Saloon League was ever hanging on their flanks to take advantage of any opportunity to vote them out of business.

But the brewery workers also feared this prohibition menace. Many of them had been brewery workers all their lives. All their hopes, they thought, were wrapped up with the continued existence of this industry. If the industry should be outlawed, they would be forced into other industries and quite likely down into the ranks of the unskilled. There has probably never been a time when the proletariat and the capitalist have had so much in common as in the long-drawn-out struggle between booze and prohibition. The capitalist not only gave the worker his job, but he also was the great defender of that job against a host bent upon destroying it. The brewery workers were militant and powerful but if they had dared to knock out the capitalist they would have "killed the job" with that same blow.

The brewery workers have an industrial union. Each craft may have its own local, but all must submit to one international authority. The three locals at Toledo unite in a District Council, which negotiates the Labor Agreement. Before the District Council can sign a labor contract, it must be approved by the General Executive Board of the International Union. The International has general standards which it requires, and so takes this method of securing approximately uniform conditions throughout the industry. So, the general features of the labor policy at Huebner's will hold true for other breweries of the country that bargained with the union.

On the employers' side the contracting is done by a Joint Executive Board representing the five brewing companies of Toledo. The agreement, therefore, is city wide. It became effective in July, 1919.

The union label is everywhere in evidence in and about the Huebner brewery. The label is on all the products that go out, and on about all the raw materials that come in.   Union labor made the Huebner beer and drank most of it.   The company had everything to gain and nothing to lose by putting the label on all its products.   So, it was specified in the agreement that the union should supply the company with labels in lots of 1,000 at a time and see to it that a label is on every barrel, keg, case, etc., that carries away the Huebner products.   But the company must see to it, in return, that the union label is on all the malts, grits, cereals, brooms, brushes, cases, which it buys.   Union preference extends to all the materials purchased by the company.   The brewery workers demonstrate their solidarity with their fellow workers of the other organized trades by enforcing patronage of the union label.

The brewery workers got their beer free.   They had it written in the agreement that "employees except drivers may receive a reasonable quantity of beer free of charge (a) before starting to work; (b) at 9:00 A.M. and at 10:30 A.M.; (c) twice during lunch hour; (d) once in the afternoon; (e) and at quitting time." And the employer had to keep the beer at the "proper temperature."   No, the drivers were not ruled out. They were to receive "not to exceed four small bottles" a day.

Once a mooted question, free beer seems now to belong to the ages.

The eight-hour day is firmly established.   Eight hours within nine hours, with one hour off for lunch and drinks—so reads the agreement.   The six-day week is enjoyed by all except the stablemen, who must work seven days, but their score is evened up by giving them four days off per month with pay.

There is no evidence of speeding up or overwork. It is not the company but the union that prescribes the conditions of labor here. No union member can be compelled "to pile up full half barrels too high alone when the average exceeds 50 one-half barrels a day"; nor can he be compelled "to pile alone three dozen pints (small) filled cases more than four high, or two dozen quarts (large) more than three high, longer than two hours each day." There must be at least three men when it comes to unloading malts, grits, rice, or sugar from a loaded car. A man who is working in a warm room cannot be transferred at once into a cold department. While the bottle worker is cleaning the "soaker and pasteurizer," he is dressed in a suit of overalls and in a pair of boots (or wooden shoes) furnished by the company. One notes that all the wagons and auto trucks have cushioned seats and "suitable tops"—this to placate the Deliverymen. They have a first-aid establishment, but it is not a "handout" from the company to employees, but a requirement from the company by the union.

Besides the usual legal holidays, they have added another,—"Brewers' Day." Some time during the summer the union and the company set a day for general jollification, and the company pays full time for the day.

The general agreement is confined to minimum rates of pay. These rates hold for the term of the agreement. While the brewery workers are upholders of the principle of arbitration, they have not, like the Amalgamated Clothing Workers, employed arbitration to effect wage increases during the period of the agreement. Flexibility of wage scales within an agreement is especially desirable during periods of rising prices.

The minimum rates ranged from $32 per week in the brewery department, which includes the wash house, cellar, and kettles, to $27 per week for stablemen. Twenty-nine dollars and fifty cents is the minimum for bottlers and keg beer peddlers. Permit card men get but $24, while apprentices receive $23 for the first year and $25 for the second.

Security of employment is the great outstanding feature of the labor policy. The company employs only union men of good standing. When the company is in need of more help it phones to the local union, who have obligated themselves to supply competent help whenever it is needed.

The company is forbidden to discharge any member "except for good and sufficient reasons." And the agreement proceeds to state what these "good and sufficient reasons" may be. They are (1) refusal to work when able, (2) neglect of duty, (3) dishonesty, (4) drunkenness while on duty, (5) disrespect to employer or foreman, (6) failure to report for duty without permission from employer or foreman.

To forestall any controversy as to what "disrespect" means, it is defined as "assuming of a defiant or impudent attitude or the use of profane language." But "there shall be no disrespect if employer or foreman by attitude or language, give provocation for same." So, it is perfectly legal in this shop for a worker to do unto the boss as the boss does unto him.

If the employe is unable to report for duty because of sickness, either of himself or a member of his family, he can retain his job by giving the employer notice of the fact on two different occasions during any month. The company must hold the job for such an employe six months. But if the employe has been injured while on duty, he is to be given back his job any time within twelve months.

Another means for making employment secure and equitable is the system of layoffs "in rotation" during slack seasons. Union members cannot be discharged by the employer no matter how slack the season. If there is work for just two-thirds the full force, the employer may lay off one-third of the workers for a week or a day, and at the end of this period lay off another one-third while taking back the first one-third, and so on until the return of normal conditions. In the Brewery Department the layoff is "for not more or less than one week at a time." In the Delivery Department workers may "be laid off, in rotation, for not more than one day at a time." In this manner the unemployment is spread out equally among the whole membership.

The union protects the jobs of its members by not recruiting its membership above the number necessary to run the local breweries in normal seasons. When the rush seasons come the employer is permitted to hire non-union men for the extra work. But, when normal times return, the company must discharge this non-union contingent. The Bottle Workers take care of such non-union influxes by requiring permit cards, which run for only one month at a time. If a member of a union comes looking for work, a permit card man must be dropped at the expiration of his card and his job given to the waiting union man. Under no circumstance can a non-union man compete with union members in this industry.

In refusing membership to this additional force, the Brewery Workers are simply protecting their jobs. If they increased their numbers during the rush seasons, then when normal times returned there would not be enough work for all and the layoff in rotation system would bring unemployment to the original membership. This condition would be still intensified during the slack seasons. This is one case where job consciousness drowns out the class consciousness of the Brewery Workers.

Again the union protects its members by forbidding the company to take in any apprentices when union men are out of work or when such apprentices would cause the layoff of union workers. The Brewery Department is permitted one apprentice for every 25 men, or two-fifths fraction thereof. The apprentice must not be less than 18 nor more than 21 years of age. He is to spend at least three months in each of the four departments, namely, wash house, kettle, fermentation, and chip cellar; and he must be taught to brew beer, and then join the union.

Prohibition came with January, 1920. The erstwhile Huebner Brewery is now making soft drinks instead of beer, with "Ledo" as its specialty. Only about two-thirds of the former labor force is required since this transformation of the plant. But the union and the Labor Agreement were still recognized by the company. The labor force could not be reduced by discharges. The company could only lay off in rotation, and thus spread the unemployment over the whole force equally.

Gradually the workers found positions elsewhere and the numbers diminished until only about two-thirds of the old force was left. This statement must not be construed as meaning that the Brewery Workers have not suffered during this transition period. Most of them have taken new jobs because these were better than but two-thirds of the former pay. Nor are the prospects bright for those who remain. There is not as much profit in soft drinks as in beer, and this fact, coupled with the expenses of transformation and of establishing a new trade, has depleted the reserves of the companies. Union leaders who ask for advances in wages to keep up with the still jumping costs of living are taken to the books and shown deficits on the new operations.

But the Brewery Workers have the militant spirit that overcomes obstacles. If they come through with their organization intact, it will be the first time in the history of modern industry that a Trade Union has been able to survive the destruction of an industry.

There is no complicated machinery here for carrying out the agreement. A member who feels that he has a grievance may try to settle directly with the management, or he may put his case in the hands of the Business Agent of his local, who takes it up with the management. Nearly all cases are settled in this simple manner. But if an agreement cannot be reached in this way, then the case goes to arbitration.

The Board of Arbitration is made up of two appointees of the company and two of the union. When the Arbitration Board fails to reach an agreement, then it selects a neutral party, whose decision is binding upon both sides.

While any dispute is in process of adjustment, there is to be no strike or "vacationing" on the part of members of the union. If any decision is made that the members feel they cannot accept, they must appeal their case to the General Executive Board of the International. Under no circumstance does the union permit members to "take the bits in their teeth."

The brewery industry was not a highly complicated one like the clothing industry. The problem of government here is comparatively simple. But what problems the brewing industry presented to labor were pretty thoroughly covered in this contract. The company had been kept busy the past fifteen years fighting Prohibition, and had had neither time nor money left to fight the union. Labor was able to secure those conditions of work which it regards its just due. Here labor comes about as near getting what it says it wants as anywhere else in the country.

The Brewery Workers' Union is one of the best disciplined in the American Federation of Labor. It can exact and does exact obedience from its members because of its complete control of employment and the co-operation which its officials get from the companies. While the union fought Prohibition to save the industry, it never sacrificed the union out of sympathy for the Brewers.

The sweep of Prohibition the past decade obliged brewers in one locality and state after another to transform their plants and make a different product. The erstwhile Brewery usually began making soft drinks, grape juice, yeast, and the like. So the union requested the American Federation of Labor to extend its jurisdiction to these new industries. The Federation did it, and added flour mills and cold storage plants. No matter which way the erstwhile brewer turns he is pretty apt to find the same old union facing him, demanding recognition anew and the same conditions of labor that held under the old brewery régime.

The union has expanded its name. It is now called "The United Brewery, Flour, Cereal and Soft Drink Workers of America." Its official organ carries notices every week about the forming of new locals in the recently wet states as well as in such states as Kansas and Colorado, where Prohibition has been enforced for years. They are unionizing the yeast plants, flour and cereal mills, and soft drink plants. Although the union has lost in membership the past few years, it is making a heroic effort to win back its former strength.

Prohibition has dashed the hopes of the old brewery worker. He is a class-conscious worker, a believer in the social revolution. Like his fellow comrades he saw society divided in two classes, the one, the possessing class who garnered the fat and honey of the land without toiling; the other, his class, that did all the work but possessed none of the tools of production. He had subscribed to the declaration that "The earth with all its riches belongs to all men. All the achievements of civilization have been gained by the work of all the peoples during thousands of years. The results belong to all in common." He was looking forward to that great day, the day of social ownership of the means of life. The second great purpose of his organization was to see that the Brewery industry was socialized along with the others. This was to be his heritage, and the heritage of his children. But alas! Prohibition has thrown a monkey wrench into the hopper of his expectations. He must begin his struggle again; must conquer a new field. And he isn't sure that he may not be thwarted in the hour of victory.

PART II. INFERENCES

XIX

THE OPPORTUNITY OF MANAGEMENT

John R. Commons

WE do not convince ourselves that the eighteen concerns which we have described are typical of industry as a whole. They seem, indeed, to be successful, with one or two exceptions, for the present, along new lines. One of these employers said that 25 per cent, another that not more than 10 per cent, would be a liberal estimate of the proportion of employers in general who were alive to the modern labor situation and were meeting it in the new way in which they themselves were trying.

Our conclusion, therefore, is statistical. From 10 per cent to 25 per cent of American employers may be said to be so far ahead of the game that trade unions cannot reach them. Conditions are better, wages are better, security is better, than unions can actually deliver to their members. The other 75 per cent to 90 per cent are backward, either on account of inefficiency, competition, or greed, and only the big stick of unionism or legislation can bring them up to the level of the 10 per cent or 25 per cent.

We see the process going on continuously, and can compare the results over a period of time. Thirty years ago two great industries, the steel industry and the newspaper industry, were working 11 to 12 hours daily, seven days a week. In the steel industry unionism was defeated at the Homestead strike of 1892. In the printing industry a strong organization grew up, based on the closed shop. Now, after thirty years, the steel corporation, under its "open shop" banner, works a large part of its employees 11 to 12 hours a day, seven days a week, but the printing industry with its "closed shop" works them only 44 to 48 hours a week (Chapters XIV and XV). In the steel industry wages go up and down like the prices of commodities determined by the import and export of labor. In the printing industry wages are "standardized and stabilized" according to humane principles, and the printer earns more money (in terms of purchasing power) for 8 hours than he earned for 12 hours' work. In both industries revolutionary improvements in processes of manufacture have been introduced, displacing the laborers or enlarging their product. In the steel industry the results of those improvements go only into profits for the owners and reduced prices for the consumers. In the printing industry the improvements have made newspapers cheaper and larger for consumers, have increased the profits of the owners, and have shortened hours and raised wages. In the one industry only the owners and the public participate in the progress of the nation. In the other, the owners, the public *and the wage earners* participate.

With such a contrast, it cannot candidly be said that the "closed shop" with its restrictive policies in the printing industry has been disadvantageous to the nation, and that the "open shop," with its unfettered policies in the steel industry, has been advantageous to the nation as a whole. The steel corporation has kept ahead of the game, not by doing better than the unions can do, but by doing worse, and doing it under the name of liberty and the open shop. We did not make a point of investigating, in this trip of ours, establishments that keep out the unions by doing worse than the unions, but those that do better than the unions. The open shop may be either a cloak to hide long hours, competitive wages, and voiceless workers, or it may be freedom for the management in furnishing reasonable hours and fair wages for manly workers. We tried to find the latter and to find out how they do it.

No one can squarely defend all of the restrictive policies of unions, but if they are carefully examined, as we have tried to do, they will be found to be not so very different from the restrictive policies of employers and of non-unionists. In all cases these policies have their source in the knowledge that there is not, at all times, enough work to go around, which is but saying there are not, at all times, enough markets to take all of the work at fair wages and profitable prices. In the summer of 1919 almost every establishment in the country was bending its energies to get out more product. In less than a year they began laying off the same workers because they were getting out too much product. A false prosperity in 1919 produced by fictitious sales-prospects, by reckless orders from retailers and generous credits from bankers, was followed in 1920 by cancellation of orders, withdrawal of credits, and drop in prices. The workers were restricting output in 1919 in order to spread out the work or make more wages out of the apparent prosperity—then the employers were restricting output in 1920 in order to keep up prices in the evident collapse. In one case it seemed to be unjust—in the other it is good business. It would seem that what is needed by both is "stabilization and standardization," and one of our chapters shows how this is being attempted on a national scale. (Chapter XV.)

We do not find that "labor" wants participation in the responsibilities of ownership or management. At one extreme our Chapters XVI and XVII show an organization of labor, strongly socialistic, which has put off its ideal indefinitely into the future, because its thousands of inexperienced members know that they are not ready, and have launched an ambitious program of education in the management of industry. At another extreme our Chapters XIV and XV show an organization of the most intelligent workers in industry, some of whom have been employers and failed, and they want somebody else to take the responsibility. Even the employers' shop unions which in two or three cases (Chapters IX, XI, XIII) have gradually taken over a large participation in shop management, draw the line distinctly at the point of financial responsibility.

In fact, the whole history of labor organization shows that "labor," as such, cannot manage industry. The older unionists have learned by experience. They have seen producer's coöperation tried. While, as consumers, their coöperatives have moderately succeeded, and while there have been successes in coöperative marketing, yet they have seen the laborers always lose out on producers' coöperation whether it succeeded or failed. For, when their producers' coöperatives succeeded, the members closed their doors to new members and began to hire wage-earners on the market, like other capitalists, and eventually went over to the employers' side of the game. If they failed, labor, of course, lost out. If they succeeded, the new members knew a good thing too well to let in anybody that came along. Labor, as such, is made up of young laborers and new laborers continually coming in, without experience or discipline. It is even immoral to hold up to this miscellaneous labor, as a class, the hope that it can ever manage industry. Labor, as such, in control of industry breaks down on discipline, on credit, on depreciation accounts, on planning for the future, on finding managers who can shoulder responsibility. But if it seems to succeed on these points, it is because certain *individuals* succeed, and then those individuals immediately close the doors, and labor, as a class, remains where it was.

What we find that labor wants, as a class, is wages, hours, and security, without financial responsibility, but with power enough to command respect. This is seen at several points. Security in a good job is the very heart of that due process of law described in Chapter XVI. Suspicion of absentee owners, who seem to take no responsibility of management, yet are there where they can take off the surplus earnings in time of prosperity, and lay off the workers in time of adversity, has been largely removed in certain establishments (Chapters I, II, IV, V, VI, XII) and this explains in part their success. The failure of profit-sharing, observed in Chapter XII, was the inability of laborers as a class to see further than present wages, and hence their inability to share in the management's present responsibility for future profit and loss.

If we are right in this, that what labor wants, as a class, distinguished from what individuals want, is nothing more than security in a good job with power to command respect, then so much the greater is the opportunity and responsibility of management. Management, then, becomes responsible, not only to the stockholders, but also to the workers and the nation.

Modern capitalism has been built up on security of investments. It is not labor, or management, or machinery that produces wealth—it is the credit system, and the credit system is nothing but confidence in the future. Without the credit system there might be production of wealth, but it would be the hand-to-mouth production of individuals who dare not trust their products out of their own hands, and society would sink back into feudalism or violence.

But, while capitalism is based on security of investment it has not provided security of the job. Modern socialism is but a reply to the old theories of political economy which practically assumed that everybody was employed all the time, and that the elasticity which brought this about was the rise and fall of prices and wages through demand and supply. Karl Marx replied that the elasticity of the system was not in the law of demand and supply but in "the reserve army of the unemployed." But he concluded that capitalism could not cure itself, and if so, there was nothing left but revolution and its overthrow. Socialism, anarchism, and trade unionism, all have their source in this fear of unemployment and the inability of capitalism to give security to the job as it has given security to the investment. They are wrong in so far as they conclude that by destroying security of investments they can obtain security of jobs.

They are wrong, too, in so far as they conclude that capitalism cannot cure itself. The outstanding fact of our investigation is the importance of Management. Instead of capitalism moving on like a blind force of nature, as Marx thought, here we see it moving on by the will of management. It is management that attracts capital through the confidence of investors, for the bulk of investors, like the bulk of laborers, do not want and cannot manage industry. It is Management that attracts laborers, but, if our conclusions are true, seventy-five to ninety per cent of management attracts labor, not by confidence in the future but by fear of unemployment. So when "labor" has no fear of unemployment, in times of prosperity, it "lays down" on the job, and when it fears unemployment, in hard times, its so-called "efficiency" increases. This is a curious paradox. In good times, when there is a shortage of products, labor enlarges the shortage by working slow, but in hard times when there is a surplus of products, labor enlarges the surplus by working hard. This is not good business, from any standpoint, and it is because management has not learned how to utilize hope and security for purposes of discipline in place of fear of unemployment.

That it can learn and is learning may be seen in our chapters. In one establishment (Chapter I) the entire policy turns on getting the employees to think and plan for the future, with the management. In others (Chapters IV, VI, and XIV) a good record has been made of balancing the sales department with the production department, so that no man is laid off in dull seasons or years. In another (Chapter XIII) absenteeism on account of sickness has been reduced one-half by health insurance. In other establishments which we visited, when the market slumped in 1920, the shop unions of employees were given the problem of meeting the situation and met it by laying off first those who were willing, then those without families, then shortening the hours all around for those that remained. One firm (Chapter VI) prepared the way in the profitable years of the war and after by setting aside an "employment fund" and then left the matter to its employees, through their representatives, to dispose of that fund and to enlarge it. In another (Chapter XII) by means of unemployment reserves, enabling them to stock up in hard times, no employee has been laid off in twenty-five years through lack of work. Others have set up old-age pensions (Chapters XII and XIII).

On the whole we have seen enough, in these establishments and others, to be convinced that management can provide security of the job if security is deemed important enough. It is, of course, not a simple matter to work out the details, and three-fourths to nine-tenths of employers cannot be expected to do it without pressure. That pressure was brought, in the case of unemployment through accidents, by the workmen's compensation laws. Those laws are, in effect, a tax on accidents, which can be evaded by preventing accidents. And accident-prevention has already, within ten years after the first laws, become a big feature of American capitalism, with its well-paid safety experts.

Capitalists have even set about the education of the children in the schools and the education of the public on the streets, through their great National Safety Council, with the indirect result of greatly cutting down accidents in the factories. In fact, capitalism, in the effort to cure itself of the insecurity of accidents, is doing more than politics, trade unions, schools, and all the rest of the public together have ever been able to do. It is simply because management, by the pressure of a tax on accidents that penalizes mismanagement, has begun to feel its responsibility to the workers and the nation.

Likewise it may be expected that a tax on absenteeism through sickness and a tax on unemployment through layoffs will bring capitalism as a whole to do what the establishments we visited have done, in reducing sickness and stabilizing employment. The tax on accidents induces investors to let the management have a free hand in preventing accidents, and penalizes management that does not prevent accidents.

So with the tax on sickness and unemployment. It induces investors to give to management the opportunity to do what management has begun to know it ought to do, prevent absenteeism through sickness and unemployment through turnover and layoff. The main purpose of accident, sickness and unemployment insurance is not the relief of the injured, nor the relief of sickness, nor philanthropic benefits for the unemployed, but is the business purpose of preventing unemployment through accidents, sickness, turnover or layoffs.

The concerns that we visited have shown that it can be done,—and the only question is, "Is it sufficiently important to require all the others to do it?" If it is sufficiently important and the insurance tax is sufficiently heavy and accurately imposed, then capitalism will find the way to do it. Capitalism can cure itself, for it is not the blind force that socialists supposed; and not the helpless plaything of demand and supply, but it is Management. And the greatest self-cure that it needs today is security of the job, for it is the insecurity of jobs that is the breeder of socialism, of anarchism, of the restrictions of trade-unionism, and a menace to capitalism, the nation, and even civilization. Our chapters have shown beginnings in this self-cure of capitalism.

XX

PRINCIPLES OF MANAGEMENT

Alfred P. Haake

I. WHAT MANAGEMENT IS AND INVOLVES

Each of the manufacturing or merchandising concerns discussed in the chapters of this book is an industrial unit, a going concern. Together with all the others in all branches of making and marketing, it constitutes the industrial world.

Each of these concerns is made up of representatives of the several factors in production—labor, materials or capital, the forces of nature, land, and management. It is an organic unit, primarily a psychic unit, for its principal parts are human beings cooperating in the use of materials and forces.

But men do not automatically combine themselves in organizations for the purpose of production. The great majority of mankind is strongly disinclined to take the initiative in thinking and planning. Most men prefer to follow the plans and directions laid down by the thinkers. It is so much easier. Imagination, constructive and foresighted thinking, is scarce, and because of its scarcity the price paid for it is usually high.

Some inducement must be offered to secure the expenditure of any effort. Bill Jones and his fellows work because they have to work to get what they want. Charlie Smith and others like him must see the prospect of some reward before they will deny themselves the full satisfaction of their wants, a denial which is necessary if capital is to be saved. They must be paid to let others have the use of their savings. Likewise with the owners of land and natural resources.

We express and measure values in terms of money, and since the possession of money carries with it power over goods, payment for services in production can most easily be made in terms of money. This results in wages, interest, rent and profits.

It takes the combined efforts of Bill Jones, Charlie Smith and many others to produce the goods which we need. It is generally accepted that to each belongs that which he produces, but it is next to impossible to determine just what that share amounts to. It would simplify many troublesome questions if everybody could agree on just how much each person ought to get, but Bill Jones has one idea, Charlie Smith has a different notion, the man who hires Bill Jones to work for him has still another notion. Here is the root of most of our industrial troubles : there is a never ending struggle to decide just how much each of the parties produces and ought to get. There is no absolute standard, and whatever scheme or basis of division an effective majority of men believe to be right will work. When they change their minds other arrangements must be made.

Industrial effort is the carrying into effect of some idea. Henry Ford had an idea, making a standardized car in such quantities that the price could be low enough to fit the purse of the great class of persons of moderate income. The result is one of the greatest and most profitable industrial units the world has ever seen.

Some one must conceive the idea, or select it from ideas presented to or available to him. Some one must plan for carrying the idea into effect. This is the rôle of the promoter, a function today assumed by the banker or financier. By granting or denying the use of funds in the launching or support of some enterprise he effectively determines which ideas shall be carried into action.

But this is only the first step. The next thing is to secure the active and continued coöperation of labor, capital and land, the agencies in production. This goes beyond the rôle of the pure promoter, and marks the rôle of active management. This is government, and it is active management which constitutes the government of the going concern.

The rôle of management then includes the following:

1. The selection of the idea;
2. The determination of the feasibility of the idea;
3. The selection of factors necessary to effect the idea;
4. The combination of these non-automatic factors into a well-proportioned organic unit, the business;
5. The securing of the active and continued coöperation of these non-automatic factors.

These five functions fall into three broad groups:

1. The idea or purpose (1 and 2);
2. Organization (3 and 4);
3. Administration (5).

Promotion is concerned primarily with the idea and the selection of the active management. Organization and administration are the tasks with which active management concerns itself, although it may also from time to time modify the purpose of the business.

This is the task and function of management. It is the organization and administration of an organic unit, a going concern. The conventional point of view considers the owner and officers the higher executives only, as constituting this management. But this view is inadequate. Authority must be distributed from its source, and filters down through delegation of power to all parts of the business organization.

The business unit is a number of human beings, co-operating in the use of materials and of human and natural forces, under the direction of a dominant will, toward the consummation of a common end. They are held together by the cohesive forces of responsibility and mutual risk.

As a unit these human agents are engaged in producing value; use-value from the point of view of their customers, exchange-value from their own point of view. It is because they want a universal purchasing power, money, which they can exchange for such goods as they want but do not themselves produce, that they are willing to help in the production of use-value which will be sold to others who are willing and able to pay for it.

The purchasing power, money, which they secure is in turn distributed among the several factors producing the product. It constitutes both remuneration for their services and incentive for their participation and coöperation in production.

Central in this business unit stands management. It secures and accepts the services of labor. It is responsible to labor for the advances of creative effort. It is in the position of both employer and employee of labor: an employer because it hires Bill Jones and his fellow workers, an employee because it assumes the task of guiding and coördinating the efforts of workers, because it assumes the responsibility of safeguarding the investment of labor.

Management is likewise responsible to land and natural resources: that is, to society which has a vested interest in the gifts of nature. It is the task of management to employ effectively these natural agents and yet conserve them for the continued use of future generations. This is particularly apparent in the oil industry. So far as we know, the supply of oil pools beneath the surface of the earth is limited, and a wasteful exploitation of these resources now would injure society by unduly curtailing the future's available supply.

It is more easily appreciated that management is the employee of capital. With the development of the Domestic System of industry, followed by the Factory System, management and the ownership of capital have usually been vested in the same persons. But today, the active administration of industry is not always in the hands of the owning capitalist; he simply hires the management as he hires other employees. He places his capital in the hands of management just as management places tools and machinery at the disposal of workmen, and naturally tries to hire the management which will make the best use of his capital, pay him big dividends and keep his capital safe. This means that the most efficient management usually gets the biggest opportunities.

Just as skill in craftsmanship once relinquished its control over industry to the possessor of capital, whose chief qualification for control consisted in bargaining ability and tne sheer possession of capital, so the possession of capital shows signs of giving up its control of industry to the possessor of managerial ability, capacity for performing the five functions summarized earlier in the chapter. There is, however, a strong counter tendency for the great banking and financial interests of the country to gain control of industry through the purchase of controlling shares of stock and majority interest. Specially qualified managers are placed in charge of the industries thus acquired. In one of the plants visited, we met a gentleman who has shown peculiar aptitude in the picking and handling of men. He is employed by a syndicate of financiers to bring back to a paying basis plants over which they have acquired control. This is but one of a growing number of examples.

It is true, then, in a real sense, that management is responsible to capital. Even though capital does not closely supervise the activities of management it can always discharge an inefficient management, as it usually does, and set abler management in its place— just as workmen are fired and hired. But we must make a distinction in the kind and degree of responsibility.

Whether the enterprise be a corporation, or partnership or individually owned, its capital will be of two kinds. There is invested capital from the point of view of the management, and borrowed capital from the same point of view. The first is represented by stock and reinvested earnings; the latter by bonds, loans from banks and credit advances by supply houses. The borrowed capital stands in relation of creditor to the business, having a prior claim on both earnings and assets. Its returns are guaranteed and the rate fixed in advance; but, except in case of failure to receive interest, has no control over the business. It is borrowed; its services are hired. It stands in relation of employee to the management, its remuneration coming in the form of interest.

The holder of preferred stock, while legally an owner of the enterprise, is actually, from the standpoint of management, in the same relation as the bondholder, since he is assured, not management, but limited profits.

It is the common stock, with neither guaranteed nor assured return, which carries control of the enterprise through its voting power. Sometimes it represents an actual initial investment, often it is simply a bonus given by promoters to themselves for their services in organizing or to the initial purchasers of preferred stock, as a capitalization of anticipated future earnings. Carrying voting power, this common stock confers upon its owners a control similar to that conferred by the actual investments of partners or individual business men. Possession of it gives control over management. It is the agency through which the dominant will in the enterprise finds expression. It takes what is left after all the obligations of the business to its creditors have been discharged. Each of these factors, labor, nature, capital and management, contributes to the creation of value: each takes a risk in the venture. The difference is in the kind and degree of risk.

Labor contributes human services, investing them

much as the capitalist invests his money although usually under disadvantages to which capital does not have to submit: the person of labor is inseparable from its investments,—it is perishable and its supply cannot be withheld from the market awaiting more favorable conditions, as capital can. Labor risks its well-being in employment as well as alternative opportunities for employment. Money wages are the measure of the value of those services and a payment for that risk.

The money furnished by the capitalist,—for every lender of funds, large or small, is a capitalist—buys the materials and equipment for making possible and increasing the effectiveness of human effort, as well as providing the means of paying for the services of labor. Therefore the risk of its being used up and not replaced. Its owner must go without those things his money otherwise would buy for him. Its owner receives, or should receive, a payment sufficient to compensate for the sacrifices necessary to saving and to encourage the saving of additional capital.

Nature contributes forces and materials in the raw state. Nature asks no pay for services and materials rendered, but society has a vested interest in the conservation of natural resources for future generations. It is entitled to a respectful consideration of that vested interest.

Management, through a selection and combination of the several factors, proceeding in accordance with the law of division of labor and specialized effort, makes them all more effective than they would otherwise be. The total value created is greater because of the control by management. Management accepts or takes the contributions of the several factors and assumes the responsibility for their effective combination and direction, for their most complete utilization. Out of the surplus value thus created it takes its reward. If management has been efficient, its product is great, and the fund for its remuneration, considerable. If not, the reverse is true.

MANAGEMENT AND EARNINGS

We may say, then, that the effectiveness of management is reflected in the net earnings of an enterprise. Where common stock has been issued, its market value becomes the capitalization of those net earnings. It is true that the vast majority of common stock is held by individuals who are not responsible for the growth in net earnings but who are in a position to appropriate those earnings because in one way or another they have secured possession of the common stock. In all justice it seems that the earnings should go to those who have produced them, and once the period of initial risk has been passed, all that the holder of common stock, who is not a part of the active management, is entitled to, is a fair return on his investment in accordance with the risk. The only real managerial function he exercises is the right to discharge inefficient management through the board of directors, a rather doubtful managerial activity in most cases. The common stockholder, as such, exercises no functions of active management. In other words, the absentee common stockholder should occupy the same position in respect to the enterprise as is occupied by the holder of bonds or preferred stock with difference in rate of return due to relative priority and the risks taken.

Common stock literally should represent capitalized managerial ability.

WHO IS THE MANAGEMENT?

The pertinent question is, "Who is the management?" Is it the initiator who has the idea and secures with his money the participation of the several factors, including the person in active control of the enterprise, or is it the person in active and actual control of the enterprise? Again, is labor, in that it exercises discretionary power and uses judgment in planning, as well as effort in executing, also a part of the management?

The answer is, any one of these or all, depending upon which assumes and performs the duties of active organization and administration. The absentee stockholder who does nothing more than risk his money, strictly speaking, is not part of the management, although he does participate in an initial step in management by making the advances of funds and selecting the management, which are necessary to get the business started. But his contribution is not a part of active management. On the other hand, if after having furnished the idea and the funds or secured both, he also selects and supervises the activities of management, we may properly designate him as management. Andrew Carnegie showed himself a genius in the selection and handling of subordinates. In selecting the type of man whom he placed in charge of the various enterprises in which he interested himself, he exercised a profound influence over each of these enterprises. Had he selected someone else than Mr. Schwab to be placed in charge of the Carnegie Steel Works, it is doubtful whether that concern would have developed to the proportions which it reached. He offered high salaries and was generous in sharing profits with his managers, leaving a trail of new millionaires in his wake, but if his labors as a manager had stopped with the selection of the men and the offering of these inducements, in other words, if he had exerted no influence in the determination and administration of the policies which were subsequently adopted, he would have fallen short of the stature of true manager.

Those individuals constitute the true management who through the exercise of observation and creative imagination maintain the requisite proportioning of effort within a going concern, whether in the position of stockholder they themselves assume the residual risk of the enterprise or are simply employed by those who as stockholders do assume this risk.

As we go down from level to level within a going concern, we find a distribution and delegation of managerial authority. This reaches even to the person of a foreman, who, while often not considered a part of the management, does, nevertheless, exercise judgment and discretionary power in the planning of work. He assumes the responsibility for the carrying out of plans, he has authority over others who execute his orders, and to that extent is a part of management. We may state it as a principle, then, that management includes all those who accept responsibility for the making and carrying out of plans, and definitely exclude from the category of management only those persons who are accountable solely for the carrying out of, plans and the execution of orders from above without any power of discretion as to the time, place, and manner in which these plans shall be carried out or orders executed. The foreman is a part of management—the skilled and unskilled workmen who have no authority over their fellows are not.

THE PRINCIPLES OF CONTROL

Active management, as we have shown, is primarily concerned with organization and administration of the going concern. This means control. The going concern is an organization, each of whose various parts has its appropriate function. If it is to function efficiently, that is, if it is to effect its purpose with a minimum of energy outlay, its management must observe certain principles of control.

The first principle is that of *individual initiative;* each part must be capable of initiating its own efforts. The energy that is necessary in handling an oar in a boat race must come from the person handling the oar as a part of the crew, a going concern; he, the individual oarsman, must initiate the effort. The individual workman, who as such is only one part of the business, or going concern, must of his own initiative perform the duties that are necessary in the carrying out of an order. If at any point this is not the case, then at that point the organization breaks down. One of the problems of management is the securing of voluntary initiative of the individuals constituting the business unit.

The second principle is that of *balance.* There must be accurate proportioning of capacity throughout the organization. No one part may be of such proportions that its active functioning produces more than another part can handle. In the Plimpton Press (Chapter XIV) the management has worked out a balance between the sales and production departments. The productive capacity of the plant for a period is determined, and such a sales force employed as can market the possible product. This is a static concept, however, and applies to capacities of individuals rather than to their active coöperation.

The third principle is that of *coördination*. Assuming that each part functions on its own initiative and that the requisite number of units has been provided for the several parts, there still remains the necessity of so determining the relationship of the various parts or activities that the work will flow smoothly from one to another without undue speed or friction, and that there is such a timing of operations that each part is functioning at its full capacity at all times. The Dennison Company (Chapter VI) arranges and trains its sales force to secure orders for the kind of product which the factory can most effectively produce at a particular time, and to educate the trade to order different varieties of goods at such seasons of the year as will permit of the steady operation of the factory. Thus the trade was induced to order jewelry boxes early in the year instead of just before the retail season, which enabled the management to keep the factory employed on these articles at a time when work would be slack. This is the dynamic aspect of balance, the properly adjusted capacities coördinated in action. With these principles realized, management has made the going concern into an efficient organization .

HUMAN RELATIONSHIP PRINCIPLES

The principles of individual initiative, balance, and coördination may be said to be only the mechanical aspect of control. They do result in an efficient organization but do not explain why or how men can be fitted into such an organization. They leave untouched the question of how the organization can be maintained at this high level of efficiency. It is easy enough to control and maintain equipment, but not so with men. The workman may put forth great efforts today, he may work with interest and enthusiasm, and tomorrow be sluggish or ill-disposed. He is a human being with likes and dislikes, sensitive or dull, generous or selfish, open-minded or prejudiced, any number of combinations and variations of these and other qualities—he is governed by emotions. It is necessary for management to observe closely and carefully the principles of control. From this point of view they are responsibility, mutual risk assumption, and inducement.

A. *Responsibility.*

To the extent that a worker accepts responsibility for the performance of a task, individual initiative will be forthcoming, he will hold himself accountable for the necessary expenditure of effort. If the power of discretion as to the manner of performance of the work accompanies the delegation and acceptance of responsibility, the worker becomes a part of the management to that extent. In that type of management where we find one man control—that is, the executive assuming all responsibility for planning and delegation of work and, on the part of his employees, not more than an obedient acceptance and carrying out of orders with an absence of discretionary power—this principle is not in use and management, limited in the extent of its personnel, must depend for effectiveness upon its personal driving qualities. In this type of management we find the executive overloaded with work, wearing himself out, and the organization under him either consisting of hero-worshippers almost blindly following his lead or, often, sullenly performing its tasks, not because of genuine loyalty to the management but because there is fear of discharge and no alternative employment. It is when the worker looks upon himself as a part of the business, one of the management, that his greatest interest can be aroused. He is helped to see that his interests and those of the management, instead of being opposed, are really in common.

A splendid example of an effective use of this principle is found in the Nunn, Bush & Weldon Shoe Company (Chapter XI). This concern has deliberately placed the responsibility for the conduct of its employees in their own hands. It has gone so far as to delegate to them the power of fixing wages and hours of work and the right to discharge. And the significant thing is that the employees, instead of running wild with the authority given them, have actually been sobered. They look upon themselves as business men interested in the welfare of the concern which employs them, being careful not to go so far in their demands that the concern is unable to compete effectively with other manufacturers of shoes. The same principle has been applied at Filenes (Chapter V).

B. Risk Assumption.

Closely allied to this principle is that of risk assumption. Labor is an investor, and if the employee can be brought to see that he takes an actual risk in devoting himself to the services of his company and that he can make the investment of his labor more or less secure according to the kind and degree of interest he takes in his work, he is far more likely to function effectively on his own initiative. It will not be necessary to drive him.

This is the philosophy which lies back of all profit-sharing schemes. The management wants more production. It can afford to pay a share of the increased product to the workers because their increased activity, distributing the overhead or fixed charges over a larger number of units, lowers the unit cost of the product. A portion of this saving is held out to the workers as inducement for greater production. They call it profit sharing because they want the men to believe that they will get back at least a portion of the surplus net value produced. They are teaching the men to visualize the effects of increased industry and loyalty, to see a connection between work, production and the pay envelope. In effect this means that the workers are brought to see that they are joint-sharers in a business venture, risking their labor now in order that they may secure returns in the near future; that they are in a position to influence the degree of returns by their individual industry and team work.

The men do not always respond to the teaching. They see wages as a payment for services sold, not invested. All too often they look upon the shared profits as nothing more than belated wages, arguing that if the management can afford to pay profits at a later time it can do so only because it has withheld a part of their wages previously. The men prefer to receive their wages from week to week instead of letting the management have use of their money, for its own advantage as they see it. Thus they fail to see any causal relation between variations of their efforts and fluctuations in dividends. This is primarily why profit-sharing schemes fail. If management would first educate the worker to realize his risk-taking function, and then suggest, or better still, let him suggest, the sharing of profits; instead of using the profit-sharing scheme to effect that education, it is likely that the sharing of profits would in many cases succeed where the method now fails.

C. Inducement.

Thirdly, and fundamentally, inducements are necessary to secure an active coöperation of the several factors. The bestowing of responsibility together with discretionary power upon the workman often proves to be the most effective inducement, for in that bestowal the worker sees possibility of future returns. This means more than monetary returns, since, as men rise to higher levels of achievement, opportunities for power and the sheer gratification of capacities make work more attractive; mere money is not the sole inducement. But, in the last analysis, men work not because they want to, but because they have to, in order to get the things which the money they secure will buy for them. If wants are few, that is, if the scale of living for the worker is low, and if he is not desirous of raising it, he will not respond so readily to financial inducement. The hope for management at this point rests on the truth that human wants are not easily satiated and have a way of expanding as rapidly as they are gratified. For most men, money is the most highly desired single thing, because it can buy almost anything the average man wants.

It is this principle which Joseph and Feiss (Chapter IV) use so effectively. Through the several bonuses which they hold out to the workers they offer the possibility of increasing income. The increased income depends upon increased quantity and improved quality of the output. The piece rate and production bonus encourage the worker to accept the responsibility for getting out the requisite quantity. The quality bonus operates almost automatically to keep the quality up. The worker, or operative, is encouraged to see the direct relationship between the amount and kind of work and the contents of his pay envelope. Individual initiative is thus secured. Through the scientific analyzing of process, motion, and time study, the correct assigning of work and the proportioning of the various parts, balance is achieved. Careful planning of work and close watch of the reaction of workers to the various inducements effects coördination.

Teamwork is simply an everyday term for the condition existing when each worker accepts his responsibility, meets his accountability, understands his relation to the risks involved in the enterprise, and finds the inducements adequate. The securing of teamwork constitutes administration of the business. It is likely to follow intelligent delegation of managerial, or planning and supervising functions down through the personnel of the organization.

STRUCTURAL AND ECONOMIC LIMITS

Since the securing of teamwork is dependent upon human relationship principles, the problem of active management is essentially a human relations problem. This is more than a good-will problem. Good-will can often be secured through so-called welfare work—and aids the management in securing the coöperation of its labor personnel. But, important as it is, it is not the whole problem. The larger part of the problem lies in the securing just the requisite action from each factor in the business, within structural and economic limits, through the appeal to action-inducing motives.

Securing just the requisite amount of action is a matter of providing proper balance of parts, whose capacity will be such that a reasonably complete utilization of each will keep all busy for the full time. Thus, it would be poor management to hire more salesmen when the factory is already unable to fill orders. It is also a matter of coördination; that is, each part, or production center, will function in such a manner as to be ready to receive work from a preceding production center, or stage of production, when that production center is ready to deliver its quota of work. This is closely approximated in both Joseph and Feiss (Chapter IV) and the Printz-Biederman Company (Chapter IX) through central planning departments and control boards which show the progress of work from one stage to another.

It might be possible to secure more work from any one of these production stages, but this would be inefficient since either men or equipment or both, somewhere, would be idle while others were endeavoring to catch up; there would be an incomplete utilization of labor even where the piece-rate wage system is in use. Men are induced to act or work not through thought, but through feeling. Thought may suggest an act, but feeling determines. Men often do things which their reason condemns up to the very moment in which feeling results in action. The effectiveness of any inducement depends upon the kind and degree of feeling aroused by the management. It is necessary then to use the various inducements as approaches to emotions, or motives. Motives are the handles by which men may be taken hold of and guided.

These can all be traced back to two fundamental motives, hope and fear. It is the motive of hope that induces the employees of the White Motor Company (Chapter I) to put forth their best efforts, to be loyal to their company. The management lays before them its plans for a coming year and even a period of years. It reveals past costs and profits as well as contemplated future costs and profits. It shows the relation between capital, production, and wages. The charts shown to the workers indicate a proportionate increase of wages with a mounting of production. The workers are helped to visualize the future, are given hope for increased income both as to amount and certainty,—and they rise to their opportunity. Hope unlocks initiative, it spurs the worker on of his own volition, taps unsuspected strata of energy and devotion.

But this is true only so long as the worker's scale of wants is in excess of his ability to satisfy them. If his income reaches the point where no wants go unsatisfied, he does not respond to the stimulus. Witness the coal miners and others who during the war earned enough in four days to live for a week and then laid off for several days each week. It has long been known that more than a subsistence wage for certain levels of workers along the Mississippi simply operates to shorten their working week. Actual experiments among the latter have shown that increases of wages above what is needful for bare livelihood have been accompanied by proportionate decreases in the number of days worked. For most workers, this is not true for very long. A period of high wages brings new wants into existence and the scale of living rises to a new level which organized labor fights to maintain.

Fear may impel the worker to effort. But it is a sorry substitute for hope. It usually is most effectively appealed to in the lower levels of employment, where men have not the vision to see future returns. It is this motive which, in times of depression, when goods are not relatively scarce, impels workers to overproduce. They work hard to keep their jobs, but not because of interest in the work itself. It is the motive which management is steadily letting go where it can, educating workers instead to respond to the stimulus of hope. Fear inhibits, hope unlocks.

AVENUES TO HOPE AND FEAR

The appeal to hope is made through holding up the possibility of wage increases, security of income, or participation in the management. The appeal to fear is made through threat to close these avenues.

Most concerns rely on the first of these avenues to

secure the coöperation of the workers—naturally enough, since values are measured in terms of dollars, and through the possession of dollars the individual can secure most, if not all, of the things he wants. While it did speed up production during the war period, the inadequacy of the method is reflected in post-war labor conditions.

The second of the avenues or methods is receiving quite considerable attention. Concerns like Nunn, Bush & Weldon (Chapter XI), Joseph and Feiss (Chapter IV), the Dennison Manufacturing Company (Chapter VI), the Plimpton Press (Chapter XIV), Hart, Schaffner and Marx (Chapter XVI), and the Ford Motor Company (Chapter II) are doing much in this direction.

The Dennison Company in 1919 had set aside $100,000 as a starter for an unemployment insurance fund. This is to be increased from time to time out of the earnings of the company and ought eventually to reach such proportion as will guarantee every worker full-time employment even in times of depression. Joseph and Feiss pay a service bonus of five cents per day for each year of service up to ten years, and encourage the setting aside of this sum, in some cases arbitrarily, as a reserve against old age. Thus, a worker who has served for ten years or more is receiving fifty cents each working day in addition to his regular pay and other bonuses, and is virtually building up a pension fund for himself.

The third method is being widely exploited; indeed, so widely as to give many an observer the impression that the time is not far distant when labor will become an important part of management. It is the method used by the Demuth Company (Chapter VIII), the Milwaukee Electric Railway and Light Company (Chapter XIII), the Printz-Biederman Company (Chapter IX), the Wayne Knitting Mills (Chapter XII), and many others with varying success. Some exponents of this method go so far as to suggest that managerial policies and methods can best be determined by agreement between the several groups of labor, capital and management, each possessed of equal bargaining power. In order to accomplish this, it is held that workers must deliberately be educated for participation in management, the process of education to be begun early in the school life of the boy.

THE LAST WORD

There is reason for some alarm as we see the growing degree of control exercised by the strictly financial interests. We see industry after industry coming under the control of Wall Street. We may well recognize the dangers in absentee ownership and particularly in absentee control. The danger in the former is potential; even when it regards itself as no more than an investment interest, it may, if it wills, encroach upon the active management. The danger in absentee control is real and ever present. It was to get away from the latter that the Dennison management (Chapter VI) adopted its present scheme of capitalization and control. It was the fear of absentee control that prompted the workers in another plant discussed in this volume to protest the threatened appointment of a new general manager.

The stupendous profits taken from industry by men

who in many cases have made comparatively small initial investments and who often have not even laid eyes on the plants which they control, are too well known to need any comment here.

But to say that we can dispense with capital is quite another thing. Nor is it likely that good business policies can be effectively determined on the basis of delibate agreements reached with capital, management and labor possessing equal bargaining power. Collective bargaining really fixes the limits, but is not the administrative source of business policy.

Granting that equality of bargaining power is desirable, or even attainable, it still remains true in a society based on division of labor and specialization of effort that advances of material, equipment, food, shelter and clothing must be made before a single stroke in production can take place. It still remains true that the pyramid of organization must have an apex. Somebody, somewhere, must have the final authority, must say the last word; and this authority cannot be a distributed authority. This is fundamental in organized effort. Participation in management by workers without capital investment must in the very nature of things be confined to limitations placed by them around the activities of management and the acceptance by them of responsibilities delegated by the higher management.

REMEDY FOR ABSENTEE CONTROL

Accepting this position, how can we remedy or prevent the evils of absentee ownership and control? If we could and were willing to wipe the slate clean, that is, wipe out existing rights, obligations, and the social and political institutions which protect these rights and obligations, it would be easy to suggest a remedy. But a new deal is quite out of the question: we must play with the cards as they lie in our hands. We are dealing with a situation, not merely a theory. And the situation at present is that capital is the most powerful and influential among the factors of production. The person or group holding capital usually has the whip hand in industry. If we are to get away from control of industry by absentee investors or owners we must have a new leadership to take their place. This new leadership, the personnel of trained management, must win its way to a position where it can make the final decisions for industry—say the last word.

From the time that control of industry began to pass from the hands of the skillful craftsman into the hands of the craftsman who was the abler manager of processes and men, capital accumulated in the possession of this manager; it strengthened and extended his control. Later, accumulated fortunes made possible the employment of able managers without capital, and opened the avenues of managerial development and opportunity to thousands of men with ideas and executive ability, but no capital. Also there developed the credit and banking system which mobilized in the hands of men having the money sense the vast number of small individual savings deposited with their banks. These bankers and financiers have come into positions of great influence and power. Men without industrial experience, they are nevertheless the dictators in industry through their ability to hire managers to run the industries over which they have acquired control but are not qualified actively to manage; they can dictate through their ability to grant or withhold financial assistance to industries in need of funds.

In the second stage of the development briefly traced above, management controlled industry because it also owned sufficient capital to finance itself. The third stage indicates that the real control is tied up to the possession of capital, and when management and capital were no longer vested in the same person, management became the employee of capital. At present management is principally responsible to capital, including absentee owners of capital because capital is indispensable in production and must be sought where it is.

That capital should hold the whip hand is almost a commonplace in economics. In the existing system of production, one not likely to change because of the manifest economies of division of labor, specialization of effort, and the consequent long-drawn-out process of production, advances of funds must be made at all points to sustain the process until the returns can be realized somewhat later. Of course this means advances of labor and management effort as well as of capital, but men must live and most men have neither the foresight nor the inclination and usually not the ability to provide for their own maintenance out of savings while investing their labor in an enterprise. Thus it comes about that practically all of the advances are made by capital. Indeed this is true, even when the workman can accept postponement of his wages— for he can do this only as he has transformed past fruits of labor into money capital. Capital can be stored, as such; labor cannot be stored, except as it becomes capital through savings: this is true of managerial effort as well as common labor.

Capital exists in the shape of money, a universally accepted medium of exchange. It is general and can be exchanged for anything—it is the storehouse of value for anything which has a money price. This is not true of labor. Labor is not only perishable with the passing of the moments in which it can be put forth, but it is also of specific and limited nature. It has a market limited to the demands for that specific effort, as for example the demand for the maker of watches, whereas capital has a universal market, limited only by the limits of demand for goods with a money price. This is true even when capital exists in the form of buildings, machinery and materials with limited use in production: for such capital can be hypothecated, and as security for loans from banks, or for bond or preferred stock issues, virtually be transformed into the universally accepted purchasing power, money.

In a world where money buys nearly everything, capital is the symbol of power. Someone must take the final risk for any business, must stand responsible for payments under contract with the several factors in production. This someone must own or have access to capital, since capital or money is the thing universally desired in payment for services. It is evident then that any scheme for divorcing active management power from the absentee owner of capital must provide for some other factor to take the final risks involved. And that factor can safely assume those risks only with capital at its command.

Of all the factors concerned active management seems best qualified to control industry. It has the initiative, the creative imagination, the organizing and executive ability. If management is to free itself from the domination of absentee owned capital, and assume the dictatorship of industry, it may do so in any of the following ways:

1. Provide its own funds for the financial responsibility of the going concern: it assumes in part a capitalistic function.

2. Encourage labor to save and invest its funds in industry thereby either playing labor-owned capital off against investment-owned capital and controlling through a balance of power, or going so far as to substitute control by labor-owned capital for control by investment-owned capital.

3. To make itself more nearly indispensable in production than any other of the factors, and thus have both capital and labor compete for the guidance of management rather than the converse.

4. To coerce absentee-owned capital through threat of inefficiency or direct action by organized management, to relinquish its active control and accept the position of bond or preferred stockholder.

5. To buy capital off, making its owners content to relinquish active control in consideration of greater security and adequate returns on investments.

A complete discussion of these alternative means of removing the active control of absentee capital would lead us into a realm of pure speculation far too broad for the scope of a single chapter. The idea is too untried to justify us in definitely committing ourselves to any particular scheme. It is still in the stage of experimentation. In a growing number of instances the managerial group is taking the initial steps in starting new enterprises, naming itself as the management, and, in addition to borrowing funds, is providing the initial stake in the enterprise. Here and there well-established concerns are sharing the actual management with the employees, particularly those exercising management functions. In several cases this is done through participations in ownership through sharing of profits.

One of the most successful of the latter type is the Dennison Manufacturing Company (Chapter VI). Indeed, it has gone well past the stage of experiment and sets a new mark in industrial development.

In this case the separation of absentee ownership from management was effected through the agency of that corporate device known as common stock. It was recognized that the period of initial risk for the owners was well past. The owners themselves, for the most part, were not so much interested in actively managing the company as they were in security and amount of income. Following the initiative of the president of the company, himself a heavy stockholder, the common stockholders were bought off. They were given preferred stock to a considerably increased par value over the par value of the common stock surrendered. They were guaranteed eight per cent on the new stock with return to active control in event of failure to receive the agreed-upon dividends. They took little chance—they had much to gain and little to lose by the change. For a time they shared control with the active management—until the accumulation of a large reserve after paying all preferred stock dividends fully justified their faith in that management.

Against this growing reserve, common stock, carrying voting power, was issued as profit-sharing dividends to the managerial employees, those whose creative imagination and management of the going concern produced the profits. When a sufficient amount of common stock had been issued, control passed entirely to the new active owners.

The rate of return on the new common stock was limited to ten per cent, and this provision together with several others insures a steadily growing reserve which, in time, if not already, will make the company independent of outside capital, and so avoid what is possibly the greatest danger of a return to absentee control.

The effect on the managerial group of employees has been gratifying. The added incentives of recognition and financial reward have brought them to a high level of efficiency. Their increased sense of responsibility, their realization of an actual financial risk in the concern, of the necessity of maintaining a strong reserve fund, the possibility of automatic loss of their power as well as profits in the event of failure to meet the preferred stock dividend requirements, have increased their productive power and usefulness—have developed teamwork and knitted them into a strongly cohesive unit. They are sufficiently close to the problems and actual situations of the industry to imbue them with a sense of responsibility to the other factors in production; they are far more likely to conserve the welfare of their industry and its usefulness to society than would be the absentee capitalists who see in their control the sheer exercise and increase of their power and profits.

While this plan does not include the employees below managerial rank in active control of the company, it does provide a share of profits for them. Also opportunity for rising to the level of employment which entitles them to participation in management is open to them.   More than this should not, perhaps, be asked for these employees of the lower levels.   It is not likely that they will for a long time be qualified or even interested in undertaking a share of managerial authority and responsibility.   At present they are certainly unwilling to assume financial responsibility.   But the proximity of fellow workers whose superior loyalty or productivity or both has brought and is bringing them within the managerial group will act as a constant goad and incentive to these lower level workers. The way to promotion into the upper group must be kept open at all times.

To just what extent and on what terms absentee owners can be persuaded to relinquish their control we can only speculate.   There is no way of surely knowing except through experimentation.   There is encouragement, however, in the example of a man like Henry Dennison.   The far-seeing owner who is also an active manager, who has sufficient breadth of vision and depth of human understanding will, in many cases, follow the lead of the president of the Dennison Manufacturing Company.   A succession of such examples will go far toward bringing absentee owners to terms, whether they are bought out, kept out or put out.

Our conclusion is that we have got to develop a new leadership of active managerial vision and capacity, which will be prepared to take the final risks in enterprise and eventually win its way to domination over the other factors in production—it must be the very heart of a vitally-functioning going concern.

II.   TRAINING THE MANAGEMENT

This theory rests for its validity on the possibility of training leadership within the concern. For unless leadership comes from within it will have to come from without; and control will be where leadership is.

It is probably fair to say that leadership developed in the past in industry throughout has not been of a very high order. Thanks to a plentiful supply of labor, especially unskilled labor, the power of summary discharge was generally sufficient to maintain discipline. If any workman failed to produce, or prove amenable to discipline, he faced discharge; and usually several others stood waiting to take his place.

But with the growing power of organized labor and its relative scarcity the threat of pending discharge has in many cases proved inadequate. There is an increasing need for effective leadership down through the ranks of industry, an increasing need for capacity to handle men. For leadership is essentially personal in nature.

Great leaders like Marshall Field have gone far because they had a canny knowledge of men which enabled them to pick for managerial employees the natural or potential leaders. They have trained their leaders. For the minor executive who has developed the imagination and judgment which enables him to use men and materials effectively within his limited vision and scope of authority, it is but a series of steps to widen this view of authority to include markets as well as departments. The essential thing is the ability to lead and utilize men.

In the average enterprise the foreman, or corresponding person in authority, is the keystone of the arch. He comes into direct contact with the men. To them, he is the firm. President, chairman of the board of directors, are but names; the foreman is a flesh and blood reality. He interprets management to the men, and the men to management. It depends largely upon his relations with the men whether they are satisfied with their wages, their security of employment and their voice in controlling conditions of employment.

Certainly the management cannot hope to have workers assume responsibility whole-heartedly, look upon their efforts in production as energy investments whose rate of risk they can influence, and see any connection between their wages, their output and profits, unless the foreman first of all sees these things.

The average foreman is a man who has been given his place on the basis of seniority or mechanical ability as well as his driving capacity. It is rather rare that the question is asked: "What can he do for his men? Can he teach them to become better workmen?" or "Has he the executive capacity which will make him a leader of men?"

Consequently he is usually a man who has been a workman. Having risen from their ranks he has never quite ceased being one of them, and therefore he feels constrained to be harsh or severe with his men to impress them with his authority. Intolerance and impatience are frequent faults. He is a technician rather than a psychologist, a driver rather than a leader, full of the old notion that the best way to get results with men is to fire them if they do not "come across." He is not a student, for it has not been necessary to learn

more than he could see with his own eyes or do with
his own hands. He has usually little patience with
books. His mind works objectively. He has not been
taken into the full confidence of his superiors and so
does not feel the same urge to loyalty that is theirs.
He is easily suspicious and quick to resent what he
terms "passing the buck" on the part of the management. He has not the vision which enables him to see
opportunities higher up and to prepare himself for
them, and so falls short of his greatest usefulness to
the concern and to himself.

This is the average man whom the management
must train to his higher capacities, to qualifications for
the task of personal administration of workers. What
is true of him is true of the average "underling" in the
managerial group.

The job of this sub-executive is essentially the job
of management brought down to its personal aspects.
It is his job to secure teamwork in the lower levels
where men are less responsive than in the upper. He
should possess these qualities:

First: he should appreciate the dignity of his job.
This is but another way of saying that he must whole-
heartedly assume the responsibilities of his function.
He must see himself an executive, the representative of
the firm.

Second: he should see the relation of his job to his
department and to the business as a whole. Without
this understanding, he may not avoid wastes and losses.

Third: he must understand his own job in minute
detail.

Fourth: he should understand the technical process
of his department and the factors employed in that

process. His attitude in supervision and inspection may lead to misuse of materials and serious losses.

Fifth: he must be square. He must be a human nature expert; lack of tact on his part can seriously disturb the morale of an entire force of employees.

Sixth: he should understand the principles of management and production involved in his work. He should not be of the type of so-called "practical" man who sneers at all theory.

How can you develop such a leader?

There is no absolute answer. But until the technical process of production can be separated from the device of personal control by foremen, no plan can ultimately succeed which does not make the foreman better qualified to perform the two-fold nature of his task, control of materials and processes, and especially of the human beings engaged in those processes.

The conference, or committee method, is perhaps the simplest as well as the earliest. Its purpose has not always been so much to train foremen in their duties as to enable the executive in charge of the group to keep in touch with affairs, to provide a means of ironing out and preventing difficulties among the foremen, to better coördinate the work of the factory. As a by-product, if not deliberately, foremen are given training as executives.

It is this method which is used in the Philadephia plant of the great Link Belt Company (Chapter III). The groups of foremen meet with their superintendent daily to talk over such questions as work routing, complaints of failure to live up to schedule, plant conditions, and frequently matters of discipline and welfare of the workmen.

In the Ford plant (Chapter II) there is an interesting development of the committee method. This is not a joint meeting of superintendent and foremen, but a picked group of thirty specialists who spend their time adjusting difficulties between foremen and men. They are "trouble" specialists whose job it is to know what is going on, to detect trouble before it ripens, and to help keep the vast Ford family at peace within itself.

The packing house of Swift and Company selected John Calder, the engineer of well-known standing and an executive of broad experience, to head its industrial work. He organized classes of foremen and other executives in fourteen plants of the company, with a total enrollment of over three thousand.

The outstanding features of the Calder method are the lectures, the standardized course booklets and the answering of questions at several meetings. The groups are large and include men of differing rank, all the way from assistant-foremen to superintendent of the plant, embracing men in different departments and branches of the work, factory and office. The course booklets, six in number, are cultural as well as practical, easy to read and interesting. There are problems and questions which are handled as in any regular correspondence course. The emphasis appears to be on the educating and inspiring of foremen more than simply training them, and the principal agency is the lecture.

A very different method is that of Robert B. Wolf, industrial engineer, who has made a series of interesting experiments in the paper industry.[1]

[1] *Amer. Soc. of Mechanical Engineers,* Publication No. 1673 (1918).

Mr. Wolf's objective is to arouse the creative capacities of workmen through appeal to what he calls the "non-financial motives," to get each man to compete with his own previous records. The basis of all these motives, he holds, is interest in work, which implies a desire to produce, actuated by internal motives rather than external discipline. His solution for the problem of training active management to increased capacity for initiative, risk, and responsibility assumption, would be to arouse interest in work. To do this involves changing the industrial environment from one which repels to one which attracts.

To arouse interest in work he uses no lectures, home-study courses or discussional groups, but relies primarily upon graphic individual progress records, for both workmen and foremen. Thus in the sulphite plant of a paper company, he had attached to the digesters, in which pulp is reduced to a mass of fibres, charts which informed the workmen about reactions in the digester, enabling them to better visualize their work. He provided other charts which showed standardized curves of what the temperature and pressure of the vats ought to be. Allowance for variation from the standard was made and the men graded on the degree to which they approximated the exact standard. An absence of deviation from standard meant perfect control of the process and a grade of 100 per cent. It meant increased product of improved quality.

A continuous progress record of performance enabled each man to see from day to day whether his control over the process was increasing or diminishing. There were no wage bonuses given, but the aroused interest of the men in their own progress, their increasing sense of power and control over their jobs, their efforts to better their own past records, brought yearly production from 42,000 tons to 111,-000 tons. For the foremen in the plant, progress records were made in terms of costs instead of quantity.

The idea above has in one plant been carried to the point of considering each of the departments as a separate team in an industrial league. Each team has both its individual and team progress charts, and each week is given a rating similar to that of a baseball team, based on this progress record. The teams are then shown in their respective standings, recorded as a baseball league standing. Rivalry and emulation are aroused as well as interest in work per se: the result is a more intelligent and productive labor personnel.

Mr. Benjamin E. Mallary, of the Department of Industrial Education of the Cleveland Public Schools,[1] attacks the same problem with a somewhat different emphasis from that of the Calder method. These methods were used in different plants, under different conditions, in response to the demands of different managements. While both strongly emphasize the need of developing foremen, Mr. Mallary apparently uses the lecture less and the group discussion to a greater extent. His is the seminar rather than the lecture method. His groups are smaller and more homogeneous, confined to executives of uniform rank, on the theory that men will talk more freely with men of equal rank than in the presence of superiors. In

[1] "The Foreman, His Training and Education," Benj. E. Mallary, *Annals Amer. Acad. Pol. & Soc. Sci.*, Sept., 1920.

the opinion of the writer, this method is the best yet developed.

The procedure is slow and careful. The men's minds are prepared for the ideas of a training course and initiative is allowed to come from them. A single group is trained first. Its members become the leaders for subsequent self-initiated groups. Entrance is purely voluntary, but subsequent attendance is required. The discussion at every meeting is devoted to the specific work of the men and is directed towards the solution of some practical problem.

The principles of training as laid down by Mallary are as follows:

First: the management must practice policies it wishes foremen to practice.

Second: system of training men must be fairly democratic, but not so much so as to destroy all distinctions of rank.

Third: the foremen must take part in the administration of the work, in both organization and administration of the classes and groups.

Fourth: if the foremen think, they will expect to see their ideas taken seriously by the management.

Fifth: the training course must result in the foremen taking greater part in the active management of the plant.

CONCLUSION

It must be remembered always that the real problem in industry is that of human relations. It is necessary to establish personal contacts at all points of transfer of authority, instructions or reports. The executives at these contact points are the important links in the organization. The executive must be developed as an individual and trained as an executive, and whether the methods used be those of Mallary, Calder, Wolf or anyone else, the principles developed in this chapter remain fundamental. The real purpose is to develop self-initiated acceptance and discharge of responsibility on the part of all executives having personal contacts with the employees. Team work, based on mutual trust, confidence and complete understanding will take us farther toward the solution of industrial relations problems than any mere industrial relationship schemes, wage bonuses or attempts at conciliation.

XXI

PRACTICE OF LABOR MANAGEMENT

WILLIS WISLER

THE proper practice of labor management strives
to maintain a balance at the point of maximum return for investors of capital and investors of labor as
producers, and for both as consumers of their common product. Ideal labor management must study so
to coördinate the productive, the financial, the purchasing, and the sales factors in its business as to promote
and to justify a sense of security among the workers.
This is no easy matter. Perhaps until good labor
management has become the rule rather than the exception no employer can hope single handed to succeed. But demonstrated good intention can disarm
much of the resentment incident to failure.

From this it would appear that labor management
is not a function that the employer or board of directors can hope to delegate properly to any subordinate. It is a responsibility peculiar to management
itself. As the business grows and becomes unwieldy
various subordinate functions of labor management
may be delegated for economy of administration.
Among these are employment management, labor maintenance, and welfare or social service work. But the
determination of the economic relations that involve

the division of the product of the industry, the employer cannot delegate without at the same time delegating with it his own authority to commit the company.

No intelligent labor policy can be set up or administered without free access to the other factors of the business. The unwise purchase of raw materials may have to be recouped in lower wages if their high cost cannot be passed on to the consumer through sales. Again, an ambitious sales campaign may necessitate such demands on a labor market already rising as to wipe out in excess wages or overtime payments all additional profits. Then again the financial conditions may be such as to make investors suddenly very critical. As a result capital may be restricted and the working force may have to be curtailed. The failure to take into account these interrelations is largely responsible for spasmodic underemployment, irregular employment, cancellations, and financial losses. Even seasonal and cyclical unemployment can be largely reduced by maintaining a due balance of these factors.

Between the investors of capital and the investors of labor lies a sort of industrial "no man's land"—a middle area of waste. In prosperous times the consumer can easily be made to bear the burden of this middle area of waste. When the consumer balks at high prices, prosperity languishes, prices fall, the demand for production disappears, and unemployment threatens. Then the employee is constrained to bear this burden in the form of reduced wages. Both are complacent in times of high prices—both are helpless in the face of declines.

If the maintenance of wage levels could be enforced

in the face of declining consumption, the employer no doubt would develop or procure the requisite managerial skill to effect compensating economies by the reduction of this middle area of waste. Experience confirms this view in those industries where organized labor has approached a monopoly. There the employer is constrained in dull times to reduce waste sufficiently to procure the means for maintaining wage scales. On the other hand, shrewd employers are using the leverage of falling prices and threatened wage levels, not so much to reduce wages, as to stimulate coöperation of their employes with them in concerted efforts at greater economies and efficiencies.

This middle area of waste is the proper field for the exercise of labor management. But until the ambitions of mere capital and of mere labor to manage *per se* can be restrained, as well as the impatience of investors for immediate large returns, labor management will find itself in the same difficulties as confront all management.

From this there seems but one hopeful avenue of escape—the liberation and enfranchisement of management on the strength of its actual achievement. Labor management as a major phase of industrial management must educate and train itself for its rightful rôle of organizer, director, and leader.

On the side of economic relations in industry labor management cannot hope to achieve standardized technique and formulæ, but must seek to remain mobile, alert, and resourceful. Like management itself, which is the policy-determining function of the Board of Directors and the chief executive, it cannot be reduced to technique and routine. It is not a profession—it is the very government of industry, its legislature which cannot delegate its legislative function of determining the labor policy along with the financial and sales policies.

The real problem of labor management is to realize as fully as possible the practical expectation of production by reconciling the human element to it. The impersonal compulsion of scientific management cannot accomplish this. On the other hand, more than simple placation or ingratiation is needed. Something more substantial than the glad hand and a genial smile are needed to keep the home fires burning. The reconciliation must go to economic foundations. The labor manager must be able to measure bargaining power and economic force; he must forecast market movements intelligently; he must be on guard against mere opportunism. All of this requires more than the keeping of records, the manipulation of forms and routine. It involves analysis and vision. All the labor manager's energies must be given to the task of knowing the truth of each situation. The keeping of records by the labor department to help him accomplish this must be designed for accuracy, adequacy, immediacy and simplicity. What they bring to the real labor manager is the raw material for him to work up into a truthful exhibit of what should be his best procedure. It is this interpretation of labor management also that distinguishes the mere glad hand of personnel relations, which workmen resent, from that sense of even participation in the problems of the business which appeals to their self-respect.

Personnel relation—the human or man-to-man relations—on the other hand, admit of very definite organization in their administration. Here technique and routine can be standardized. Employment management, labor maintenance, service or welfare work —all have to do with these personnel relations. Common shop practice, ordinary decency, and minimum legislation have brought these personnel relations into the non-controversial field of labor management. What constitutes a safe place to work can be authoritatively determined by the safety engineer and not by the contest of opinions. What constitutes decent treatment of workers as human beings, public opinion and universal practice have determined beyond the need of debate. These matters are settled by trained and experienced experts in accordance with well established rules and standards. What is needed here is machinery to collect data, and organization to assure performance.

When trouble arises in this field of personnel relations, it is usually because economic issues have been injected or because this distinction between personnel management or its subordinate function of employment management, and labor management itself is not recognized. The term "labor manager" has in a number of instances been loosely given to personnel officials. This is a dangerous practice. It needs only an economic or financial crisis in the business to uncover the inability of such misnamed officials to deal competently with economic issues.

In one of our largest clothing markets this weakness disclosed itself in a very dramatic and disconcerting fashion. The employers—the real labor managers—had, during a period of great prosperity and of powerful labor organization, permitted their "labor managers" to exercise full powers in making and administering collective wage agreements. The performance of these so-called "labor managers" was marked by a fine tolerance and largeness of humane vision. They had won the good will of the workers and the friendly esteem of the union officials. But when the balance of economic power slipped suddenly toward the employers' side, these same "labor managers," in an endeavor to maintain the equitable balance needed for the continued functioning of the joint government of their industry, found themselves thrust aside and discredited. Their true function then appeared. All along they had exercised the administration of economic relations only on sufferance. The men who paid the bills, when they saw an opportunity to impose their economic will upon the situation, summarily withdrew from their "labor management staff" all power to deal with economic issues. The staff resigned. They felt that they had been repudiated. As a matter of fact it would seem rather that all along they had misconceived their real place.

On the other hand, the supervisor of personnel, the employment manager, or the welfare director constantly finds himself in the precarious position of having to impersonate the third person in industry. Where no collective agreements or machinery for negotiations exist it is the personnel official who finds himself put into the impartial arbiter's place. Paid by the employer he is called upon to create among the workers the illusion of impartiality. This is by no means impossible of achievement. There are many employment managers and other personnel officials who by their personal integrity, the enlightened labor policies of their employers, or by their tact and personal charm accomplish this difficult feat.   But at best the personnel man as the impartial agent between employers and employees is in a precarious and an unsound situation. He is forced to be both advocate and judge.

In his proper place the personnel or the employment manager can do much toward guiding his corporation along sound lines of labor management.   But this he must accomplish by suggestion and advice.   He certainly exceeds his right when on his own initiative he sets up decisions and determinations in the field of economic relations.   It is a great deal better for him to concern himself mostly with the effective administration of the personnel machinery and with the data, records, and exhibits necessary to its effective administration.   Arising out of this material for the consideration of the management in setting up or in modifying labor policies analytical reports will be of the utmost value.   Most of these records and exhibits will have to do with the management's efforts to reconcile the will of its employees to the profitable fulfillment of production standards.

The labor manager in his efforts to harmonize the mechanistic and the human factors of production finds himself divided between two conceptions of labor: labor as a commodity and labor as human beings.   Having set up, by investigation and analysis, what seem to him in his engineering capacity reasonable standards of production, his natural impulse is to release labor into production just as he releases raw material, power and machinery.   From the engineer's viewpoint labor is essentially a commodity.   It differs from other com-

modities, however, in being animate. The commodity
is inextricably tied up with the human being who is
marketing it. He controls it in a manner far more
intimate than the other commodities of industry are
controlled. The worker's good-will becomes a determining factor at this point. The labor manager at
this point must shift from the position of engineer to
that of bargainer. He must meet labor as one business man dealing with another.

This he does not always do. He may persist after
the fashion of the more short-sighted of the scientific
management school in an effort to coerce by the force
of mathematical fact. But such coercion ordinarily
breaks down at the crucial point, i. e., the point where
the employer urgently needs or desires maximum production. This very urgency gives to the worker the
economic advantage with which to force virtual aban-
donment of scientific management standards. Many
instances of alleged successful scientific management
have been studied and so far none has been found in
which concessions, open or concealed, have not been
made by the management.

Only after repeated failure and the effective resentment of workers has scientific management come to
recognize the animateness of labor. It conceded then
that the laborer should be treated as a human being;
that his well-being and contentment are essential to
good production control. Thus was ushered into industry the era of organized welfare work.

It has been repeated within the last years to trite-
ness that workmen resent being patronized, that paternalism is un-American. The real offense of welfare work has been its calculated substitution of wel-

fare work for economic freedom and wages, and the studied evasion of the fair administration of the economic relations between employee and employer.

Had scientific management concerned itself more with the human than with the mechanical factor, had it worked toward mechanical efficiency through the human factor by giving to workers a sense of economic participation there might never have been occasion for our present segregation of labor management from executive management. Again had the functional foremanship provided for under scientific management operated properly through its "disciplinarian" or had the foremanship of the old type been free, able, and willing to work toward production through the worker instead of imposing the job upon the man, there might not now be this present much resented encroachment on the foreman by the personnel and employment manager. One of the most significant things in foremanship training is its effort to retrieve its lost or at least its greatly impaired position in labor management. When foremanship truly finds itself, and employers by their own insight or by the economic compulsion of organized labor assume their proper functions of the real labor manager, our present preoccupation with labor management as a specialized field of management will probably pass away.

While, then, the contest between the employer and the employee in this bargaining process must be a continuous and should be a progressive contest, labor management, which on its economic side must be the chief executive management itself, must remain fluid and elastic. This is no argument for that opportunism which is the worst kind of mismanagement. The employer must know his business well enough to have a set of definite policies. These policies it is that give character to his particular industry. But in the application of his policies to changing economic conditions he must be prepared constantly to modify and revise his behavior with a view of getting for his policies their greatest possible realization in practice. In the bargaining encounter he must know as accurately as possible not alone his own force but the force of his employees.

In short he needs an "intelligence service"; he needs organized machinery to supply him with records that are immediate, simple, accurate, and adequate. This is not an easy matter; but it is not too hard of accomplishment for the smallest concern. And it does not need to be complicated even for a business of increased size.

A careful study of about three hundred typical employment management systems seems to disclose that much of the needless elaboration in employment and personnel forms is the result of incomplete analysis of personnel functions. Forms have been designed often under the pressure of emergencies, hastily and short-sightedly. A proper grasp of fundamentals in most cases would have forestalled the emergency, or a careful review of existing forms would have prevented the perpetration of an additional form by passing some existing form through an additional manipulation. The evil of this indiscriminate multiplication of forms is not merely one of increasing clerical or administrative burden. The more serious evil is the loss of effective coördination of records. In this fashion records come into being without their proper relation to other vitally associated forms being considered. Not only are opportunities for error greatly multiplied but the detection and discouragement of abuses and fraud are greatly impaired.

The more compactly the data-collecting and record-keeping machinery is designed the more economical will be its operation and the more effective will be its performance. The very physical adjacence of forms minimizes neglect and error. The very simplicity of the forms themselves discourages omissions and faking. It is obviously absurd to encumber forms with self-incriminatory questions to an applicant. Some of the forms examined may have been excellent sociological questionnaires. But the employment manager or even the personnel director have no call to be sociologists except as it serves the definite needs of labor management. Why ask a man eager for a job whether he is a drug fiend, an epileptic, or of unsound mind? If these facts are essential to his working with the company, let an expert examine the applicant and determine these things. If blood pressure, venereal disease, or defective eyesight are vital matters, they deserve the use of a qualified doctor to carry on a competent investigation.

There are really only four stages in the cycle of employment, (1) engagement, (2) follow-up supervision, (3) adjustment, and (4) termination. Labor should be issued with even greater care than tools and stores. The labor requisition should be tied in with the proper job specifications on one side and with the engagement notice on the other. This can be readily accomplished by having the original engagement record placed on the back of the labor requisition memorandum. A three by five card is a convenient size. Attached to this should be the duplicate engagement record for the foreman's file. This duplicate should be tied in with the completed record of the employee's career in that department. For this reason the termination record should be placed on the back of the duplicate engagement record. When notice of termination is given either by the foreman or by the workman, the latter returns with this termination notice to the hiring agent for adjustment, for transfer (which is a form of adjustment), or for separation from the company payroll. By the proper arrangement of these two pairs of employment forms the engagement record can be typed with carbon duplicate. Transfers are combinations of departmental terminations and departmental engagements. Labor departmentally dismissed had best be reissued (unless separated from the plant payroll) just like any other labor.

Fads also play their part in complicating forms. Every caption should undergo the severest scrutiny before it is allowed to be incorporated into a form. It is better to err on the side of simplicity. It is better to use captions that will permit of variation in the entries made under it, e.g., it is better to have for general purposes one captain—Education—than to list a half dozen or more degrees or types of education. If one particular degree or type of education is essential to employment that is a different matter. The procedure in such cases is clear enough. Often personnel directors are carried away by the zeal of the statistician. They refine and refine their forms to the point of utter impracticability. Usually the enthusiasm of the originator gives a semblance of successful operation to machinery so intricate that it must collapse as soon as its designer passes away. There are personnel and employment managers unfortunately who take pride in this very defect. They surround their function with elaborate hocus-pocus. Such misguided men should be vigorously reformed or driven out; they are a real menace to all concerned in industry.

The forms described above can be conveniently made up into pads with a stub for (a) keeping a count on the number of labor requisitions used, and (b) for entering a brief follow-up report on the new worker by the foreman. At monthly intervals these stubs can be called in for consideration by the personnel or employment manager and entered upon the worker's individual record folder. Thus the work of four forms is condensed into two and these combined into one. The manipulation of this one "5 x 6" sheet parallels physically the steps of the cycle of employment through which the worker passes while with the company. The files for these forms had best be kept numerically.

The employee's individual record folder serves as the alphabetical or directory file. This form should be designed to hold in one central file all pertinent facts regarding each employee. The face may be designed to carry the identification data—name, age, sex, race, etc., and the pre-employment record needed for determining his suitability for employment. The back of the folder—which can now be folded into a five by eight container is arranged to carry, in the form of successive entries properly distributed under columnar headings, the post-employment history of the worker. When the applicant selected to fill the foreman's labor requisition has been accepted by the foreman the receipted engagement record with this labor requisition on the reverse returns to indicate a completed hiring. These data are posted to the first line of the post-employment record, and to the daily labor record. The engagement record is then filed numerically, the individual employee's record folder is filed alphabetically, and a carbon of the daily labor record, showing engagements, terminations, transfers, and rate changes, is sent to the paymaster for daily adjustment of the payroll. If the paymaster makes such adjustments promptly and makes adjustments only from these daily labor records, many of the troubles of the time office and of payoffs will be removed. A perpetual labor inventory can be kept by posting daily to a monthly form the totals from the daily labor record. Both these summary forms should be designed to show reasons for engagements, transfers, and terminations.

From these four blanks embodying the essential employment processes in compact interlocking fashion, six closely interrelated forms can be designed and operated to satisfy all the personnel necessities in the largest plant. For plants of less than five hundred the Individual Record Folder and the Perpetual Labor Inventory alone would be sufficient.

The condensation and simplification described above was actually made in a company employing nearly five thousand. They represent the boiling down of forty-six separate forms into six forms. Most of the forty-six were already inoperative, although carried along. The number needed for plants of less than five hundred employees is only three forms. The aim of this procedure was to achieve accuracy, adequacy, immediacy, and simplicity of records.

The practically minded employer will naturally want to know just how the keeping of labor records can help him to improve his labor management, how individual records of performance, of attendance, of behavior can affect him. Their general desirability he is usually ready to acknowledge, but the special applications to his own business are not so apparent to him. Much of the employer's hesitancy in adopting such forms and record keeping arises out of the feeling that these are theoretical refinements which big business alone can afford. For this the complexity and elaboration of forms described above is largely to blame. More of this, however, is the result of bad accounting tradition. Much of our accounting practice rests on the ancient traditions of mercantilism— that values inhered in the things of wealth and that their behavior lies beyond human control. Accounting under such a conception can be merely an investigation of past experience in order to arrive at the results of accomplished facts. Even when the conception of "standard costs" came along, the mechanical processes were too cumbersome to achieve the immediacy of records which all accountancy should strive for.

Ingenuity has now contrived a variety of machines to accomplish this immediacy. Employers need no longer grope their way by the feeble and uncertain light of last year's cost figures. But in spite of this, progress is slow. Employment management, largely having its origin in cost accounting, has a chance to achieve this immediacy. When the employer-manager can see moving before him day by day the current behavior of his business; when he can follow with graphic charts the fluctuations of markets, of production, and of finance, he is well guarded against errors of negligence or oversight.   He knows at every turn where he is.

Formerly in dull times manufacturers shut down their plants as soon as their books showed no profit. More recently shrewd employers have come to recognize the advantage of working their plants even at a loss. Just where the shut-down point in each case lies is the problem of accounting practice.   Undoubtedly it lies near the point where the net loss equals that overhead expense which will continue even if the plant is idle—rent, interest on capital, depreciation, taxes, insurance, etc.   Even when this point is reached it may be well to continue operating to keep intact a well-organized working force of employees or a smoothly working staff of executives.   To determine the wisest procedure, to avoid the needless irritation of employees, to decide how far to go in maintaining the good-will, the sense of security, and the contentment of the working force requires the aid of the most accurate, adequate, and immediate records of all phases of the business.

One prominent mid-western company in such a situation decided to encourage greater economies by acquainting their employees of what reduction in the unit cost of production was needed to enable the company to continue its full working force.   When this reduction of production cost was not achieved lay-offs occurred of those employees whose individual records showed a consistently poor performance.   To enable the workers to readily grasp the situation these records of unit cost and per capita performance were kept graphically. Delinquent or defective workers were warned and placed on probation, and when some of them were finally dropped there had been brought about a general feeling of fair play and mutual confidence between company and operatives.

But it is not only in times of unusual depression that records become of vital importance to good labor management. Periods of unusual prosperity need the wholesome discipline and the foresighted safeguarding which effective record-keeping alone can give. The dramatic collapse of the clothing industry in the last quarter of 1920 is an excellent example of ill-advised overproduction which might have been prevented by accuracy and immediacy of records. Manufacturers, deceiving themselves with the mass of fictitious orders from equally eager distributors, purchased raw materials and engaged labor indiscriminately. Ignoring the threat of permanently high wage levels they bid up labor higher and higher. The pervading complaisance on all sides during this period of fictitious prosperity changed almost over night into one of the most bitter industrial conflicts the clothing industries have known. Cancellations precipitated the situation. But in any event the deflation must have come. Here the whole of labor management has been basically affected by misguided or vicious purchase and sales policies.

Viewed in more detail we find that in the individual shops poor production control played an analogous part. The flow of production in most cases was spasmodic. In some cases, through defective supply, poor routing, or bad dispatching; in other cases by deliberate intent, operations were being thrown out of balance. To recover the "balance of the shop," workers were subjected to constant alternations between layoffs and overtime. Shrewd and none too scrupulous foremen dammed up the flow of garments to "rush" strategic operations. With stacks of garments piled up on one side and with clamorous operatives calling for work on the other, the operatives between were stampeded into top speed production. Thus there was created in many shops a state of nerves no less than a state of mind that readily exploded into violence on slight provocation. The presence of impartial adjustment machinery in some of the larger clothing markets provided a safety valve for much of this tense discontent. But where such machinery was lacking or where it functioned inadequately, labor management broke down under the strain of poor production control unchecked by proper record keeping.

Sometimes a business grows large and unwieldy so suddenly or so imperceptibly that all manner of confusions and abuses arise in its various departments. One large shirt and collar manufacturing corporation found that its wage levels had gone alarmingly high. It was found that this was due to two causes: first, the bidding of departments against each other; second, workers using the highest rates in other departments as the fulcrum for prying their own rates higher. The first of these causes was disclosed in the transfer records, the second in the paymaster's records. The only sensible way to check this confusion appeared to be to arrange all the operations in a sequence of relative

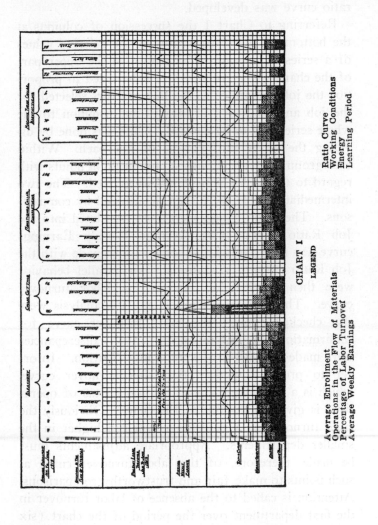

CHART I

LEGEND

Average Enrollment
Operations in the Flow of Materials
Percentage of Labor Turnover
Average Weekly Earnings

Ratio Curve
Working Conditions
Energy
Learning Period

value.   A thorough job analysis was made and a job
ratio curve was developed.

Referring to Chart I the succession of columns at
the bottom of the chart represent the relative values
of a series of operations as named in the upper part
of the chart.   The columns are subdivided to proportion the job valuations to the three factors selected for
the job analysis.   An arbitrary unit common to the
whole series had to be devised.   This was done by dividing the series into groups of five each.   Within
each group the highest, lowest, and medium points with
regard to the factor considered were fixed.   The two
intermediate points were then determined by comparisons.   These job values were then translated into the
Job Ratio curve.   The Average Weekly Earnings
curve was then plotted and comparisons made with the
Job Ratio curve.   Variations from parallel behavior
were then checked up against the labor turnover
curve.   The factors covered in the job analysis were
also checked against the labor turnover curve for
confirmation or discrepancies.   Such discrepancies
were made the object of special investigation.   In order to properly qualify the labor turnover curve,
which is a percentage curve, the job quotas of operatives is given at the top of the chart.   Obviously the
labor turnover as a percentage will run higher in the
smaller departments.   Appropriate adjustments must
be made, therefore, of the labor turnover curve at
such points to make fair and trustworthy comparisons.
Attention is called to the absence of labor turnover in
the first department over the period of the chart (six
months) in the parallelism between the job ratio and
the average weekly earnings curve.   The flattening of

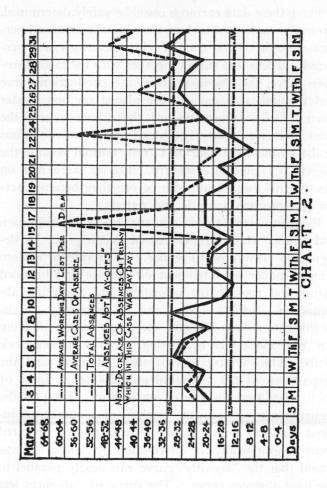

CHART · 2 ·

the latter curve is a natural tendency but none the less
interesting as a wage phenomenon.

From these data earnings could be safely determined.
From the same data a chart showing the standard personnel needs of the company by operations was prepared. These two curves together with the labor turnover curve, the absentee curve, the production curve
and the unit cost curve were placed on one master
chart. Daily adjustments of these curves kept the
chief executive constantly advised of current conditions
in the business. Departures from normal became the
objects of immediate inquiry. Losses were met on
the threshold and dealt with before they became facts
for post-mortem analysis and regrets.

Even in normal times industry is full of congestion
and abuses which proper record keeping can be designed to prevent or to reduce. A prominent eastern
tannery under an intelligent directorate had installed
forms and routine for recording and analyzing absenteeism. Such a system can be extremely simple.
In this case a daily absentee sheet was drawn off from
the "out" clock rack by posting to it the unrung clock
cards. The investigation of these absences and the
preparation of the analytical exhibits for a force of
six hundred took the time of one person. The periodic
recurrence of prominent "peaks" of absenteeism invited further investigation. A chart was prepared
showing graphically the distribution by causes. It was
found that the "lay-offs" curve ran nearly parallel to
the total absentee curve. The curve of "absences less
lay-offs" was then constructed with the lay-offs curve
shown in dotted line above. Referring to Chart 2 the
curves are arranged with the calendar scale horizontal

and the numerical scale vertical. The solid line curve indicates absenteeism after lay-offs have been subtracted. The dotted line curve indicates total absenteeism including lay-offs. The space between these two curves indicates absenteeism due to lay-offs because of lack of work. These curves reduced to absentee percentages for the month are straightened out into the parallel horizontal lines. The upper of these two, 29%, covers all absenteeism; the lower, 12.5%, covers only absenteeism from which the lay-offs have been subtracted. It will be seen that the loss by lay-offs amounted to 16.5% of the total possible working time for the plant. When 5% is considered a fair normal of absenteeism it will be seen that the condition here shown was unusually dangerous at a time of labor scarcity. Many of these lay-offs found their way into the labor turnover. Employees could not afford to remain with a company where so frequent interruptions of earnings were occurring.

The loss of time by lay-offs was so conspicuous that a conference of executives including foremen was called by the management. The conference was a lively one. The discussion located the cause of these lay-offs in the management's policy of buying hides in small lots. The management excused itself on the score of lacking adequate storage facilities. But the records had disclosed so dangerous a situation in so unmistakable a fashion that the management pledged immediate steps toward having additional warehouses put up.

A further investigation of these absentee curves showed that not only the "frequency" of absence because of alleged sickness but the "severity," i.e., the duration of absences, decreased periodically on Friday of each week. This proved to be pay day. On the following Saturday there was always a pronounced rise in frequency. The company promptly changed its pay day to Saturday forenoon. Another company in a similar instance shrewdly changed its pay day to Monday, aiming thereby to reduce habitual Monday absences. The resourceful labor manager will see many opportunities for using such absentee data.

It does not follow, of course, that all types of industry will have like needs and like experiences. But the matters touched on in the foregoing examples are pretty common to all manufacturing concerns. There are many special points equally valuable but of more limited application. Two rival Ohio firms in one of the larger cities made labor surveys of the communities around their plants. As a result they found that they were hiring out of each other's territories. The result was inconvenience to workers, transportation troubles, tardinesses, absenteeism in bad weather and usually ultimate increases of labor turnover. They solved their problem by giving their employees the chance to exchange plants at no loss of income. They went farther. They arranged for transfers from one plant to the other for promotional purposes when no opportunity offered within reasonable time in their own plant. This required some courage, but they found it paid in increased good-will and confidence among their employees. Another plant made an analysis of its working force by ages and found that the accurate character of the work required could be best supplied by men past forty. Another company with a monopoly in an automobile essential found they could reduce all their operations to automatic machinery. They invested in a staff of high class supervisors and ran their plant most profitably with hoboes and transients. Another corporation manufacturing kitchen supplies found by a special job analysis that they could operate most profitably by hiring only cripples.

The superintendent of a large furniture factory will hire only Scandinavians. Another will hire any north European stock except Finns. The General Superintendent of a large railway repair shop "mixes" his foreigners to obstruct their organization by agents of the unions. Another "balances" his nationalities so as to effect the same purpose by grouping workers in proper proportions of races antagonistic to each other. All such plans to achieve any success, even according to their ideals, need to be based on data that are accurate, adequate, immediate, and simple.

Because a business is small is no good reason for assuming that these things are not equally important for it. If anything, the small business needs to be more minute in its records. It may be that the employer in the small concern carries these facts and records in his head. Well and good so long as he is on the job. But to guarantee continuity of labor policies there must be continuity of machinery. The machinery should be designed for the business. The outside expert can help a great deal in giving proper proportion to those factors and facts which lie too near the employer for him to focus properly. But if the outside expert strives to cram the business into a ready-made form or routine, trouble is sure to follow. Each establishment must work out its own industrial salvation in its own way.

A careful consideration of the foregoing chapters will bear out this conclusion. Here are a variety of types of labor management, no two alike, ranging from the benevolent autocracy of Ford to the courageous democracy of Filenes. And yet all appear to have been successful to an unusual degree. The reason is not far to seek. It is that each of these establishments has a definite labor policy, each has created the appropriate machinery for administering its labor policy, and each has procured for its labor policy the widest and frankest publicity among those affected. It can hardly be the particular form of industrial government, nor any one device that has achieved this uniform success. These are but the tools with which to work out well defined labor policies.

The White Motor Company seems to have come nearest to a realization of these truths. Without making any pretense of democracy and without recourse to any unique device or method, on a straight unmodified day rate, they have developed a remarkable shop morale. This they have done almost entirely by keeping their eye intently on their business and designing the entire machinery of their labor management to accomplish their one avowed purpose—the ultimate survival of the White Motor Company. To this fundamental purpose they give the widest publicity among their employees. Thus they have created a community of interest in the business itself that arises out of the practical self-interest of each. The management is interested in survival and financial returns; so are the workers. In such a situation data collecting, record keeping, and report making are of as great concern to the workers as to the employer. The investors of capital and the investors of labor alike look to those charged with their company's management for the essential facts—they want them to be accurate, adequate, immediate and simple.

If each instance of successful labor management is carefully examined it will be bound to rest on three conditions: (1) a definite and consistent labor policy inaugurated and backed up by the chief executive or board of directors; (2) the organization of machinery for putting into effect these labor policies, and (3) the competent administration of such machinery.

XXII

INSTITUTING EMPLOYEE REPRESENTATION

O. F. CARPENTER

SHOP organizations of employees are not a new and sudden discovery. In the early period of trade unionism committees of workmen were frequently selected in the shops to seek wage adjustments or the settlement of grievances. Local government makes its appeal in the industrial as well as political field. Many of the trade unions of today have made the shop committee a part of the structure of the union. To such committees are usually entrusted the maintenance of the union organization and the enforcement of its rules, the negotiations with the management for the settlement of purely local questions, and the duty of observing the compliance of the firm with the trade agreement and of reporting any violations.

Shop committees of various types have been making their appearance in non-union shops. Some of these committees were informal and but temporary, while others have become permanent. A great many of them have been developments from purely social activities on the part of employees. Some employers who had sensed, during the past twenty years, the need of social and welfare work and who were aware of the necessity of avoiding paternalism, had urged the employees to form committees or clubs of their own choosing for participation in or direction of that work. The safety campaigns have been often conducted in the factories by committees of the workers, and there has been a tendency in some instances to vest these committees with other functions. Several of the organizations described in the preceding chapters have developed by this gradual and pragmatic process. When an industrial problem looms up it has been only natural and logical that the employer turn for consultation to some shop organization with which he has been coöperating on some other shop problem. Successful experience in such mutual efforts has led to the extension of the functions of such organizations of employees, and, quite frequently, to the creation of new agencies for handling the questions arising in the field of industrial relations.

The Milwaukee Electric Railway and Light Company (Chapter XIII) affords an example. At first the works organization was a joint council which was concerned with the administration of a benefit program. So it continued for seven years, when departmental committees were elected by the employees to perform the usual functions of collective bargaining. The Filene Coöperative Association (Chapter V) is another example of gradual growth. Its beginning was an Insurance Committee elected in 1898. Several other committees were soon at work. The increasing number of employees and their increasing participation in store affairs soon rendered it impossible to transact business at mass meetings. Then a council was elected, having one representative from every fifty employees. This council is a legislative body. In the meantime a board of arbitration, elected by and from the employees, was set up. From time to time, as occasion showed the need, there have been extensions of the authority of these bodies. From the early participation in insurance, social and recreational activities, the participation of employees has been extended to practically every question that concerns company and people, or individuals or groups among the employees or management. A variation from this line of development is the Nunn, Bush and Weldon Company of Milwaukee. (Chapter XI.) Its first council represented only those employees who had been three years or longer in the service of the company. Today a shop committee represents all the regular employees and is exercising larger functions than the original joint council.

The plants that had established employee organizations for participation in the settlement of factory questions prior to the period of intensified unrest that has swept the country since the spring of 1918 seem to be the least affected by this unrest. The machinery has been at hand for meeting those problems and, what is more to the point, management and employees had gained that experience, understanding of and confidence in each other, which are a prerequisite of a successful endeavor at joint shop government. In several instances the existing organization had to be modified or enlarged to meet the greater needs, but this is not difficult to accomplish with going organizations.

But where this organization and experience are lacking, the firm that desires to organize its industrial relationship finds itself confronted immediately with the problem of how to introduce employee representation. The National Industrial Conference Board has well said:

"The employer who has determined upon the introduction of a works council into his establishment needs to exercise great tact and wisdom in initiating the project. The success of a works council is frequently endangered at its inception by the manner in which it is instituted." It cannot be too strongly emphasized that the *method* of devising and instituting a shop organization of employees is of prime importance.

Employee representation has been introduced in nonunion shops, as a rule, by the initiative of the management. It is obvious that, in these shops where the firm is in complete control, the first step toward popularizing the shop government is "to sell" the idea to the directors of the firm's policies. Oftentimes the urge has come from within the management itself. Some responsible official has read an account of "Industrial Democracy," or of the workings of some shop committee or works council, and has been convinced of the wisdom of such a policy. He has advocated such a policy in the inner councils of the company and has succeeded in getting the firm to make the move. In other cases employers have been persuaded by some advocate like John Leitch. In still other cases the company has made the move to circumvent the efforts of the unions to organize the employees.

The employer who is contemplating such a move should give the proposition thorough consideration before acting. He should have estimated the probabilities of the move and should know to what extent he is prepared to share his industrial power with the employees. The employer should realize that his sanction of employee representation implies faith in the integrity, capability, and good judgment of the workers. It goes without saying that he should be sincerely convinced that the new arrangement will prove advantageous to the employees as well as to the firm in the solution of shop problems. The employer who conceives employee representation as a means to beat the unions, or as a clever device for putting over certain policies advantageous to the firm, is bound to bring discredit upon the organization sooner or later and will thereby nurture in the employees that scepticism and mistrust which militate against further efforts looking toward coöperative action.

The employees are the critical factor. Their approval and confidence are necessary conditions of success. During periods of unrest and class antagonism they are suspicious of the moves of employers and their coöperation cannot long be expected unless concrete evidence of the advantages of the new arrangement are promptly forthcoming. It is highly advisable to acquaint the employees, at the very start, with any plan that is to require their coöperation. No pains should be spared in making the employees understand the full significance of the proposal. The firm that ignores the employees, works out the representation plan and adopts it, and then posts notices of that fact in the works, acts upon a bad psychology. Under such circumstances the workers will be asking each other: "What's the company trying to slip over on us now?"

If the employees are trade unionists, and, especially, if their union or unions have previously been recognized and dealt with, the management will act wisely to take into consideration the policies and attitude of the union or unions involved. Trade union leaders are on the lookout for what they term "company unions," which they regard as subterfuges for "real unions" and as the greatest menace to their trade unions. Rightly or wrongly, the trade unionist feels that such a move on the part of the company is a challenge for a fight to a finish (Chapter X), as many industrial tragedies of the past few years bear witness. The employer who does not wish thus to challenge unionists is confronted with the problem of getting the sanction of the union or unions concerned for the proposed shop organization. The approval of the local union officials is sufficient for those unions that provide a large measure of local autonomy, while for unions of the more centralized type it will be necessary to negotiate with the international officials.

The *foremen* are a factor second in importance only to the employees. Foremen are the point of contact of management with workers. Being face to face with the problems of management every day, they see these problems in the concrete; and their judgment and counsel cannot safely be ignored. It is the foremen who interpret and apply those policies that affect employees. The foremen, also, should know from the very beginning what is being proposed in the way of new policies. They are just as insistent on participation in what is transpiring as are the more militant among the workers. The conditions that make necessary the change in policy, the purposes sought to be attained under the new plan, the new responsibilities and the changes in methods that will thereby devolve upon the foremen, should be thoroughly explained to them, and their coöperation and approval should be sought at every step in the development of the new plan. They must be thoroughly trained and prepared for the change when it comes.

Too much emphasis cannot be placed upon this preparation of foremen. The foreman has been aptly characterized as "the key man of industry." He actually is that. In order to measure up to his job he must know the features of the firm's policy, and must know well in advance any proposed changes in policy. He must be prepared to explain, to defend, as well as to apply the new policy. The adequate training of foremen and consultation with them is thus seen to be a part of the problem of instituting employee participation in shop affairs.

The *first step*, then, in the introduction of employee representation is the approval of the move by the three factors: company, foremen, and employees. If the shop is trade union, then there is a fourth factor, the union or unions affected.

All the factors concerned having agreed upon the first step, the next "step in order" is the preparation of the plan, the constitution of the shop government. There are a few organizations, however, that deferred the drafting of a plan or constitution until after experience had shown what the constitutional requirements should be (Chapters V, IX, XI), but the great majority have followed the political precedents of formulating the constitution first and getting the experience under the constitution, after which amendments to the constitution can be made as experience shows their advisability.

The preparation of the plan should be entrusted to a council or committee made up of representatives from the several factors already enumerated. Attention has already been called to the inadvisability of the management's submitting a plan of its own devising at an election of its own calling. This is not affirming that any plan so formulated and introduced is foredoomed to failure. There are several plans in operation that were introduced in this manner and are considered successful, but there are equally striking failures on the same score. None of those so introduced escaped a period of distrust, while, at the same time, they were laid particularly open to the charge of being purely a "company union."

The methods used in introducing employee representation in America range all the way from that of formulation of the plan by the company and submitting it to the employees for their approval to formulation of the plan by the employees and submitting it to the management for the latter's approval.

The method followed by the Goodyear Tire & Rubber Company, Akron, Ohio, exhibits a wide joint participation in the move from the start. The decision for the new shop organization was made by the management, but immediately all factors were given representation in the preliminary organization designed to prepare a plan and introduce it. The following excerpts from the announcement in the *Wingfoot Clan* (the factory paper), March 29, 1919, describe the initial step and give the purpose in view:

"The ending of the war has brought to our Akron factory, as well as to others, the need of a program of reconstruction. . . . Probably the greatest change will be the initiation and progressive development of employees' representation on all subjects of industrial relations between the factory management and the men. The *first step* will be the establishment of a council of industrial relations to meet with the factory manager, composed of five members of the executive council, the manager and assistant manager of the Labor Department, two foremen elected by the foremen, and six non-salaried employees, of whom two will be elected by the Service Pin Association, one by the Flying Squadron, one by the Engineering Division and two by the Production Departments. All important questions of industrial relations will be passed on by this council and it will formulate a plan to establish a legislative body somewhat along the lines of our national federal Congress to give representation on matters of industrial relations to all Goodyearites over eighteen years of age, who are American citizens, understanding the English language, who have had six months' continuous service or one year total service with the factory. These Goodyear INDUSTRIANS will have a large voice in shaping the policy of the factory in the future on such subjects as employment and working conditions; housing and living conditions; safety; sanitation; health; restaurants; employees' transportation; recreation, athletics, and entertainment; continuous work and reconstruction problems. The efficiency and permanence of this plan, as in any democratic form of management, will depend on the interest taken by those eligible to vote, and we have every confidence that you will measure up to the opportunity."

This announcement has the merit of setting forth briefly and definitely what is involved in the proposed move. It shows also to what extent the management is prepared to go in sharing its powers with the representatives of the employees. The announcement indicates the management's preference for a plan of organization and the qualifications it expects to establish as the requisites of industrial citizenship. It might have been better had the management refrained from this incidental injection into the announcement of its views on these two particulars.

Then followed the election of representatives from the several departments to the Council of Industrial Relations. In its issue of April 5th, the factory paper announced the coming elections. Industrial citizenship was explained, and the requisites were given for this citizenship and for voting, in the Goodyear elections. Registration lists were posted in each department and the workers were urged to see that they were not omitted from the lists, if qualified.

Different methods of conducting elections were used in the different departments in order that the resulting experience might aid in the formulation of that section of the constitution. The foremen held a meeting and made nominations from the floor. The election of their representatives took place by secret ballot at this same meeting. The procedure for Plant No. 1 illustrates the method of election in the Production Departments. The registration lists were posted and one week was given for employees to obtain corrections, The Plant was divided into twenty precincts, and the voters in each precinct were instructed to vote for three persons. The person who received the highest vote became the electoral representative for that precinct. The twenty persons thus elected constituted the Electoral Committee for the department. The Electoral Committee elected one representative on the Council of Industrial Relations. "By this system the man who obtains an office should obtain it on merit and ability and not on account of popularity." The Service Pin Association, a group of 2,000 workers who have been five years or longer with the company, conducted its election by mail. Nominations were made by petition, the names of ten members being required. A ballot was prepared with the names of the candidates thus nominated and the "past history of each nominee." Voting booths were placed at one of the gates, and the members were permitted to leave and vote at any time on the day of election.

The Council of Industrial Relations was now chosen. The *second step* was the preparation of a plan for the Goodyear factory. At the initial meeting the Factory Manager amplified the earlier announcement. He analyzed the present industrial situation, pointed out its weaknesses, especially on the side of industrial relations, called attention to the great factors of modern industry and dwelt on the duties and responsibilities of each. He indicated again the extent to which the company was willing and able to curtail its powers in favor of the representatives of the employees. This address to the Council shows that the Factory Manager had thoroughly considered the proposition before launching it and knew definitely what position the company would take on the many questions that were bound to arise.

At its second meeting the Council studied and discussed the plan of employees' representation of the Youngstown Sheet & Tube Company; at the next meeting it was the plan of the Printz-Biederman Company, and so it continued. A recent publication of the Goodyear Company summarized the work of the Council as follows:

"This organization, purely temporary, studied all forms of employees' representation, shop committees, House and Senate plans and the like as they found them in America. They obtained statements from workmen and managers in various plants where these plans were operated. They studied the good features and the bad features and dissected and criticized all the plans very thoroughly and finally set themselves to the task of creating a Goodyear plan.

"Publicity was given out on all actions of this council and each of their meetings was reported in the shop paper, so that all workers in the factory could know what was going on."

In this manner the Goodyear plan was formulated. The *third* "step in order" was to get the plan approved by the board of directors and by the "industrians"— employees having the right to vote. The Council showed its good judgment by giving considerable publicity in the factory to the proposed plan. Every employee got a copy of the plan. It was discussed in the shop, explained. Discussion and explanation were the major topics of the factory paper. The board of directors of the company acted first and approved the plan. Ten days later came the referendum among the industrians. Only eight per cent of those voting voted in the negative. The Council then appointed an Election Committee to supervise the nominations and elections of employee representatives, then signed the Constitution and adjourned sine die.

The Goodyear people have appreciated the necessity of extreme care in the manner of conducting elections. The elections to the Industrial Assembly followed promptly. The Australian ballot system was used this time for both the nomination and election of representatives. The factory was divided into forty precincts and ten senatorial districts. Four precincts were grouped to make a senatorial district. One representative was to be elected from each precinct, and two senators from each senatorial district. Each voter in the nomination election was entitled to vote for two persons for representative and two persons for senator. Not more than three candidates for each office were placed on the ballots. At the regular election the industrian had his choice among three candidates for representative, and his choice of two candidates out of six for the Senate. These elections are conducted with the same care and precautions that characterize our political elections. The elected representatives and senators then organized the two houses of the Goodyear Industrial Assembly. This completed the fourth and last *"step"* in instituting employee representation in this factory.

Another large firm proceeded in the following manner to set up its Industrial Representation plan:

A. A committee representing equally the workers and the management was sent out to visit a number of representative plans in operation. The committee noted the successes and shortcomings of these plans, the character of the industry in each case and the racial composition and the spirit of the workers. The committee made its report to the Industrial Representative and was then dismissed.

B. A second committee was then selected, with equal representation for management and workers, for the purpose of formulating a plan for their shop. This committee studied first the observations, descriptions, and recommendations embodied in the report of the first committee, then studied the conditions in the factory, and prepared a plan which they thought squared with experience elsewhere and was, at the same time, adapted to their own situation.

C. The plan was then submitted to a vote of the workers and was accepted. A majority vote was required for approval.

D. In accordance with the plan, the workers in each voting division chose their own committee to conduct the elections for representatives.

The Labor Agreements between the Metal Trades Department of the American Federation of Labor on the one side and the Bethlehem Shipbuilding Corporation and the American Shipbuilding Company on the other side are examples of the articulation of employee representation with trade unionism. Take for example the Bethlehem plan. By decree of the War Labor Board a shop committee system had been established, which excluded union recognition. The representatives were elected on a numerical basis. Crafts were ignored. When the war ended the company was faced with the question of union recognition. The award would soon expire and to attempt to continue without an agreement meant a conflict with the trade unions. The company decided to deal with the unions collectively.

With but slight modifications the same method was used in revising the War Labor Board's committee system in the plants of the American Shipbuilding Company.

To consummate such an agreement the unions that compose the Metal Trades Department authorized the officials of the Department "to enter into an agreement with the Company providing for the relations of employees affiliated with said unions and employed by the Company." [1]　The agreement between the company and the department provided, that:

1. The unions affiliated with the department select a committee of five members, to be called "The Internationals' Committee"; the company appoint a committee of five, to be called the "Company's Committee."

2. "The employees will select local or plant committees that will function in the same manner as provided for in the Shipbuilding Labor Adjustment Board Awards, subject to such changes or modifications as may from time to time be agreed upon by the Internationals' Committee and the Company's Committee."

3. The adjustment of all questions affecting wages, hours, working conditions, or grievances shall be first attempted by the local or plant committees.

4. The Internationals' Committee and the Company's Committee sitting as a joint committee shall consider all questions that failed of adjustment in the lower committees.

Six weeks later this general joint committee of company and union adopted the rules and procedure for carrying out the agreement. The big problem was the revision of the old shop committee system to harmonize with the structure of the unions. It was agreed that craft committees should be substituted for the existing series of joint committees. Each craft committee was to be composed of three members, while the Internationals' Committee was to determine how many of such craft committees were to be formed. Each craft committee elected a chairman. The chairman of the craft committees compose the new Plant Committee. All questions that concern but one craft are dealt with by that craft's committee. There are no joint committees, under the new plan, in the shop. The

[1] Agreement with American Shipbuilding Company.

committee takes its grievances first to the foreman, and failing there they meet the management's representative. If there is still a failure to adjust the difficulty, the President of the international craft union sends in a delegate to aid the craft committee in further negotiations with the company. If there is still no agreement, the case goes to a joint session of the Internationals' Committee and Company's Committee. Questions that concern more than one craft come before the Plant Committee. The procedure and line of appeals are the same as those already outlined for the craft committee.

A unique method of introducing employee representation is that used by the employees of the Dennison Manufacturing Company (Chapter VI). In this case the employees took the initiative, formulated their plan, and submitted it for the approval of the company. We have asked the employees who had this matter in charge to outline their method of procedure. They have submitted the following statement:

"In order to understand the evolution of the Dennison Manufacturing Company Works Committee, it is first necessary to have a slight knowledge of the construction of the plant. The factory is divided into several divisions each under the supervision of a Division Superintendent. These divisions are divided into departments, each department taking care of its own kind of work. Each department has its own foreman.

"The employees of the Framingham plant number about 2600 and consist of about an equal number of men and women. Twenty per cent of the employees are members of trade organizations; fifty per cent of the employees have been with the company five years or over.

"Early in the month of July, 1919, a flyer was distributed

by the Management to the employees announcing the calling
of a mass meeting of the employees to discuss the question
of Works Committee. This flyer contained a statement of
some of the possibilities of a Works Committee in order to
help the discussion and particularly impressed on all that
the discussion at the mass meeting was expected to be absolutely free from all angles.

"This announcement created great agitation in the plant.
It was the great topic of discussion and a various number
of impressions were formed, some of indifference, some
of skepticism, and a great deal of expectation. The prevailing idea among the employees at that time was that
a Works Committee was a plan to prevent affiliation with
trade unions. It was not until after the employee representatives had drawn up the plan in which it was made very
plain that it had absolutely no interference with trade unions
that many of the workers commenced to be interested.

"The War Industries Committee acted as a Ways and
Means Committee until the Works Committee was finally
launched.

"On July 2nd, the mass meeting took place in the yard
between the buildings and about eighty per cent of the employees were present. The meeting opened with a short
address by the president of the company, stating the object of the meeting and inviting an absolutely free discussion of the question. After the newness of the situation
wore away, there was quite a general discourse. The meeting was finally adjourned after it was voted by a majority
to have a committee elected by the employees according to
departments to look into the subject of Works Committee,
and to bring in recommendations for the formation of a
Works Committee in the Dennison Manufacturing Company. The conduct of this election was put in the hands of
the War Industries Committee—a committee of employees
previously created to assist in putting the plant on a war
basis.

"After an allotment of representatives according to departments was made by a committee appointed by the man-

agement, on July 14th an election by secret ballot was held and the person receiving the largest number of votes in each department was designated as the representative of their particular department.

"On July 18th this committee, which numbered fifty-four men and women, met in a place provided by the management. This gathering of representatives was started on its task by an address of confidence by Mr. Henry Dennison, President of the company. He spoke briefly on the object of a Works Committee and offered them any assistance they might desire financially or any other assistance possible in the solving of problems which they had before them. He then started the organization by the election of a Chairman and from then on the committee was left to shape its own destiny.

"After organization, a general discussion ensued in regard to the different phases of Works Committees. Realizing that the committee as a whole had a very hazy idea of the question, it was voted to adjourn to a future date, so that the gathering would have a better opportunity to study the subject before voicing a further opinion in the matter. Each went away with literature on the subject provided by the management.

"The second meeting took place July 29th. The members had gained some knowledge and were ready for a more intelligent discussion. An endeavor was made at this meeting to start the plan on the way and several articles were agreed on after debating each article pro and con. Fearing to consume too much time at a sitting the meeting was adjourned after a session of about two and one-half hours.

"August 5th found us together again and the work was taken up again in the same way. Before the meeting was over, it was decided that the first big proposition was the districting of the plant and the allotment of representation. A sub-committee was appointed to take care of this job.

"At the next and fourth meeting, August 12th, this sub-committee reported and brought in the following plan which was accepted. The plant was divided into twelve districts, including the Worcester plant employing about 200 people. These divisions consisted as near as possible of 200 employees, each division containing the allied branches of work. The allotment of representatives was made according to occupations, trades, and departments. The work of this small sub-committee brought pressure to bear on the fallacy of such a large committee as the entire recommendation committee trying to formulate a definite scheme of operation, and a sub-committee of seven was appointed to delve more deeply into the subject and bring in some well-thought-out scheme of operation, based on the discussion of the large committee.

"Immediately the sub-committee set to work and at the next and fifth meeting brought in a partial report which was then thrashed out and amended to better advantage by the committee as a whole.

"Fourteen days after the sub-committee was appointed it had the constitution and by-laws ready for final consideration of the whole committee. The plan, with a few alterations, was then passed at the sixth meeting, August 29th, and the sub-committee was instructed to engross the plan for presentation to the employees in general and to the management. The engrossed plan was accepted by the Recommendation Committee at its seventh and last meeting, September 4th.

"The plan was then presented to the management for their approval and was accepted by them with no alterations. Booklets of the plan and recommendations of the committee were then printed and distributed to the employees and a mass meeting called September 18th, at which the plan was accepted by the employees in general, with but very few minor amendments.

"As soon as permissible after the mass meeting, the Central Committee, as called for in the plan, was elected and our Works Committee held its first meeting September 23rd and organized as a full fledged Works Committee, ready to cope with any proposition brought before it by either the employees or the management."

The management must not forget the foremen after the plan is introduced. There must be opportunity for them to meet and to find out and discuss what is going on. The contact of the management with the foremen should be as regular and' as frequent as with the workers. In the Leitch system the mistake was made of making the foremen and other executives a link in the governmental system between company and workers. Foremen and workers get enough contact with each other in the shop. There does not seem to be any real need for further provision in the industrial representation plan. But, on the other hand, the management needs to take the foremen into its counsels and confidence. A paper manufacturer meets with his foremen every week to counsel and coöperate for the success of their plan. The foremen are a part of the management and their participation in the shop councils should be limited to the managerial side. They may well be an organized element within the management.

The mistake should not be made of regarding the constitution and the machinery set up to carry out its provisions as something sacred and an end in itself. If there is anything to be venerated it is the successful attainment of the purposes in view. Experience will dictate changes, and these should be made promptly. Especially in the beginning should both sides keep alert as to modifications that will improve the plan.

Governments are a growth—usually a growth out of lively participation in affairs by the classes involved. It is quite generally conceded today that the best governments, the most practical and satisfactory, are those which are the products of such participations. The stress of experience is a wonderful adapter. Industrial governments, therefore, should be as practical as possible at all times.

Someone has asked these questions: (1) To what extent and how quickly should the employees be given control over the business? and (2) What safeguards should an employer set up? and (3) What pitfalls should he avoid in order to prevent his industrial experimentation from wrecking his business?

No categorical answer can be given to questions of this kind. The answer depends upon the character and ability of the employer on the one side and of the employees on the other side. If the employer has a strong personality and is a natural and capable leader of men, the more control he entrusts to the employees, the more coöperation he will be able to get from them. An able employer ought to have nothing to fear from going it fifty-fifty with his employees. But, of course, this is assuming capable employees. If the employees are uneducated, wholly inexperienced in business affairs, a shifting and irresponsible element, or alien to the language, institutions, and customs of our country, then the employer, no matter how capable he may be, has a problem of Americanization, of education, and of reformation on his hands before he can expect any reliable coöperation from his workers. To such a class of employees responsibility should come very limited in scope at first, and no extension of power should be granted before they demonstrate their trustworthiness and capability.

If the first question assumes a shop organization already in operation, then the answer to the second and third will depend in part upon the amount of control that was initially given to the employees. Many an employer has withheld power from the employee representatives not so much because of doubt of their ability as because of mistrust. Such an attitude on the part of the employer, persisted in, has strangled a number of these efforts at shop government. In other cases the employer was quick to see that his misapprehension was not well founded, and the limitations were promptly removed. If a shop committee or council is not to be permitted ·to exercise the responsibilities of which it is ·capable, it had better never have been called into existence. Capable employees will not serve on committees or councils when they are restricted and suspected and when opportunity is denied them to deal with problems that challenge their abilities. It is not long until a committee or council thus restricted becomes inactive and an object of contempt.

Granting the capability of the employees, they should be permitted to deal with all the problems that affect them. There is no necessity for passing on to them problems that do not necessarily concern them. The field of industrial relations within the shop is the legitimate field for employee participation. Every employer ought to know what are the fixed obligations of his company. If his company is a corporation, there are certain powers and responsibilities specifically vested in the board of directors. No employer can lawfully consent to compromise or circumvent these legally fixed duties. There are, furthermore, certain conditions of business survival, of which the employer is better aware than his employees. These conditions are the prerequisites of industrial progress as well as of business survival, and it is therefore in the public interest that such conditions be adequately safeguarded. No employer can honorably connive at or permit the dissipation of the industry.

There are great differences in industries. Some are simple of operation, others are highly technical. The character of the industry is another factor determining the extent and rapidity with which employees can be initiated into control.

The rapidity with which employees are to be given control depends, then, upon three obvious factors:

1. The capability of the employees.
2. The intricacies of the business on both its technical and financial sides.
3. The legally fixed obligations and responsibilities of the company.

The particular safeguards that the employer should concern himself about center around the fixed obligations of the company and the conditions necessary for the survival and progress of the industry. The capability and character of the employees, the character of the industry, and the ability of the employer, are all elements in the problem. It is impossible to write a recipe for such a compound. We put this question about "safeguards" to the Proctor & Gamble Company. Their reply runs: "There is certainly no royal road to the so-called Industrial Democracy." This is about the most that can be said at the present time.

Joint industrial governments cannot succeed unless there is mutual confidence between management and workers. If it is the employer who is taking the initiative, he should keep constantly in mind that this kind of a move implies faith in the proletariate. If he undertakes the adventure with but a limited faith in his employees, he will soon discover that they resent a fifty per cent faith. "Aye, there's the rub." It would be better for the employer if he could proceed slowly, feeling the way. Yet he can hardly afford to be slow about it in this period of intensified unrest. Nor is it good policy to be in a hurry, for the employer who steps out like a King with a Royal Proclamation to announce his conversion to democracy in industry arouses at once suspicion and scepticism among the workers. This is the second rub.

Extremists in both the capital and labor groups are agreed upon uncompromising hostility to joint industrial government. Bourbon and Bolshevik stand at the opposing poles of human thought and activity. They both agree that they have nothing in common. The industrial struggle between them takes on the character of an unending dog fight, but in spite of this they hold in common a deep contempt for the men and women who stand somewhere in between the extremes trying to reform, construct or reconstruct human institutions and relationships in order that civilization may continue as a going concern. Joint industrial government is an impossibility with such extremists as Elbert H. Gary and William D. Haywood. In our harassing the "Bolsheviks" we have overlooked the very significant fact that the Bourbon is as great a revolutionary menace as the reddest of the reds.

It is important that the employer see this situation when he begins contemplating a move in the direction of industrial democracy. If this employer has allowed the newspapers and professional "leg pullers" to get him excited about "reds" and "Bolsheviks," if he has lost his restraint and indulged in violent denunciations, in hurling epithets such as Bolshevik, traitor, free lover, etc., if he has gone as far as some of them and has outspokenly advocated the firing-squad treatment for dissenters and domestic troubles, *his first step* toward industrial democracy is to take a vacation, to cool off and cut out puerile nonsense. He needs to be born again into the good old American spirit of toleration. An employer has everything to lose and nothing to gain by undignified "slopping over." Let the employer quietly dismiss all his spies and spotters (if he has them) months before he begins to talk about a "new day" in the shop. By thus removing the causes of irritation and mistrust he will pave the way for confidence and coöperation when the effort is put forth to establish a joint shop government.

XXIII

JOINT CONTROL

JENNIE McMULLIN TURNER

In October, 1919, we sent out a questionnaire to the firms we had visited, asking for their experience in the matter of per capita production since 1914. The following replies were received:

Reply No. 1 (Men on straight day rate.)

"We have 20,000 more employees than in 1914, and we are producing only a few hundred units (cars) more per day now than we did then. This is not to be attributed to lack of efficiency on the part of employees, but is due to the fact that we are running a great many more operations now than in 1914 and producing some things which we did not then produce, but which were made by other companies.

"The work done in our branches today is practically the same as that done in 1914, and the efficiency in our branches at the present time is higher than ever before. We are aware of the fact, here at the Home Office, that there is a certain tendency on the part of employees to slow down a bit, but on the whole we do not believe it has been to as great a degree as has been experienced in other concerns."

Reply No. 2. (Men on straight day rate.)

"The character of our product has changed so much since 1914 that there is no way that a comparison can be made such as you mention. Not only this, but the shoes that we are making now are very much different from what we made a year ago and the shoes we made a year ago were very much different from those we made the year before. Our product has been undergoing a gradual change since we started business, making a higher grade shoe all the time.

"While it is true that we are not running as many hours as we did in 1914 and it is also true that we do not get the quantity of work from the operator that we did then, I believe that the average efficiency of the operator has increased very much. In other words, I believe that he is working more conscientiously than he did in 1914.

"There are two places in the factory where the character of the work has not changed a great deal. That is in the upper cutting room and the sole cutting room. In both of these places we are getting more work per hour than we ever did before. There is only one reason for these things and that is that we have today to a much larger extent the good will of our workmen and I know that every executive in our factory will agree that we have less soldiering in the job today than we ever had before in the experience of our business."

Reply No. 3. (Employees on piece rate.)

"In 1914 the average hourly production of tags per employee was 100. In 1918 it had dropped to 90. In 1919 it was up again at 112. The great increase in 1919 over 1914 is due chiefly to improved methods of supervision."

Reply No. 4. (Employees on straight day rate.)

"I am finding a very general feeling among manufacturers to the effect that employees everywhere are letting up in their work as compared with 1914. We are receiving very hearty support from our employees' representatives in combatting such a tendency that may develop among our working force."

Reply No. 5.

"Pieceworkers and workers in rubber factory have increased about 50% since 1914. Common labor and members of building trades have fallen off about 50%; bricklayers and carpenters 50%."

Reply No. 6. (Employees on straight day wage.)

"The average per capita output of our employees has increased 111% since 1914."

The National Association of Credit Men have made an investigation of the present efficiency of labor. Their report says:

"Replies were received from 169 manufacturers located in all sections of the country, and an analysis of the answers led the author, Dr. Whyte, to conclude first, that there is a good deal of exaggeration in the oft-repeated statement that labor in this country is only 50 or 60 per cent as efficient as it was before the war, and second, that the year 1920 is so far showing an increase in efficiency.

"In reply to the question, 'Is your labor more efficient now (March, 1920) than it was three months ago (December, 1919), 57, or 34 per cent of the 167 firms replying reported an increase in efficiency; 72, or 43 per cent, reported no improvement; and 10, or 6 per cent, reported a decrease in efficiency, while 18 companies thought that, although there was no improvement shown, labor was as efficient as in pre-war times, and 10 stated that old labor showed as much efficiency as in the pre-war times but that new labor was inefficient. Since more than one-third of these firms believed that conditions in this respect had improved, as against 6 per cent who reported a reduction in efficiency, altogether an increase of production for the three month period was shown.

"On the other hand, the replies to the question comparing the present with the so-called normal period (1913-14) show that production is not yet up to the pre-war standard.

Seventy per cent of the 169 companies answering this question stated that they did not believe that labor is as efficient now as it was in 1913-14. Thirteen of these attempted to make a percentage comparison which when averaged showed a relative efficiency at present of 73 per cent, and while the number reporting was too small to form a general estimate it was considered that it refutes in a measure the charge that the relative degree of efficiency reaches as low a point as 50 or 60 per cent. Twenty-seven, or 16 per cent, believed that labor is as efficient now as formerly, but only three per cent considered that efficiency has reached a standard beyond that of normal times.

"The reasons assigned for lowered production show that a large number of employers attribute it to labor shortage. The causes next in order of importance are given as industrial unrest, high rate of labor turnover, high wages, reaction from the war, and high cost of living, while in a few instances the blame was laid upon organized labor, the high wages paid by the Federal government during the war."[1]

Some of the employers we visited kept careful statistics of per capita output. Their testimony is therefore more reliable than the sweeping statements we sometimes see in the newspapers. We can probably place little reliance upon general statements concerning output by either employers or employees, unless the statements are accompanied by figures. At a recent conference of representative employers and employees in the state of Wisconsin, at which four employers were present, the latter were asked if they could furnish figures showing their average per capita production. Each one of the four asserted that he was keeping no such figures and that he knew of no employer in the state who could furnish such information.

[1] "Efficiency of Labor Increasing." U. S. Bureau of Labor Statistics, *Monthly Labor Review*. June, 1920, p. 219.

If these employers were correct in their belief that no such statistics are available, and if this Wisconsin experience is indicative of conditions in other states, then much of the criticism of labor must be admitted to be based upon general impressions.

But whether per capita production is increasing or decreasing at any particular time, the productive power of labor could probably be greatly increased by the recognition of a few significant principles in industry. These principles are to be found, not in the spoken and written literature of economists and experts, but in opinions of the workingman himself when he feels free to speak his mind. The best place to find them is, therefore, the labor press.

The labor press is necessarily the organized labor press. Unorganized labor has not and can not have any effective means of expressing its opinions on industry. Unfortunately many employers shut themselves off from this reliable source of information, the labor press, in the mistaken belief that when a man joins a union he changes his views and no longer speaks for the unorganized mass.

A careful study and analysis of this kind of literature and of labor phenomena for the last five years, leads us to the conclusion that labor conditions its whole-hearted contribution to production on four main items: (1) the form of management of industry, (2) the fairness of the distribution of the proceeds from the sale of the product, (3) the possession by labor of a fair share of power over both production and distribution, and (4) the right kind of education.

The philosophy of labor on the question of production is summed up in the Reconstruction Report of the Wisconsin State Federation of Labor:

"The worker must share the responsibility in the administration of government. He is under an equal obligation to share in the burdens of administration of industry. We referred earlier to increased production as one of the elements involved in the raising of wages. We believe that greater production ought to be the basis of increased happiness. Many of us would like to have more to eat and wear; most of us would like to have better homes, better surroundings, more opportunities for recreation, travel and study. Can we produce enough so that the things now enjoyed by only a few will in the future be sufficient for all? Can we do it without injury to the worker?

"We cannot do it without a reorganization of industry, which, though gradual, must be thorough. We cannot do it as long as men, women and children are permitted to undermine their strength through long hours of toil; so long as they are permitted to be idle, when they have produced for the profit of an individual so much of an article that their services are no longer needed. We cannot do it so long as children are permitted to leave school and go to work before they have found the work or have been trained for the work for which they are best fitted. We cannot do it so long as workers are in fear of the introduction of improved machinery and resist it because they realize that instead of giving them a better living it will take away from them the meager living they already have.

"The standard of living can be raised to the highest possible level only when the workers so control industry that increase in production brings better living for all, instead of increased luxury for a few and unemployment and poverty for many." [1]

The American Federation of Labor at its annual

[1] "Next Steps for Wisconsin. A Program of Construction," Milwaukee, 1918.

convention in 1920 held at Montreal adopted a program which expressed the same ideas:

"Industry to-day requires these remedial measures:

"It requires greater democracy in order to give to the workers full voice in assisting in its direction.

"It requires more intelligent management and acceptance of the principle that production is for use and not for profit alone.

"It requires full and free acceptance and use of the best that invention has to offer.

"It requires bold and audacious reconstruction of method and process in the conduct of basic industries.

"Labor does not oppose introduction of improved methods in industry. It courts and encourages improvements in processes and in machinery. What it will always resist is the introduction of these processes and this machinery at the expense of the workers.

"There is a knowledge of industry among the workers in industry of which society has not begun to avail itself. The effort has been to suppress use of that knowledge and to demean those who possess it. The workers know their work as none but the workers can know it. The shoemaker knows his last and the engineer understands the capacity of his engine.

"The workers are appalled at the waste and ignorance of management, but they are too frequently denied the chance to offer their knowledge for use.

"They decline to be enslaved by the use of their own knowledge and they cannot give of it freely or effectively except as equals in industry, with all of the rights and privileges and with all of the stature and standing of employers.

"Adoption of the principle of voluntary effort, of full coöperation in industry, will bring to the industrial life of the Nation such an impetus that production will cease forever to be a problem in American life.

"Adoption of the principles we here urge will inevitably result in a rapid decrease of the number of nonproducers who at present live by fastening themselves in one useless capacity or another upon the industrial life of the country. Proper absorption of non-producers into useful channels would be but a simple problem.

"The welfare of the workers must be a paramount consideration. There can be no progress and no gain in production volume if there is not such consideration. But a greater mutuality in industry would insure proper safeguarding of the rights of workers.

"Only by such methods and under such principles can there be an advance in production which does not penalize the worker for his own industriousness and for his own alertness and inventiveness.

"Autocratic industry kills incentive. It punishes brilliancy of attainment. It warps the mind and drains the energy from the body. We have repeatedly condemned the principle of autocratic control of industry, and we now declare that short of its complete removal from our industrial life there is no industrial salvation and no hope of abundance in our time.

"We urge the setting up of conference boards of organized workers and employers, thoroughly voluntary in character and in thorough accord with our trade-union organizations, as means of promoting the democracy of industry through development of coöperative effort. We point out to employers the fact that industry, which is the life blood of our civilization, cannot be made the plaything and the pawn of a few who by chance today hold control. Industry is the thing by which all must live, and it must be given the opportunity to function at its best.

"Labor turnover is but one of the evils which will disappear in proportion as the workers are given voice in management. This is proven by statistics which show the lowest turnover in those industries where the workers exercise the most effective voice by reason of the highest degree of organization.

"We propose the salvation of industry. We propose the means whereby the world may be fed and clothed and housed and given happiness. We have service to give, and

if permitted to give freely and on terms of manhood and
equality we will give in abundance. We cannot be driven
as slaves, but we can give mighty service in a common effort
of humankind."[1]

MANAGEMENT

The idea that labor should share the burdens of
administration is comparatively new. The old attitude
of labor was one of indifference to the effect of their
demands upon industry. "We want wages," they used
to say. "Where are they to come from?—That's the
employer's business. Let him worry."

Their attitude coincided with the employer's own
feeling in the matter.

"My business is my own, and I can manage it
without any interference from my employees or from
the public," is a sentiment that has a familiar sound.
But when he *has* managed it to suit himself for a long
time, shutting his ears to the complaints and the suggestions of employees, fighting every attempt by the
State to mitigate the bad conditions prevailing in his
plant, the employer has sometimes come at last to the
point where his employees refuse to go on with production. Sometimes then he forgets that this is *his*
business, run to suit himself. He appeals to the public,
whose advice he formerly despised, to protect him by
injunctions, by police and by moral pressure against
his erring employees. He appeals to his employees to
come back and save the business. He is eager to show
them what before he considered to be none of their
business, the financial conditions which make it impos-

[1] U. S. Bureau of Labor Statistics, *Monthly Labor Review*,
August, 1920, pp. 168-169.

sible for him to meet their demands. He would gladly call in the leaders among his employees to see if their superior intelligence would be able to grasp his point of view. Then he finds there are no leaders among them who have any great influence with the others, no tried and trusted men disciplined by years of collective bargaining and compromise. He himself has seen to it that none such have ever developed.

It is in such a crisis as this that the possible contribution of the employees to management sometimes appears. It was out of such a crisis as this at the firm of Hart, Schaffner & Marx that there has developed in the clothing industry a machinery which makes possible such a contribution.

Before we discuss this machinery and its contribution to management, we need to study the industrial conditions which are making necessary the adoption of a new science of management.

As industry grows in size, we are passing out of the stage when management was identical with capital, into the stage when management is more nearly identical with labor—when management is simply a body of employees hired by the owners of capital to discipline and supervise the work of the other employees. The fact that the members of the managerial force are frequently stockholders in the corporation, sometimes with considerable holdings, does not alter the general employee-character of the managerial force, which depends for its livelihood, not primarily upon the profits of the industry, but primarily upon fixed wages.

The employee-manager in modern industry is not in a particularly enviable position. Forced by absentee owners of capital to find dividends for them, tormented

by his fellow wage-earners for wage increases, harried
by competitors, dictated by bankers, he finds himself
in the position of a statesman who knows himself what
is good for his country, but who has no solid public
opinion back of him to enable him to stand out against
its enemies.

Who are the enemies of industry? That depends
upon what we consider the purpose of industry.

Many people have the idea that the purpose of industry is production of goods. Capital is inclined to
encourage this idea when by doing so it can demonstrate the iniquity of the strike. If the purpose of
industry is production of goods, then the strike is directed against the public which uses the goods. The
stockholder has been wont to represent himself as the
defender of the public against the delinquencies of
labor. He has been wont to shout "Production! More
production!" as if that were his main object in living
and in investing his money.

But now the courts come along and strip the glamour
of public benefactor from the stockholder. In the
case of Dodge vs. Ford Motor Co. (170 N. W. 668,
1919.), the Supreme Court of Michigan tells Henry
Ford that benevolence is not for him as a manager.
Profits for the shareholders, not production for the
public is the object of a business corporation. "There
should be no confusion (of which there is evidence) of
the duties which Mr. Ford conceives that he and the
stockholders owe to the general public and the duties
which in law he and his co-directors owe to protesting,
minority stockholders. *A business corporation is organized and carried on primarily for the profit of the*

stockholders.[1] The powers of the directors are to be employed for that end. The discretion of directors is to be exercised in the choice of means to attain that end, and does not extend to a change in the end itself, to the reduction of profits, or to the non-distribution of profits among stockholders in order to devote them to other purposes. It is not within the lawful powers of a board of directors to shape and conduct the affairs of a corporation for the merely incidental benefit of shareholders and for the primary purpose of benefiting others, and no one will contend, that if the avowed purpose of the defendant directors was to sacrifice the interest of shareholders, it would not be the duty of the courts to interfere."

According to this decision, industry exists primarily for the benefit of one factor of production, and only incidentally for the benefit of the other factors and of the public. Wages of labor and prices of products are to be determined solely in consideration of their effect upon profits.

Management being now responsible only to capital must determine its conduct of the industrial enterprise primarily by its effect upon profits. If high wages and low prices are conducive to high profits management must lend its efforts toward high wages and low prices. If low wages and high prices bring high profits, it must work toward low wages and high prices. If greater output means greater profits management must try to secure greater output. If restriction of products brings greater profits, products must be restricted. Management must produce profits rather than goods.

According to this philosophy, we are today totally

[1] Italics are the author's.

dependent for the satisfaction of our needs upon organizations the main object of which is profit, not production. According to this, under the present joint stock system of private industry, the public cannot benefit from low costs unless the benefit would result in high profits.

There is steadily growing everywhere a conviction that this philosophy is wrong, that production is the vital thing to all; that industry exists primarily for something more than the benefit of one class or group. There is steadily growing this notion of the public purpose of industry and of all the factors in industry, and of the equal interest of all of these factors and of the public in efficient production.

In the majority of cases, machinery for the control and direction of industry is based on the theory of the Dodge decision, that capital alone selects the management, and to capital alone management is responsible. The interest of the other factors is ignored. Management must answer the demands of labor in accordance with the interest of profits. Labor may make itself a nuisance when its demands are not met, but management is not responsible to labor.

But as industries have grown in size to the dimensions of small cities, management is coming to feel that in the interest of profits, there is one duty which it can no longer perform efficiently and which it is willing consequently to delegate to the workers. This is the function of discipline.

Even the employer who is the most hearty exponent of the theory of the independence of management of both labor and capital, and who is extremely jealous of the prerogatives of management, admits that he uses the shop committee "openly and purposely, as told to them, for the purpose of making them more responsible for those things known as shop discipline, shop service, etc., which they can accept and must accept for the common good, and when they do accept it, they are making themselves 100 per cent responsible for its enforcement."[1]

This disciplinary power also rests with the employees at Filene's (Chapter V), though here it is joined with policy making power. In many union or preferential union shops disciplinary regulations are likewise established by joint agreement or consent.

One device which has been adopted to protect management against labor and against the tendency of labor to organize against the power of capital is "scientific management." By employing experts to study the business and by insisting upon the infallibility and scientific nature of all their conclusions and arrangements, they have attempted to make labor accept as infallible the order of things which is found to be conducive to profits. They have taken refuge in the happy theory that their experts are searching for truth, and that when the truths are found, it is the duty of all to conform.

But labor is not a good conformist. It refuses to accept as inspired the word of the expert chosen by management. To labor, management itself is simply another group of employees, a subservient and sometimes rather contemptible group, obedient to the will of the absentee stockholders upon whom they depend for

[1] Richard A. Feiss, Address before the Economic Club, Boston. *The Consensus*, July, 1919.

the tenure of their position, and acting as a buffer to protect capital against the demands of labor.

The study of labor expressions discloses a difference of opinion among workers as to the methods by which democracy in management is to be obtained. To one group, the only hope appears to be public ownership and management by the state. To others, the solution is management and ownership by all the employees. To others it is ownership by the state and management by the state and all employees jointly. The Plumb Plan for railroad administration is an expression of this idea. But we are interested here chiefly in the ideas of those who believe it possible to bring about the four conditions under which labor will work unreservedly under private control and ownership of industry. Some of these talk of membership of employees on the boards of directors; of the selection of the foreman by those who work under him, and the necessity for publicity concerning the methods of management.

There is more experimentation along these various lines than is ordinarily suspected. Filenes' have for years had representation of employees on their board of directors. As a matter of policy, the wishes of the employees are often consulted when a department head has proved unsatisfactory and a new one is found to be desirable. In one place we visited, the employees by threatening strike had saved a popular general manager from official decapitation by the absentee directors. In a certain closed union shop, while there is usually no formal election of the foreman, the latter must nevertheless be acceptable to the men. The King of England chooses the prime minister, but his choice is limited to one man, the leader of the party which is in the majority in the House of Commons. So the company chooses the foreman in the closed union shop, but the foreman must be one who has the good will of the men. No management can be truly "scientific" which expects men to give their best in production under the direction of a man whom they dislike.

The expressions of organized labor on these various devices for introducing some degree of democracy into the management of private industry show that labor is alive to the danger of accepting any of these responsibilities in its present state of organization. The Wisconsin State Federation of Labor went on record against the bill introduced in the Legislature of 1919 to require an employee member on every board of directors. They insisted that one lone member on such a board would be either a dupe or a cat's paw of the company unless he had an invincible organization behind him to help direct his policy and to hold him responsible for his acts. Under any circumstances, one labor representative would be at a disadvantage in that he would have no acceptable witness to prove his integrity and faithfulness to the cause of his constituents. They felt that there should be at least two employee representatives on every board. There was also the feeling that too much inside knowledge might discourage employees from trying to improve their conditions at the expense of a tottering business, and that the persistence of inefficiency in management might thus be prolonged by labor's fear of upsetting the industry. There were many individual members of organized labor, however, who believed that they should seize any opportunity to get the inside facts

of the business and that while the privilege would be
of no value to unorganized labor, it would not harm
and might really be useful to organized labor.

But while workers may hesitate to allow themselves
to be saddled formally with responsibility for the ac-
crued mistakes of the management of privately owned
industry, and while they may entertain considerable
differences of opinion concerning such devices as representation on the board of directors and election of
foremen, organized labor, wherever it is allowed to
function, is steadily contributing to the science of
management.

Suppose that in every industrial or commercial
plant, a great mirror could be hung which would so
reflect the events of the day as to magnify all the
strong and the weak points in administration. That
mirror would be invaluable to the management in check-
ing up its own defects.

Such a mirror has been provided in every industry
which has set up a machinery for continuous collective bargaining and for the continuous consideration
of grievances and disputes. Among the most important pieces of machinery of this kind are the Trade
and Arbitration Boards of the Men's Clothing industry
(Chapters XVI and XVII) and the Board of Arbitration at Filenes' (Chapter V). These boards, dealing
as they do day after day with all the dissensions and
dissatisfactions in factory and store, can scarcely fail
to find out the weaknesses in the plant, and the source
of trouble, the mistakes and frailties of management
and employees. These are all disclosed in the questions
which come up over making and keeping the wage

agreement, over the impoliteness of employees, over dishonesty and over standards of efficiency.

The criticism has sometimes been offered of the system at Hart, Schaffner & Marx that it offers to the employee who has a tendency to grumble, a constant temptation to relieve himself of petty complaints which might better be left unexpressed, and which tend to become exaggerated in the telling. There are two answers to this. The first is, that these petty complaints often are the key to the real inefficiencies of the plant. Similar and frequent complaints from a certain department or by a certain individual frequently lead to the location of a trouble center, and the recommendation perhaps of the removal or transfer of the person responsible or the complete reorganization of the department. In the second place, the constant fear of publicity has a good effect on manners. The knowledge that everything he says or does is likely to come up for review before a body which has great power has a strong tendency to make each official of the company attentive to his duties and polite to his subordinates. His self-controlled behavior, in turn, has a good effect upon the employees under his direction, and goes far to secure their good will and similar self-control and politeness. All this is not lost on production.

Management cannot afford to be without such a mirror of its strength and its weakness as a board of this kind affords. But simply setting up a board will not accomplish the purpose. Such a board cannot be made to reflect truly the strength and the weakness of the management unless complete frankness of employees before the board is secured. This is secured in the case of Filenes' by the knowledge of the employees that the company is perfectly willing to listen to criticism and that they themselves are perfectly safe in offering it. It is secured at Hart, Schaffner & Marx by the knowledge that the union is strong enough to protect its members. In the one case, it is the will of the employer, in the other the power of the unions, which makes it possible for the employees to render this great service to management.

It requires courage for management to accept a check like this upon its work. There are still comparatively few employers who have dared or who have been forced to do so. The majority would rather bury their heads in the sand and imagine that everything they do is right than to meet the daily criticism and suggestions of the men whose work they direct. Many firms which have established joint committees of company and employees have not dared to face this criticism, and have saved themselves by restricting the subjects with which the committees can deal. In one place which we visited, not reported in these chapters, the superintendent deliberately ignored the existence of the representative body which had been set up, and went ahead settling every complaint himself. As the ordeal of facing him appeared to the employees to be considerably worse than most of the hardships of which they might complain, it was obvious that he received very little light on the way his employees regard the activities of himself and the other managerial employees.

Our conclusion, then, is that the kind of management which secures the best production from labor is management which is kept closely in touch with labor through machinery which forces both parties through their representatives to sit together, constantly listening to mutual criticism, and to discuss constantly the problems of the industry.

DISTRIBUTION

The second great influence upon labor's part in production is the distribution of the earnings among the factors of production.

Labor literature and labor tactics demonstrate that "labor" is growing less and less inclined to work cheerfully and effectively: first, when it knows that someone else is getting the lion's share of the product; second, when it does not know but merely suspects that someone else is getting the lion's share; and third, when the terms on which the product is divided among the factors of production are determined by one or more of the other factors with labor unconsulted.

"More production means more profits for Coats" was the slogan of a crowd of angry men and women employees outside a hall in the city of Glasgow to picket the meeting of the stockholders of the Coats Thread Combine called to declare a big stock dividend.

The American worker is less demonstrative than his English brother and sister but he feels very much the same.

"Through the whole period that has elapsed since November 11, 1918," says Mr. Gompers, ". . . there has been an abandon and ruthlessness worthy of high seas piracy. Buccaneering tactics have been used in the conduct and management of industry without regard to the needs of society and to the needs of the workers. . . . Out of this repression and out of this ruthless exploitation and profiteering, there has been bred among the working people a deep and stern resentment." [1]

"The meek shoe clerk who tries on your shoes, . . . is bitter about conditions today. When he sees a woman buy seven pairs of shoes at $20 a pair, while he can not afford good milk for his children at home, his thoughts turn to dangerous channels." [2]

The fact that labor is vociferous in its outcry against profiteering does not in itself prove that labor would work harder under a non-profiteering system. There are few firms, moreover, which afford the opportunity to watch the effect upon labor of a limitation of profits. We are able to see it, however, among the managerial workers at the Dennison Plant, and among the shop workers of the Wayne Knitting Mills and the White Motor Company.

There is probably no place in the United States where the employees have shown greater zeal for efficiency and for output than at the Wayne Knitting Mills, where we found the closed union shop of the Full Fashioned Hosiery Workers working steadily on high, straight day wages (Chapter XII). These men pointed with pride to the record of their company having never paid annual dividends in excess of 12 per cent on its stock, all of it unwatered. They pointed also to the emergency fund, built up from what might have been turned over to the stockholders in the form of profits, and to the liberal old age pensions provided

[1] Samuel Gompers. *The American Federationist*, June, 1920, pp. 523-524.
[2] John Francis Neylan, representing *The Public*. "Capital, Labor and the Public. Transactions of the Commonwealth Club of California." September, 1919, p. 349.

out of another fund that might also have gone as profits.[1]

At the White Motor Company, the policy of voluntary limitation of profits is likewise pursued. "Our policy has been in the past, and is now, to limit payment of dividends to 8% on capital stock," says the blue print flier which contains the maxims of the company.

There are other factors than this at work at the White Motor Company but this limitation no doubt has something to do with the 111 per cent increase in per capita production from 1914 to 1919 on a straight hourly wage basis.

We find, then, a growing recognition among managers of labor's resentment against the constant flow of a stream of profits into the hands of absentee stockholders, and a belief that this resentment results in restricted production. We suspect that this feeling is really a reflection of management's own resentment of this state of affairs. According to our observation, labor's resentment is directed at exorbitant profits. It makes no fine distinctions as to who gets them.

"The coal miner gets 25 cents more a ton for digging coal; the consumer pays $3.00 a ton more than he did last spring. When you are ordering your next winter's coal and the dealer tells you the price is $2.00 to $3.00 higher, 'because of the increase in wages to miners,' smile pleasantly and say something about coal miners driving to work in limousines."[2]

When labor has no way of knowing whether the dis-

[1] The strike discussed in Chapter XII has little significance for the point made here concerning efficiency. It resulted from a controversy over profit-sharing and reduction of wages.
[2] *The Worker* (Ft. Wayne, Ind.). April 23, 1920. Quoted from the *Butcher Workman's Advocate*.

tribution of the product is fair or not, its suspicions
fall alike upon the just and the unjust. Distrust of
capital where the facts are not known may result in
a bad spirit among the employees, and in as low production as if the distribution were actually known to
be unjust.

Every protest of capital against making known the
facts simply confirms the suspicions of labor. Such
incidents as the protest of the coal operators against
having the President's Commission entertain as evidence the figures which the miners' organization had
collected relative to the organization, capitalization,
earnings, and profits of the anthracite companies, and
the constant fight to prevent publicity of individual
and corporation income tax returns convince labor that
they are being wronged, and that they have no duty to
produce more until this injustice is righted.

Many employers are beginning to feel that con-
cealment leads to exaggeration, and that the policy
of secrecy is a mistake. They feel that if what employers do is justifiable, they will be able to explain
it to the satisfaction of their employees; and that in
the interest of production, it is their duty to make the
attempt.

"Employers," says the Cleveland Chamber of Commerce, "should recognize the need of informing their
employees on the subject of business principles as
affecting their mutual interests, especially the relation
of wages and expense to costs and prices, and the necessity for an equitable return on invested capital. Frankness is advised on the part of employers in placing
before their employees business details necessary to
prove these economic facts. Employees should be

equally frank in discussing with their employer matters affecting their conditions of employment and the interests of their industry. Such an attitude on the part of both employer and employee will tend to remove the barrier of suspicion and distrust which often is the cause of labor disputes, and establish a spirit of mutual interest and confidence." [1]

"A good many things," says Charles Edison,[2] must be cleared up in workers' minds (just as a good many things must be cleared up in employers' minds) before anything like ideal conditions can be developed in American industry. Workers do not always realize the exact relationship between their product and the employers' profits. Take a man who gets $20 for a certain job and sees his output sold for $100. He is likely to imagine that the employer makes $80 profit on the work. He doesn't realize the extent of overhead charges against his product, the amount of raw material, the thousand and one things which enter into the production and selling end, the many prices which affect costs and profits. Often he has no conception of the fundamentals of competitive business. He doesn't realize that very likely the employer who seems to be making a fine profit is walking the floor nights wondering how he can meet his obligations. . . . Capital, the employer, has fallen into the habit of secrecy, and it may be that this habit has grown out of knowledge that there have been things in by-gone days about the conduct of business which must be kept under cover for safety's sake. . . . It is our belief that business should not make itself mysterious."

[1] "Declaration of the Cleveland Chamber of Commerce" (*The Survey*), March 13, 1920.
[2] *The Saint Paul Pioneer Press*, Sept. 7, 1919, p. 5.

We have seen several places where an attempt was being made to clear up some of the mysteries of business. The White Motor Company, for example, does not stop with simply announcing that its profits are limited to 8 per cent. In the classes described in Chapter I, officials of the company instruct their employees in the costs of production and in the principles of distribution. Their employees are dependent, it is true, upon the integrity of the firm for the truth of what they are told, but they can verify the statements given them by comparison with the annual report of the Board of Directors to the stockholders. At Filenes' (Chapter V), the employees, being represented on the Board of Directors, have access to the books of the company. That they have not, however, always trusted their own ability to interpret correctly what they see is evidenced by their employment at one time of an accountant to go over the books and determine whether they were receiving the profits agreed upon between them and the company.

These firms are both open shops. Among closed union shops, we know as yet of no actual demand on the part of employees to see the books of the company. The railroad employees and the mine workers, however, have gone ahead and calculated costs and profits, without access to the books. The employers of the Photo-Engravers are under agreement with their employees to keep accurate accounts, but the latter have not demanded to see the accounts. That will probably, however, be the next step.

"We have reached a status in our craft," says Matthew Woll, President of the International Photo-Engravers, "where our interests relate not alone to wages and hours. The necessity of our time demands that we have full and complete knowledge of all trade and business relations. We need to know the cost of production—the selling price—the overhead charge— the division of the income jointly produced by our employers and ourselves." [1]

The shop employees of the White Motor Company have a good deal of information as to the distribution of the product, but they have no authority over it. Yet the two bad principles which are absent at the White Motor Company, namely, unjust profits, and secrecy concerning distribution, are less important so far as production is concerned, than the third principle that distribution shall be by agreement between the parties to production, rather than by the simple dictum of one factor, capital, or one small group of labor, management.

Just how much wages labor should receive is not a matter which can be settled by an appeal to reason or to justice in general. Reason and ideas of justice are individual, not general. To one person it appears reasonable that the laborer should receive the "full product of his toil" if anybody can find out what that is. To another it looks as if labor should have a "living wage." The trouble begins when any group comes together to try to determine what a living wage is. To one person, a living wage for a family includes an automobile, to another it includes only the bare essentials of food, clothing and shelter—that is, the smallest sum on which anyone is found to be living at present. A man is likely to have one idea of a liv-

[1] *American Federation of Labor Weekly News Letter*, June 28, 1919.

ing wage for himself and a different idea for other people. A reasonable rate of any kind must be a compromise. But no rate can be considered reasonable or just when one side has all the power, or sufficient power to coerce the other into accepting its idea of reason.

There are two considerations involved in the wage question. One is the amount of money which an individual receives for his work, the other the amount of work he gives in return for his wages.

We have found among certain scientific management employers a tendency to claim that while the amount of wages paid is a matter for bargaining and agreement, the amount of work to be given in return for the wage is a matter for scientific measurement. Thus while they might agree with their employees to pay a minimum wage of sixty cents an hour on certain operations, they would reserve to themselves the power to determine through a time study the amount of work to be given. (Chapter IV.)

The control by the employer over the "scientific" expert or time study man has been the source of much friction in scientific management plants, and of criticism by organized labor. Its undesirability is gradually being recognized, and a system of joint control by employers and employees is being inaugurated in union and "company union" plants. (Chapters IX, XVI.)

The determination of wages by agreement is gradually coming to involve the classification of occupations by agreement. There was a time when the employer who dealt with trade unions had to make his agreement with each one individually, no matter how many unions were represented in his establishment. Each union went after all it could get, regardless of the others.

Fortunately, that method of collective bargaining is giving way to something more equable. The unions within the plant are in some cases federating and working out their scales together. Shipyard workers, railroad employees and clothing workers have adopted this method.

So far there are few expressions of labor on the wages of management. So far as we know, the great body of the employees have no control over the wages of management except in those firms in which they exercise it through their representatives on the Board of Directors. At the Milwaukee Street Railway Company (Chapter XIII) the company organization includes all the employees from the President down, but the salaries of the managerial force are not brought up for discussion when the wage schedule for the other employees is being made out. At the White Motor Company, where the distribution of the costs is discussed with employees, the salaries of individuals in the management have not been discussed. There is noticeable, however, some general uneasiness and suspicion concerning the wages of management as well as concerning profits. In the interest of production, this suspicion should be allayed by a frank discussion of the matter with all employees. If the salary paid is justifiable, there is little doubt that labor would consider it a legitimate charge on the business. There should be the same publicity and mutual understanding with regard to the wages of clerical workers and scientific experts. The whole body of employees, in other words, should understand the obligations and the compensation of all, and should thus be in a position to exert a wholesome influence in keeping up the standards of performance of all.

It is not merely wages in this wider sense, that is, wages of management, of scientific experts, clerical and shop workers, but the rate of profits also which must be subject to agreement between both the parties in industry, taking into consideration the money market, the necessary reserves, the condition of the industry and justice to employees and the public.

To make a statement of this kind is to lay one's self open to immediate attack from the whole profit-receiving world. But the profit-receiving world has reached a point where it is necessary to set up some effective protection for the industry, for its own employees and for the public.

The Dodge vs. Ford decision, mentioned above, sets up a theory of business which recognizes no equality of power or of interest between the factors of production or the public. It goes against the growing belief that labor and the public have an interest in industry equal to that of capital. It goes against the notion that profit, wage and price should be reasonable. It is opposed to the new philosophy which makes the industry or production itself, not the factors of production, or any one factor, the important item, and which recognizes the right of the public to demand that equal responsibility be exercised by all the parties in production to produce needed articles at a reasonable rate.

An antidote to the theory of irresponsibility expressed by this decision is to be found in the organization of all employees and the assertion by them of equal power with capital over profits, wages and prices. If management is bound by the principle of this decision to take into consideration only the interests of capital, then the employees must protect themselves and the public by refusing to work except on conditions of reasonable wages, reasonable prices and reasonable profits. The directors who represent capital and their servants, management, under this decision, cannot of their own initiative, take notice of the interests of labor and the public until labor by demanding consideration as a condition of continued service, or the public by demanding it as a condition for the permission of continued existence of the industry, threaten the profits of the stockholders if their terms are not considered.

The need for some control by labor or the public over profits is clearly demonstrated by recent events in the industrial world. Throughout the war and the prosperous post-war period, capital justified the taking of enormous profits by the "rainy day" argument. Profits must be large in order to accumulate a fund to tide industry over the coming period of depression and to prevent unemployment and suffering.

But when the depression actually came, where was the "rainy day" fund? When they found that demand was low and the supply great, many employers forgot their duty of preventing unemployment, forgot their "rainy day" fund and shut down.

The trouble with the "rainy day" funds is that they are voluntary funds—elusive funds that can be spirited away. Capital, which manages the industry, is responsible to no one for maintaining them for the time when needed. Some firms, like the Wayne Knitting Mills (Chapter XII) do conscientiously maintain and use such a fund. But the continuance of that policy depends solely on the will of the owners of capital. At the Dennison Plant (Chapter VI), employees have never secured any agreement from capital to continue it, and even if there were an agreement, there is no organization of employes with sufficient power to enforce it against the will of the management. So far as we know, no powerful union in the country has ever secured an agreement for such a safeguard. The Amalgamated Garment Workers have suggested it as a matter to be worked out. This is as far as labor has gone. There is a precedent for some such promise in the public utility acts of the various states. These acts safeguard the industry and protect the management of public utilities from the rapacity of the stockholder by requiring that a sum sufficient for depreciation be set aside before any dividends are paid.

Labor is slowly beginning to see that its comfort and happiness depend upon many more things than wages and hours. The preservation and healthy expansion of their own industry and of industry as a whole are matters of real importance to all workers. All industries, not merely a few selected ones like those which furnish electricity or water, are public utilities. The worker in any industry and the consumer of the product of the industry have an interest in the industry which precludes them from sitting down and leaving the insiders to loot or to wreck it, or even to pocket excessive profits at the risk of wrecking it. It is their industry as much as capital's, and in self-protection they must insist on the maintenance of funds for its preservation and expansion.

POWER

But labor cannot do this without power. As long as labor is engaged in a struggle for the right of organization it has little time to devote to the stabilization of industry. It cannot become a peace-time constructive organization until it has established firmly its right to existence. When the American employer realizes as clearly as does the English employer that labor organization is as inevitable as capital organization, then organized labor can become a conscious factor in the improvement of industry. Labor must have approximate equality of power before it can be held rightly to any responsibility.

Equality of power is a vague term, and may cover a variety of meanings. In this connection, however, it means equal ability to stop production and to stop the other factors from contributing to production; and equal ability to hold out against the others. It means also, equality of opportunity for the individual, according to his native or acquired capacity.

When capital can arbitrarily take a job away from a man who is doing satisfactory work, and the man has no power to take the business away from capital, that is, to prevent capital from producing and taking profits, there is no equality of power. When capital can shut down industry without consulting labor, there is no equality of power. Capital is free, so far as labor is concerned, to go where it can obtain the highest profits; labor is ofttimes prevented by capital from changing over to a place which pays a higher wage. When capital can, by a gentleman's agreement not to "steal" the labor of another firm, prevent a workman from taking a better job, and thus create an industrial serfdom for labor, while labor cannot retaliate by chaining capital to a service which pays less than the competitive interest, then there is no equality of power.

On the other hand, when employees are so strongly organized that they can prevent capital from taking the job away from an individual arbitrarily, and that they can prevent capital from getting others to fill their places when they strike, there is approximate equality of power. When labor is so organized that it can, by means of the strike, prevent capital from producing, we can say there is an approach to equality of power.

Capital is often able, by means of the profits it obtains from the product, to finance itself over a long period of waiting through a strike or lockout or unemployment. Labor can only attain equality of waiting power by means of organized saving in the form of union dues and strike contributions. Capital is also able to use superior weapons in fighting. It has its own newspapers or the money to attach newspapers to its cause. It has the money to tempt capable men from the service of labor to that of capital. It usually has control of the government and consequently the advantage of police protection.

Suppose labor obtained this equality of power. What effect would that have on production? Is equality of power really in the public interest?

The best way to determine this is to see how the unions have used and are using their power; whether or not they are using it in the public interest, especially in the interest of production. We have to remember, however, that real equality of power has never been generally attained in the United States. As long as any considerable groups are unorganized, so that they can be used as a threat against organized labor, the coercive power of capital over labor is stronger than that of labor over capital. Universal organization is necessary to real equality of power. We can only, therefore, show examples of cases in which labor is approximating this equality of power with capital.

In the first place many of the constitutions of trade union organizations contain the statement of a desire for more efficient workmanship and increased production as a result of their organization. Labor periodicals and newspapers are full of similar sentiments. A few examples can be given:

"The objects of this union shall be the fostering and encouragement of a higher degree of skill and efficiency." (Constitution Federal Labor union, affiliated with the A. F. of L.)

"Both employers and employees are getting their living out of the shoe factories. The more efficiently the factories are conducted, the better living all of them can get." (*Shoe Workers' Journal.* Date not given.)

"No fair employer can long guarantee the sale of union labor's product if that labor is deficient in skill, and members of a contracting union who contribute to such deficiencies are enemies of the union, of fair conditions of employment, and traitors to the cause they glibly espouse." (*International Steam Engineer.* "A duty we owe." Editorial, Nov., 1919, pp. 352-353.)

"Where organized labor is employed, where conditions and wages are satisfactory, where the workingman knows he cannot be dismissed unless the cause for such dismissal is furnished by himself, he then comes to look upon the factory, shop or store in which he is employed from the same angle as does the owner or manager, evincing the same lively interest in its success as does the latter. The result is that the worker concentrates and there is a decided improvement in the quality of the output." (*Stove Mounters and Range Workers' Journal*, April, 1919, p. 100.)

The labor press is full of expressions of this kind but the employer seldom sees them in the public press. They are worth studying. The employer who is having difficulties with his union men will probably smile cynically when he reads them. But he must remember that the employee also smiles when he reads the employer's benevolent expressions of solicitation for the general public. It is wholesome for both to see themselves mirrored each in the literature of the other.

One real test of the effect of organized labor on production is to be found in the testimony of employers of union labor. Those who were interviewed on this subject all claimed that the existence of the union had not hindered, and some of them believed that it had actually improved production. They considered this not so much the result of conscious effort on the part of the union employees to increase production, as an indirect result brought about as follows. First, the struggle of organized labor to force wages upward has led employers to put in more and better machinery, and to reorganize their whole administrative system on more efficient lines. Second, opposition by workmen to the introduction of new machinery has been overcome where they have confidence in the power of the union to prevent the new machinery or the administrative change from having a bad effect upon any worker. (Chapter XVI.) Third, in those union establishments in which a court is in continuous session for the hearing of all complaints, as at Hart, Schaffner & Marx, and the Rochester clothing industry (Chapters XVI and XVII), the knowledge of all that the grievances of all can be aired tends to make each one careful to conduct himself properly. Grievances that would smoulder and become more bitter if hidden away, tend to become less important in the face of a continuous session of the court, and the morale of the whole establishment is greatly improved. Fourth, the knowledge of the worker that through his organization he has power to force his employer to give him whatever he is able to produce, and not cut piece-rates unreasonably, makes him anxious to produce as much as possible. With a powerful union, the worker can protect himself against his employer. His only danger under the piece-work system is that his own desire and need will urge him on too fast, to the detriment of his longtime, future production.

The union has protected and increased production in still other indirect ways. Organized labor has carried on a relentless fight against child labor, against exhausting hours, and in favor of better education for the worker, and protection against dependency due to accident, unemployment and sickness. It has worked for better housing, for protection of the health of the worker, for fairer taxation methods, a higher standard of living. All of these things, in their turn, have helped to lengthen working life and to make labor more productive.

It is thus true, that while the unions have been accused of indifference and hostility to the introduction of devices for increasing production, they have all along been steadily working to destroy some of the great causes of individual inefficiency. They have everywhere forced improvements upon the unprogressive employer.

Really, when we come to look at it, labor's definition of "production" is different from the capitalist's definition of production. The capitalist defines production as the amount of output per day or hour. Labor defines production as the steady output for a life time of production. By the capitalist's definition efficient production per day or hour is not inconsistent with idleness through over-production, and not inconsistent with incapacity at forty. By the laborer's definition of production, efficient production, is not consistent with cycles of over-production and under-production, and not consistent with premature old age. By the capitalist's definition, production must be speeded up while the hunting is good. By the laborer's definition it must be spread out so that the hunting may always be good. The difference is perfectly natural, considering the differences in their situations. The capitalist can set aside his surplus as reserve funds to carry him over dull times or seasons. If he does not do so he goes bankrupt and falls to the level of a wage-earner. The laborer cannot set aside a sufficient surplus for unemployment and old age, and when he goes bankrupt he has no lower level to ease his fall except poverty and charity. It is not surprising that they have two definitions of production and do not understand each other when they talk of efficiency. The capitalist's idea of efficiency is big profits to take care of no-profits. The laborer's idea of efficiency is a life-time of steady wages for all.

Protection of the public health through demands for sanitation in hotels, in barber shops, and other public places, and the abolition of sweatshops are forms of service to the public. Protection of the public against exorbitant prices is a new development. The icemen's demand in Chicago that their wages be raised without increase in the price, and the British coal miners' recent demand for lower coal prices are examples of this. Organized workers have sometimes exercised their power in self-restraint. In the men's garment trade there has been a conscious effort, on the part of the leaders at least, to have regard for the future needs of the industry and to restrain their members from demanding and taking all that the traffic will bear at any one time, regardless of possible disaster to the industry in the future. The Amalgamated Garment Workers, for example, secured an agreement with employers to which the latter agreed not to pay more than ten per cent above the union wage scale. With the intoxication of high prices and high profits upon them many employers disregarded the agreement and bid wildly against each other for labor. The union went to the extent of sending committees of the union to bring back their own members who were accepting higher wages, and thus prevent the violation of the agreement and the demoralization of the workers.

Organized labor has not only helped production by securing humanitarian legislation, but it has also been found invaluable in administration. What if during the war there had been no labor unions and no labor leaders? What if there had been no workingman who stood out before the country as one who was in touch with the workers, one who had their confidence, one who could speak for them with authority? What if there had been no Samuel Gompers, no representative of labor upon the councils of the nation, upon the employment boards, upon the boards which fixed the prices of food products? And what if now in times of peace, there were no great labor movement to work for education? What if, when a labor bureau or industrial commission needs assistance from employers and employees in working out standards of safety and compensation it had to take as a representative of labor a man who could communicate with no groups of employees and speak for none of them?

Sometimes, the process may seem slow and painful, but after all it is through labor organization, through negotiation, through representation, through delegation and acceptance of responsibility that order is evolving in industry. For, last of all, the union is serving a great public purpose for which it is seldom given credit. It is a real school for citizenship in a democracy. This is especially true, where, as in the clothing trades, there is in existence machinery for the constant settlement of grievances. Here in their own industry the people are in daily contact with the workings of representative government. Here they learn to look for justice to an established industrial government; they learn to join with the employer in paying the expenses of their machinery of justice; they learn self-restraint. They learn also to be upstanding and fearless when they are right, knowing that they have all the means of publicity at their command. They learn to formulate their desires and their discontent into constructive proposals which will be able to stand up under the criticism of fellow workers and the hostility of employers. They learn to present their demands in an orderly and dignified manner, and to practice self-restraint and group-restraint for the good of the whole body of workers.

This contribution of the union to training for citizenship is also a contribution to the cause of production. It tends to reduce and has reduced in the clothing and printing industries, strikes and stoppages and the losses consequent upon them. It is solving the problem of discipline which is another important factor in production. It adds greatly to the interest in the day's work. It supplies the best kind of an antidote to the dangerous monotony resulting from extreme division of labor and of processes. It makes the worker feel himself a self-respecting human being instead of a beast of burden.

Attempts to introduce orderly government in an industry cannot be expected always to succeed immediately. The system which has worked smoothly for years at Hart, Schaffner and Marx has broken down time and again in New York City. The thousands of petty firms in New York with their corresponding thousands of degrees of efficiency do not unite easily for negotiation and coöperation with their employees. It need occasion no more surprise if, in the process of setting up industrial government, as many failures and periods of reaction will be recorded as in the process of setting up political government. Out of the very failures of political governments have grown the improvements of succeeding governments. Political government has had a long history. Industrial government has had a short history. The final form of neither will ever be reached. Each is a changing, developing process.

A phenomenon which brings much criticism upon labor is the increase in per capita production during periods when there is much unemployment. The burden of criticism is that if labor can produce more at such times it can surely do it all the time.

The answer to this is twofold: First, in periods of unemployment, holding the job becomes almost a matter of life and death for the workman and his family. It becomes at least a matter of bread and butter, and medical care. The employee therefore speeds up in competition with his fellow employees, sometimes at a rate which he could not keep up indefinitely without injuring his health. Secondly, if laborers could keep up this pace all the time, we ought to be able to work out some form of industrial government which will encourage them to do so. As long as human wants keep ahead of human needs, which are all the time increasing, there can be no such thing as general overproduction. Mistakes in production there may be, due to lack of statistics or faulty estimation of expected consumption of particular articles, and to lack of co-operation between the various firms in the same industry. But as long as the workers throughout the world continually seek to raise their standard of living there is an incentive to greater and greater production.

Why, then, do they not have regard to this incentive all the time?

Simply because there is now no guarantee that greater production will mean a higher standard of living for the worker. There is no guarantee that all wages will rise in proportion to production and will consequently be able to buy back the increased product. Labor will speed up, either unconsciously or unwillingly, when it faces loss of a job as an alternative. It will only speed up consciously and willingly when it is organized so that it faces sure reward in proportion to its efforts.

Can a company union do just as well as a national union? This is the question which many employers answer affirmatively.

Organized labor does not see how it is possible. The company union might strike, but it has no way of reaching other workers to prevent them from breaking the strike. It cannot provide itself with strike benefits and so assure its waiting power. It cannot protect its own employers by exerting pressure on their competitors to come up to the standards demanded. It cannot exert influence in favor of legislation for better conditions for all employees. It cannot, except in the case of great corporations with plants throughout the country and by means of a consolidation of the unions of these plants, develop great leaders in whose power and sagacity employees have confidence.

Industrial problems are no longer local problems. The labor policy of one great firm may affect labor conditions and sentiment throughout the country. Credit has become a national problem, and the credit policy of the nation is of as much importance to labor and to the consumer as to the employer. The distribution of credit must be in the interest of the public, and the machinery must be invented by which that interest can be ascertained and secured. That machinery must be such that not merely one factor in production, capital, but all are able to offer information and suggestions. One of the greatest obligations of organized labor in the future is the securing of representation upon the bodies which determine who shall have credit, and the protection of the credit of firms which give a square deal to labor and to the public.

We are beyond the feudal stage, economically and politically. A little group organized within an industry but separated from its fellow workers by the wall of a company union, and without machinery for regular communication with them is an anachronism in present-day society as much as would be an isolated manor of feudal times or a former slave plantation surviving as the unit of farming, manufacture and exchange.

It is not merely an anachronism. It is practically impossible to carry out consistently. For in those industries in which there is a shop organization we find employers and employees constantly consulting conditions in other industries or in other firms in the same industry as an aid to the solution of their own problems. At the Nunn, Bush & Weldon Shoe Factory, the employees' organization sent a committee to study the rates paid on certain operations in another shoe factory (Chapter XI). At the White Motor Company we were told that they were paying rates above the union scale (Chapter I) ; that is, they were actually accepting as their minimum the rates fixed by agreements of organized employers and employees of other firms.

It is conceivable that the plant organizations in the steel industry may, for the sake of equalizing conditions in the different plants, federate into one industrial organization. If other employees throughout the country were not also organized, this amalgamation might constitute a menace. There would be a real danger to an otherwise unorganized public if the employees and the corresponding group of employers were thus organized in some industry producing necessities and having a monopoly upon the product. The two groups could then form a conspiracy to raise the price and divide the spoil. In fact, we have had in the past many examples of collusion between capital and labor to do that very thing when a group of skilled laborers, completely organized in an industry, have ruthlessly pushed up their own wages out of proportion to other workers, in the same or other industries, and have allowed the cost to be passed on to the consumer.

The remedy for this dangerous situation is not less organization, but more organization. Such a conspiracy can be effective only when the other industrial groups, either of employers or laborers, are not organized for retaliation and creating and enforcing a public opinion which will condemn and ostracize them as profiteers. We see how this principle has worked in the case of the railroad employees. The four brotherhoods in the early days of their organization, were able to raise their wages far above the level of the average workers. The public paid the bill. The trackmen and other railroad employees, unorganized, were at the general wage level of the country, or a little below. But when the war aided the organization of these poorly paid groups, and their representatives began to deal with the representatives of the brotherhoods, the latter pushed the claim of the others, and moderated their own claims. In the days when the trackmen were unorganized, when they were not working with the brotherhoods for their common good, when they had no means even of becoming well acquainted with them, the brotherhoods had little sympathy for them. When they came into association with the brotherhoods the latter could see the righteousness of their claims and their greater need.

Employers testify that when their employees are called on to make a distribution of a bonus, they divide usually on the basis of need—the larger amount to the lowest paid. This principle is at work among trade unionists. As workers organize and are able to communicate with each other, they come to have more understanding of the point of view and needs of the others. When all labor is so organized that every man and woman who works with hand or brain has an opportunity to have his case heard by his fellow workers, we may expect less grabbing on the part of individuals and groups and a greater regard for the rights of the public—that is, of all the other workers.

The organized worker, when he secures power, also must accept responsibility. As his power increases, he comes more and more into the light of publicity and criticism. He must be more careful about his actions or he has the "general public" upon him. If the "general public" is also organized, that is, if it becomes the whole group of organized employers, organized employees and organized farmers, it will not allow him to take more than his fair share of goods.

Capital organization is inevitable. No firm can live unto itself without regard to the policies and activities of other firms. Each must be influenced to some extent by conditions in the other. Labor organization, too, is inevitable. And no one group of employees can or should for any length of time improve the condition of its members at the expense of the public; that is, of employees in other occupations.

Fortunately, organization is not merely inevitable; it is really desirable for the sake of securing the greatest possible increase of production and consequently the highest standard of living for all. It is necessary for capital to organize, as it is doing, on a national and international scale. It is necessary also for labor to organize on a parallel scale. For this purpose labor organization must mean the shop unit, but it must also mean the union of shop units in great national organizations; and even federations with foreign unions. It must also mean organizations parallel with the political units municipal, state, national and international federations or councils of all trades and occupations. There must be machinery for influencing legislation in city, state and nation. There must also be machinery for aiding administration in city, state and nation.

Since organization is in the interest of production, under modern conditions, it ought to be encouraged, rather than discouraged. It ought to be made easy rather than difficult. If it were possible to give "the public" an understanding of the public purpose of the union it would be made easy. Since this is impossible it would be well if those who do see the point would go out with organized labor in a campaign to bring the others in, and perhaps to secure the passage of legislation protecting employees in their right to organize. Similar laws in the past have been declared unconstitutional,[1] but new facts have come to light since those decisions, or were not brought to the attention of the court, which put the whole matter on a

[1] Adair v. U. S., 208 U. S. 161 (1908); Coppage v. Kansas, 236 U. S. 1 (1915).

different basis. The courts were unable then to discover the public purpose of the union. The attorneys for the union seem themselves not to have seen it. They took no notice of the lengthened working life due to its own activities and the protective legislation which organized labor has helped to secure. They took no notice of the need for a check upon the power of absentee owners of joint stock companies over production. They knew nothing then of the coming war emergency in which the union proved to be of immeasurable service in aiding the nation to utilize labor to the fullest extent. They were apparently unaware of the increasing complexities of administration and the necessity for crystallization and expression of labor's peculiar knowledge and sentiment. In the light of these facts the courts would today, we believe, be inclined to reverse the Coppage and Adair decisions, against which, even then, vigorous minority opinions were offered. New legislation, however, should be more carefully worked out than the earlier legislation. There should be added machinery for enforcement, probably a local board representative of employers and employees where each case could receive immediate consideration. There should have been a better recognition of the reciprocal rights and duties of corporations and unions than was recognized in the laws declared unconstitutional.

With labor organized, and capital organized, with each group and individual comparatively safe from arbitrary action on the part of other groups and individuals, and with the knowledge that the principles of distribution are in their own hands, jointly with capital, there is nothing to distract the attention of labor from the possibilities of increased wages and comfort through increased production. There is nothing to keep them from taking an interest in the efficiency with which the business is conducted. In fact, there is everything to induce them to take such interest. There is everything to make them desire careful cost accounting systems, such as those which the photo engravers are now considering (Chapter XV), and careful studies of possibilities of improvements in production, such as the International Ladies' Garment Workers' Union of Cleveland are having made in coöperation with the employers.[1]

When they have secured what they consider a fair division of the existing product, then they must turn to increasing production as their only means of raising their wages.

Even if we had not been able to show that labor has a great contribution to make to the process of management and that it should assume some control over distribution, there would still be no good reason for believing that labor could not assist production in this way. For labor has not been educated with these objects in mind.

EDUCATION

The assumption of current theories of educators has been that the rank and file do not take part in management. Education in a knowledge of the problems of industrial management and finance has therefore

[1] "Report of Miller, Franklin & Basset," in the matter of the Cleveland Cloak, Suit, Skirt and Dress Industry. Published by the International Ladies' Garment Workers' Union and the Cleveland Garment Manufacturers' Association.

been entirely neglected except in colleges, where the future shop employee is seldom found. The high school does not give it. The trade school does not give it. The trade school assumes that the boy who learns a trade is so fortunate that there is no use in preparing him for the higher managerial and technical positions. These higher positions often go, consequently, to the young inexperienced college graduate. The bright young fellow in the shops is passed over, not because he is lacking in intelligence, but because his parents could not afford to finance him through high school and college, and he himself was not sufficiently impressed with their value to make the sacrifices necessary to put himself through.

The remedy for this situation is pointed out by Henry Ford and by the Goodyear Tire and Rubber Company. Each of these firms has established a part time college for the promising men among their shop workers where the latter can be prepared for the engineering, the scientific and the managerial work of the plant.

Not all employers can do this. Neither should they. This is the job of the public schools, and they have failed to work out a flexible school system to meet the higher industrial needs of training the boy who must help himself through school. They have failed even to give adequate training for the trades or those mechanical processes which can scarcely be dignified by the name of trade. They have failed utterly to comprehend the lines of promotion in industrial life and to prepare each child to go up the line. If they have failed to grasp the idea that education must mean, first, training to earn a living and, second, preparation for promotion, it is not to be wondered at that they have failed to comprehend the possibilities of participation by all workers in the management and financial policies of the industry for which they work.

It is not to be wondered at that they have failed to give us a population of bright young workers, well informed on all phases of industrial organization, finance and management. We have allowed our youth to waste their time in schools on inanities and non-essentials, and then we insist that they have no interest in the management side of industry. Naturally! They are totally in the dark about the workings of industry and finance. They have studied with little interest a detached geography, detached arithmetic, algebra and geometry, a detached economics, and while they have been tiring themselves out with this abstract stuff, they have been neglecting its application to the industries with which they are familiar. They have not studied the financing of an industry at the outset, the needs of expansion, the processes and costs of production, the processes and costs of marketing, the labor policy, the methods of improving efficiency. Here and there, as in the University of Cincinnati, we find signs of an understanding of the relation of the public school to industry and of the real possibilities of public part-time education with a practical industrial atmosphere. In the public continuation schools of numerous states the opportunity exists, but the possibilities are not developed.

But since our schools have thus failed, we have no ground for assuming that the employee naturally has no interest in such things—that he is interested only in his pay envelope. We might just as well say that the child aged two has no interest in reading.

The foregoing is intended to show that for the sake of production, employees must have a share in management, and that education must therefore include education for participation in management; that education in order to be democratic, must give all who want it preparation for promotion to managerial or technical positions. Now we come to a third demand upon education, namely education for industrial citizenship.

If labor organization serves a public purpose, then it must be made easy and effective by means of careful preparation of the child for its future citizenship in the industrial as well as in the political world. Hence every child should study the organization of industry as carefully as we are beginning to think he should study the organization of the political unit. He should become acquainted with the types of industrial organization. He should examine the various stages of industrial government, from monarchy to democracy. He should study methods of management, including "scientific management." He should study the various types of labor organization, their accomplishments and their failures. He should study critically their constitutions, methods of organization and methods of negotiation. Whether he is in the future to act in the capacity of owner, manager, or shop employee, he needs to be taught how to put his side of the case in an orderly, self-controlled manner. Whether he is to belong to the rank and file of labor or to be a leader, he needs to learn to have respect and regard for the reputation of his organization, of his fellow workers and for public opinion. He needs to learn to make use of his facts before he acts. He needs, in short, to add to the physical force of organization all the other powerful adjuncts of moderation, caution, self-control, dignity and intelligent conviction. This is the kind of training which we need on both sides of the table at which capital and labor meet. This is the kind of education which we can demand from our schools when society recognizes that democratic government of industry is better for production than autocracy, however benevolent the autocrat.

"But is it?" says someone who is still unconvinced that the positive evidence for industrial democracy outweighs the positive evidence for industrial autocracy. "You have given some cases to show that employees do work well under management that is growing more democratic. But how do you account for the fact that in some shops where there is absolute monarchy or autocracy they are actually getting out more product than in some of your 'democratic' places? You cannot dodge Henry Ford."

That is quite true. We cannot dodge Henry Ford. He gets production. He gets it on a straight day wage. He gets it without strikes. He divides the work up into simple processes which violate all our theories about the bad effect of monotony. He employs men as they come, even to the lame and the blind. When the wheels and the belts of his great factory start, they push the work on steadily and inexorably from one worker to another. Each worker takes it as it comes and must finish his process while it is on its way to the next process.

Henry Ford gets production. He makes an honest

product. He aims to cut the price to the consumer as much as he can. Still he makes millions. He uses those millions for expansion, for scientific research and experiment. He pays wages to his men which he believes will enable them to live decently and he insists that they shall live decently. The men may hate the process they perform, but they respect Henry Ford. So does the public.

Will it last?

Marcus Aurelius died. He was a good emperor while he lived. But his mantle of statesmanship did not fall upon his heir. Neither did it fall upon his people. There was in them no wisdom, no discipline, no tradition of self-control that enabled them to stand up against the attacks from outside, the weakness and mismanagement within.

An empire held together by the force of one great will, one magnetic personality, one man or a few men glorying in the use of their power and genius for the benefit of their fellowmen, compelling submission by force of respect for the man who conceives such a great enterprise, such an empire is a wonderful thing —while it lasts. But suppose that the genius which built up this empire dies with the emperor. Suppose his successors lack it. Suppose that the people in the empire learn to rely on the emperor and forget to use their own wisdom and power to perpetuate the gigantic institution which genius has set up.

It is the old question, whether it is better to have benevolent autocracy and submission resulting temporarily in tremendous production, or growing democracy and self-control accompanied by steady and interested production.

The employer dreams of a world in which he will not forever be engaged in the struggle to discipline labor, a world in which all his energies will be freed for the mechanical problem of production. But while he is dreaming, labor is also dreaming. And the industrial world of which labor dreams is also a world of peace and production, and of a comfortable standard of living for all. It is a world in which all capital and all labor are organized for the purpose of carrying on industry efficiently and distributing the product justly; a world in which the desirability of labor participation in legislation, and of labor contribution to industrial management is fully recognized; a world in which all the elements in industry are trained to negotiate in an orderly and civil manner; a world in which adequate machinery exists for constant consultation and negotiation upon all problems of production and distribution; a world in which labor, secure in its power to obtain for itself its full share of the product, freed from the necessity of spending its energy upon the fight for existence, is able to devote its time and attention to the production of wealth; a world which recognizes the right of society and of the individual to the greatest possible material comfort; a world in which each human being is afforded the satisfaction of using and developing his powers of imagination and planning for the future, as well as his powers of accomplishment upon the industry by which he earns his living.

INDEX

Absentee ownership, 60, 62; evils, 32, 267, 295; remedies, 296.

Absenteeism, 150, 270, 334.

Accidents. *See* Workmen's compensation.

Adair *v.* U. S., 410.

Adjustments. *See* Arbitration.

American Federation of Labor, 55, 82, 122, 132, 186, 259, 370; company unions, 115, 119, 122.

American Shipbuilding Co., labor agreement, 353.

Americanization, 11, 19, 80, 83.

Anarchism, 268.

Appeals. *See* Shop committees.

Apprenticeship, 168, 172, 177, 192, 208, 219, 245.

Arbitration, 55, 111, 118, 131, 157, 165, 178, 183, 197, 200, 207-210, 213-220, 231, 258; Australasian, 225; efficiency, 53; Filene's, 49; justice, 48; legislative, 225; Rochester, 240.

Belgium, 191.

Benefits. *See* Insurance; Workmen's compensation.

Bethlehem S h i p b u i l d i n g Corp., labor agreement, 353.

Boards of directors, representation on. *See* Employees.

Bolsheviks, 363.

Bond, Albert S., 70.

Bonus, 6, 12, 69, 99, 143, 159, 161, 215, 253, 290, 294; attendance, 41; cost of living, 89, 93; economy, 73, 75, 79; excuse, 41; expectancy, 140; factors, 152; notice, 43; production, 39, 90, 100; quality, 39; retainer, 40; service, 42, 101.

Bookbinders, 161.

Boot and shoe workers, 128, 133.

Brewery workers, 259; prohibition, 25; Toledo, 252.

Building trades, England, 200.

Business agent. *See* Employees; Shop committees.

Cafeterias, 10, 44, 48, 80.

Calder, John, 308.

Canada, printing organization, 170.

Carnegie Steel Works, 282.

Citizens League, Indiana, 136.

Cleveland Chamber of Commerce, 387.

Cleveland Federation of Labor, 2, 9.